Society and Change in the Contemporary Gulf

Society and Change in the Contemporary Gulf

Edited by
A.K. Ramakrishnan
M.H. Ilias

New Century Publications
New Delhi, India

NEW CENTURY PUBLICATIONS
4800/24, Bharat Ram Road,
Ansari Road, Daryaganj,
New Delhi – 110 002 (India)

Tel.: 011-2324 7798, 4358 7398, 6539 6605
Fax: 011-4101 7798
E-mail: indiatax@vsnl.com • info@newcenturypublications.com
www.newcenturypublications.com

Editorial office:
LG–7, Aakarshan Bhawan,
4754-57/23, Ansari Road, Daryaganj,
New Delhi – 110 002

Tel.: 011-4356 0919

First Published: **July 2011**

ISBN: **978-81-7708-275-3**

Published by New Century Publications and printed at Salasar Imaging Systems, New Delhi

Designs: Patch Creative Unit, New Delhi

Cover Design: P.M. Sadiqali

Cover Photo: Althaf

PRINTED IN INDIA

About the Book

This selection of essays addresses the general aspects of social change in the Gulf on the one hand and the specific contours of transformation in different milieus of the region on the other. The volume goes beyond the paradigms of security and rentier state to capture state-society linkages, women's role in knowledge economy and social reforms, the directions of democratization, changing dynamics of cities like Dubai, the interplay of sacred and secular in the Gulf. It shows the multi-layered manner in which Arab societies of the Gulf have responded to the phenomenon of globalization.

The interconnectedness of political and economic dynamics and social change is brought forth in the volume by locating specific spaces, issues and moments of such transformation. Scholars from diverse disciplinary vantage points provide the reader with a multi-dimensional perspective of the societies in the Gulf.

Editors

A. K. Ramakrishnan is Professor at the Centre for West Asian Studies, School of International Studies, Jawaharlal Nehru University, New Delhi. Earlier, he was Professor and Director of the Centre for West Asian Studies, Jamia Millia Islamia, New Delhi, and Director of the School of International Relations and Politics, Mahatma Gandhi University, Kottayam, Kerala. He was also a Distinguished International Scholar at Bucknell University, Pennsylvania, USA. He has published widely in English and Malayalam. His recent book is entitled *US Perceptions of Iran: Approaches and Policies.* His articles and reviews have been published in national and international journals such as *International Studies, Scandinavian Journal of Development Alternatives and Area Studies, Millennium: Journal of International Studies, Contemporary South Asia,* and *Inter-Asia Cultural Studies.*

M.H. Ilias is Associate Professor at India-Arab Cultural Centre, Jamia Millia Islamia, New Delhi, India. He completed his doctoral research from the Centre for West Asian Studies, Jawaharlal Nehru University, New Delhi. His current research addresses social and cultural issues in the Gulf countries. Areas of his research interest also include film and popular culture in West Asia, Hadrami diaspora on the Malabar Coast, Islam and International Relations and Muslims and New Media. The books he has published include *Space Memory and Jewish National Identity; India-West Asia Relations: Understanding Cultural Interplays* (co-edited) and *Arabs in India: Society, History and Culture* (co-edited). He has been the recipient of Ford Foundation Fellowship for Post-doctoral Research (2007) at Oxford University and Post-doctoral Visiting Research Fellowship (2008) at the Centre for Modern Orient, Berlin. His articles and chapters have appeared in many collections as well as internationally reputed journals.

Contents

Acknowledgements

First, we wish to express our sincere gratitude to the contributors of this volume. We are thankful to Gulshan Dietl, Girijesh Pant, A.K. Pasha and P.R. Kumarswamy of the Centre for West Asian Studies, Jawaharlal Nehru University and Zikrur Rahman, the Director, India-Arab Cultural Centre, Jamia Millia Islamia for their support. Sameena Hameed, Aftab Ahamad, K. Deepa, Sivakeerthi Raveendran, Anas. S., Anju. J., P.K. M Jaleel, Rajeesh, Aneesh K., Jabir T.K., Limsheer P and Moinuddin Ahamad offered valuable assistance in preparing the manuscript.

We also benefited from the emotional support of our friends Mathew Joseph. C, Sreekala Sivasankaran, M.S. Sreerekha. Our publisher Sandeep Sury supported the publication process with a great amount of enthusiasm and patience. We would like to underline our thanks to Althaf for cover photograph and P.M. Sadiqali for cover design. We are also indebted to *Middle East Journal* for providing consent to reprint Amelie Le Renard's article "Only for Women: Women, the State, and Reform in Saudi Arabia".

Contributors

Mohamed Al-Thani was Qatar's Minister of Economy and Commerce (December 2003 to March 2006). He is currently a visiting fellow at Oxford Centre for Islamic Studies. He holds a post-graduate Diploma in General Studies from Denver community college, a B.Sc. in Industrial Management and Supervision and a minor in Public Administration, from Central Michigan University in USA. He holds a Senior Executive Certificate from London Business School and is currently a member of its Global Advisory Board. His main activities now are consulting and research in the energy sector and the GCC political economy.

Edward Burke is a researcher at FRIDE. He has an M.A. in War Studies from King's College, London. His research addresses political trends in the Persian Gulf region, including the GCC states, Iraq and Yemen. He has also undertaken research on civil-military relations and stability operations in Afghanistan and Iraq. He is currently working on a project to evaluate the politics of energy in the Middle East. Some of his recent publications include "The Gulf Takes Charge in the MENA Region" (FRIDE, April 2010) and "Iraq in 2010: The Dangers of European Complacency" (FRIDE, February 2010).

Gareth Doherty is a doctoral candidate at Harvard University Graduate School of Design. His dissertation is an ethnographic study of contemporary landscape and urbanism in Bahrain. He spent the 2007-2008 academic year in Bahrain on Sheldon Travelling Fellowship from Harvard University. He has worked with Chora in London and taught at design schools in Europe, North America, and Australia. At Harvard, he has been an Instructor in Landscape Architecture and Head Teaching Fellow. He has received a Harvard University Certificate of Distinction in Teaching in 2007. He has an M.L.A. and Certificate in Urban Design from the University of Pennsylvania and a B. Agr. Sc. and M. Agr. Sc. from University College, Dublin.

Shelly Johny is a research scholar at the Centre for West Asian Studies, Jawaharlal Nehru University, New Delhi. He completed his

Masters in International Relations from Middlesex University, London and did his M.Phil. in West Asian Studies from Jawaharlal Nehru University. He is presently a recipient of the Ryochi-Sasakawa Young Leaders Fellowship Fund awarded jointly by the Nippon Foundation and Tokyo Foundation. He has previously worked in the Centre for Air Power Studies and the Institute for Defence Studies and Analyses. He has published research papers in journals of repute. The title of his Ph.D. Thesis is *The Decline of Oman's Maritime Empire in the Late Nineteenth Century.*

Elena Maestri holds a Ph.D. degree in Political Science, with an emphasis on History and Institutions of the Arabian Peninsula, from the *Università Cattolica del Sacro Cuore* (Italy). She is currently tenured researcher at the same university and lectures on "History of the Arabs" as assistant to the Chair of History and Institutions of the Muslim World. Her research focuses in particular on state-formation and state-building in the Arabian Peninsula, on non-oil industrialization and human resources development, with special reference to Bahrain and Saudi Arabia. She has contributed to specialized studies, research papers, articles and books both in Italian and in English. Her recent book is entitled *The Gulf Cooperation Council (GCC) Region: Development and Human Security in Arabia.*

Stephen J. Ramos received his doctorate from the Harvard University Graduate School of Design. His book, *Dubai Amplified: The Engineering of a Port Geography,* is published with Ashgate Press. He has published in various journals, including *Volume*, *Harvard Design Magazine*, *Built Environment,* and *Neutra*. Ramos is a founding editor of the journal *New Geographies,* which focuses on contemporary issues of urbanism and architecture.

Amélie Le Renard is a post-doctoral fellow of the Graduate School of Muslim Cultures and Societies at Freie Universität, Berlin. She completed her Ph.D. in political sociology at Sciences Po, Paris in 2009. Between 2005 and 2010, she spent eleven months in the Saudi capital as an invited researcher at King Faisal Centre for Islamic Research and Studies, during which she conducted ethnographic fieldwork on young Saudi women. In Fall 2009, she was a visiting doctoral student at Columbia on a Columbia-Paris Alliance Doctoral Mobility Grant. Her Ph.D. dissertation is entitled *Urban Lifestyles* *and the Reinvention of Femininities: A Political Sociology of Young Saudi Women's Access to Public Spaces in Riyadh.* Her recent publications include chapters on "Engendering Consumerism in the Saudi Capital: A Study of Young Women's Practices in Shopping Malls," and "From Qur'anic Circles to the Internet: Sex Segregation and the Rise of Female Preachers in Saudi Arabia" in edited volumes.

David B. Roberts is a doctoral candidate at the School of Government and International Affairs, University of Durham. His thesis is on *The Search for Security in Qatar*. His areas of interest include state and politics in Saudi Arabia, UAE business culture, Gulf politics and international relations. He has several publications to his credit.

Rushda A. Siddiqui is a Research Fellow at the Indian Council of World Affairs, New Delhi. Earlier, she worked at the National Maritime Foundation, New Delhi, where she was also the Associate Editor of the bi-annual journal of the foundation, *Maritime Affairs*. She received her Ph.D. in 2005 from the Centre for West Asian and African Studies, Jawaharlal Nehru University. Her doctoral thesis is entitled *State and Political Islam in North Africa.*

1

Introduction

A.K. Ramakrishnan and M.H. Ilias

For more than three decades, the Arab Gulf has been on a distinct historical trajectory that stands apart from the rest of West Asia. The societies in each Gulf state respond to the forces and institutions of various socio-economic processes, like globalization, post-liberalization institutional mechanism, nationalism and new pattern of migration and these responses collectively set in motion an interesting and unique social change. The region at present is an arena of new sorts of social expressions that are critical and vibrant. The social reconfiguration is also central to contemporary economic transformations that are generally appropriated and grouped together under the overtly generalised rubric of globalisation'. But the story of 'globalization is not a simple straight-line trend; it rather indicates a process under way in the Gulf today-a complex interaction between global and local, tribal and other cultural identities. These experiences, of course, speak of a plurality of related tendencies.

The contemporary situation is more fragmented at the same time it embodies a mosaic-like appearance of several new phenomena. However, at the epistemological level, there is a perceptible lack of rigorous critical works that assess the contemporary dynamics in some detail. Academic writings that deal with various angles of economic development are seen in large quantity. But, in spite of numerous works on oil economy and certain elements of politics, foreign policy and strategic affairs, writings on changing social processes and phenomena are scanty. It would seem a sad irony that an area with such remarkable changes has not been written about adequately by scholars in social science. This volume addresses some of the issues relevant to an understanding of society and change in the contemporary Gulf. It draws works from multi-disciplinary vantage points in order to record the changes and dynamism that characterise the societies in the region.

In the last few decades, the region has witnessed a series of diverse yet shared movements that affected the social relations, economic exchanges and political institutions. The major development in the Gulf in the last few decades has been resistances in the domains of gender and class and a newfound expression of marginalized people in politics. The first incident in this line in the early 1990s was an extraordinary move by a group of forty seven Saudi women who kicked their foreign male drivers out of their cars and drove through the streets of Riyadh, disregarding the ban on female driving. The recent South Asian labour unrest in Dubai adds more to a vast body of unprecedented developments that go into the making of contemporary history of the region. This general mood is equally shared by stories appearing in local dailies on issues which are previously untouched. Reports ranging from domestic violence to gross human rights violation at work sites, women battering to sub-human conditions in labour camps find expression in the new context. These developments may not seem surprising for outsiders, but the trend has been of a significant social advance, making possible new avenues of expression that were previously unavailable.

In a society like Saudi Arabia, where women had no public forum, no opportunity to express themselves, internet became a way of making themselves publicly visible and expressive. Through their personal narration, women bloggers from Saudi Arabia transgress several socio-cultural boundaries. With many themes of love and sex, blogs always push the boundaries of permissible expression. Throughout the Gulf, blogs proved to be an invaluable tool, not just for regular communication, but women seem rather free to speak through such networks. And what seems to be happening in the Gulf society today is the formation of such socially distinct 'spheres' of women, minorities and expatriate labourers. These new communicative spaces have the ability to form a new public sphere in which discussions about the so-far taboo subjects are substantially being raised.

Renard's work in this collection, *"Only for Women": Women, the State, and Reform in Saudi Arabia* revolves around the traditional female sphere in Saudi Arabia which is largely a product of gender segregation. Saudi women have appropriated this segregated organization and reproduced it daily and in their own terms, by developing activities and discourses that are by women and for women. This segregation, however, can't be understood in terms of basic binaries of 'tradition' and 'modern'. It rather refers to a mosaic of new female spaces forbidden to men.

This separation constitutes women as a particular category for which a particular discourse has been developed. Renard seeks to understand how this specific spatial and ideological categorization of women has emerged together with discourses of national development and how it has been both transformed and reinforced through the more recent discourse of reform. Maestri in her chapter *Gulf Arab Women between Cultural Resistance and Knowledge Economy* takes a different position in discussing the matter of rising role of women in Gulf society. Apart from presenting a brief outline of the evolving role of women in the light of transformations generated by the oil era, this article sketches out the cultural factors that hinder the development of women. Education along with exposure to the world of knowledge has acted as crucial modernizing agents among both men and women during the second half of the last century in all the Gulf Arab societies. In Maestri's words, "they enhanced female self-consciousnesses as well as female willingness to gain a dynamic public role in their societies". However, the education system represents a clash between the agents of modernization on the one hand and the factors that try to curb liberal values on the other. Putting more emphasis on "the necessary respect for local culture", school curriculum turns a deaf ear to the infringement of women's freedom. The Arab Gulf governments' efforts in expanding women's education and integrating them progressively into the economy often meet stiff resistance form cultural factors deriving from custom and tradition.

The Arab part of the Gulf has also been engrossed in discussions over a single word 'reform' over the last one decade. Reform with its wide ranging imperatives like democratization and liberalization has been a serious point of concern in the political discourse of the entire region. However, it is doubtful that the multiplicity of alternate socio-political expressions has resulted in a serious structural transformation. Burke's chapter *Reaching a Threshold: The Stagnation of the Reform Process in Bahrain* critically notes the reform process in Bahrain. With the lack of institutionalised mechanisms, concrete legislation and independent judiciary, the King's attempts to introduce reform couldn't yield the desired result. There is the issue of lack of 'international pressure' also. Burke exposes the reason why the US does not want to spoil the party by exerting unnecessary pressure over Bahraini administration to open up further. Even though the country has a relatively better track record,. it is becoming increasingly obvious that the reform process has reached a bottleneck. The developments amply indicate the failure of the government to address institutionalised discrimination against Shia citizens.

New technologies have also brought a change in the pattern of political discourses and the ways in which they have been received. The newfound popularity of websites and blogs represent new communication genre for variety of purposes like political mobilization and opinion building. The extensive application of the Internet as a means of disseminating religious opinions is another striking phenomenon signifying a technologically adept integration of religious symbolism and traditional notions. Furthermore, there is the emergence of a new class of preachers with target audiences (mostly the educated class) different from those of the classical *ulema*. This new Islamic televangelists make their message relevant in ways different from the traditional *ulema,* by making their topics more appealing to the educated public. Thc new means of communication have provided many Muslim groups with an intermediate space and new means of sharing experiences on a "virtual space" beyond their limited conceptual and physical spaces. In the Arab societies of the Gulf, the multiple uses of the Internet, both as an enhancer of state power as well as a promoter of new conversations in civil society have been noted by keen observers.

As these changes occur at the open public domains of media operations, the role of traditional Islam as a legitimating ideology of the Arab states of the Gulf is still operative. But at the same time, traditional ways of conceiving state and society in religious and tribal terms on the one hand and the new transformations on the other do create tensions both in the way states function in the region and the manners in which societies interact with them. There are, therefore, new issues of state legitimacy and control. New mechanisms need to be in place in order for individual states to achieve this from their societies.

Roberts in his contribution, *The Change of Society in the Arab Gulf,* deals with the shifting idioms of legitimacy and control in the last two hundred years. His work sketches out the trajectory of metamorphosis that Gulf societies witnessed responding to two profoundly affecting phenomena in the recent history--colonialism and the discovery of oil--which culminated in a thorough socio-economic transformation. In pre-colonial society, family, clan and tribal bonding were the political reality that determined the functioning of the monarchies. Colonialism brought significance to territory and borders and the creation of notions of political separateness led to the strengthening of the ruling family. The discovery of oil and the emergence of rentier economy supplemented this with the extreme importance given to the land. The meaning of legitimacy also changed with the changing nature of society. In order to attain legitimacy for the rule, the governments of the region engaged in massive sets of welfare schemes, which of course marked the ruling elites' attempt to facilitate a transition from tribal society based on *jus sanguinis* or the criterion of inherited blood connections, to a true Westphalian state.

Siddiqui's chapter, *Responding to the Challenge of Change,* makes an attempt to comprehend the shifting dynamics of the socio-political and economic change within the framework of the state responses to these changes. From the 1960s, the Arab states of the Persian Gulf have been in the middle of change. They have been partly responsible for the changes that swept over the regional and global levels and at the same time, being tremendously influenced the dynamics of global and regional politics. With the shift in the socio-economic base of these states from being nomadic, feudal to sedentary-petro, the challenge for the governments has been to re-negotiate the power equations between the state and the society at the domestic, international and regional levels. The variables of change remained economic, external and religious. "It is within the parameters of petro-economy, the increasing military and economic presence of Western powers and the clash between Israel, Islamists and the Western ideas, that the dynamics of changes that the Arab states of the Persian Gulf underwent, will have to be evaluated", argues Siddiqui.

The Gulf is a major participant in the post-liberalization economic order and it adopted the strategies and practices of global capitalism. The shibboleth of 'economic diversification' has a spill over effect all over the region despite the exclusive character of each state. Nonetheless, the picture is not as rosy as portrayed outside. In his contribution, *Economic Diversification in the Gulf Co-operation Council (GCC) States,* Al-Thani addresses some serious concerns over the content of economic diversification in the oil-rich Gulf. He is of the view that the recent re-investment spree which has encapsulated 'economic diversification' can more realistically be viewed as a form of 'portfolio diversification'. Major avenues that have seen massive diversification drive are: natural gas, real estate and construction, financial services and tourism. Switching over to an economy dependent on natural gas can't be regarded as a shift in production. The development in the real estate field is not need-based and the demand that comes largely from the highly paid guest labour living on oil rents gets diminished as oil rents decrease. So is the case with financial services, another sector with significant growth over the past decade. It is, to a certain extent, true that through the sovereign wealth funds, GCC states could recycle their hydrocarbon revenues into external financial assets. Nonetheless, Al-Thani argues that by switching resources into external financial assets, what the government does is serving to perpetuate the existing structure of the rentier state. It is argued that much of the income that will arise as a result of these investments will be in the form of rents or quasi-rents. The economic diversification, thus, represents a cosmetic measure in the form without a substantial change in the content.

Neoliberal globalization and its attendant market orientations and capital investments, the contestations between religion and nationalism, the processes of immigration, movements for reform and new imaginations of space and cities, contribute to the re-defining of traditional identities in the Gulf's socio-political arena. The Gulf societies have been engaged in the discussion of nationalism in newer ways in this context. With its wide ranging imperatives like new immigration policy, nationalization of labour and introduction of quota systems for reducing the over dependence on expatriates and cultural homogenization, they are actively into the re-imagining of a non-differential national community. But it is doubtful how far this nationalism fit with the realities. We see some tensions between imagined state and real state.

Ramakrishnan in his piece *A Note on Transformations of Gulf Societies in the Neoliberal Context* argues that neoliberal transformations in the Gulf did not result in the sidelining of the state. There is a visible re-imagination of everyday life in the diasporic communities. He argues that there are also tendencies of the emergence of a transnational Arab public sphere with new imaginations of democratic citizenship. Such democratic transformational clams from the society confront a monarchical system that at best offers its citizens a calibrated evolutionary change.

Johny's chapter sees the changes that are taking place in the Gulf societies not as a product of the present phase of globalization. *Globalization and Cosmopolitanism in Omani Society* takes readers to a sort of Oriental globalization which existed alongside a system of interlinked trade between the east and the west with Oman playing a pivotal role in such a system. Much before the present phase, the process of globalisation began to have its impact on Oman which had been a part of the cosmopolitan maritime networks of the Indian Ocean at least since the early Islamic period if not before. This has resulted in the creation of a cosmopolitan society which truly reflected Oman's extensive commercial and cultural linkages with regions as wide apart as East Africa and India. Johny's piece tries to establish a link between the past and the present and makes an enquiry into how the present phase of globalisation has influenced Omani society in the context of its nation building project that began in the 1970s. In the course of its attempt to build an all pervasive 'Omani national identity', the Omani nation is grappling with complex issues like the limitations that the ruling dynasty has in projecting Oman's traditional identity.

The influx of oil revenues and investment in the Gulf has a major spatial impact also. This is being manifested most clearly in the socio-spatial pattern of the development of cities. As is now widely noted, there is an increasing tendency to dismiss the conventional spatial imaginations for their inability to define new geographical practices. Developments in Dubai speak eloquently of this radical re-imaging of space and it is interesting to discuss about the nature of 'religiosity' in treating the city. Ilias in his piece *Dubai: the City and Sacredness* argues that Dubai occupies exactly the space, function and exclusiveness once reserved for 'sacred spaces' of religion. Interestingly, Dubai's recent fame comes from its projection as a 'politically neutral' city in the Gulf region. Ilias argues that the use of this adjective may be to make a new strategic asset and thereby to attract business people and multinational corporations and to give the city an added edge over other cities in the region which are trying to emulate its success. Political neutrality, no doubt, is a strategic asset of profound value and it is being employed in rewriting the spatial history of the land and in disengaging old 'socio-political' narratives that the land possessed. With the similar sort of independence and autonomy once given to holy places, Dubai is more or less free from constraints of the local political units and their spatial determinations.

In his contribution, *A Gulf Merchant Synoecism: Dubai before Oil* Ramos traces the evolution of Dubai as a trade metropolis. He tries to disengage the myth that Dubai's trade vocation is a post-oil development lacking a long history and attempts to establish that Dubai's development blueprint was being layed out while the city was still a Gulf outpost and British protectorate. All through modern history, Dubai has maintained the status of 'trading state' with the ruling family, the Maktoums, playing the role of both ruler and chief merchant. European powers seldom maintained interest in the regional trade as they were concerned about the profit which was considered to be not tallying with the effort. So the Europeans allowed other trading communities like Indian merchants, Persians and the Arabs to capitalise the situation and to wield their own positions of power and influence. European involvement in the societal affairs also remained scanty. The squabbles among the local tribes and European power rivalry for hegemony led collectively to the emergence of a third genre of trade, piracy. "The piracy... in very basic terms, represented a kind of cultural disagreement on trade customs", argues Ramos. The British patronage of the commercial activities came only with the growth of the pearl sector. Increased incursion eventually established a more direct protectorate relationship with the Sheikhdom. Discovery of oil furthered the British involvement as the British firms began to enter the region more actively.

The new economy and the new life style it has engendered have hardly wiped out everything that is traditional. There is, of course, an element of mismatch between existing social reality and the new forms of life. The new architectural spaces it created are reminder of how the region has been transformed. Whilst some new structures offer as a counteract to the clichéd image of the Arabian desert, some are to compensate for the loss of old ones of pre-oil days. Medinat Jumeirah in Dubai, which has been reproduced in the form of a heritage village, is an attempt to recreate the pre-oil town with the purpose of reconstructing the cultural past.

In his work, *Changing Hues of Green in Bahrain,* Doherty looks into this aspect of new urbanism in the Gulf. For Bahrainis, green colour primarily means the most iconic date-palm trees, though the gray-green of the native date-palm plantations are being replaced massively with bright grass greens of roadside shoulders, roundabouts, and the lawns of new residential and leisure developments. Replanting date-palm trees on the roadside, therefore, has a distinctive social meaning and it marks not just the 'pull of nostalgia', but 'a resonance of a bygone era that can never be recovered'. The date-palm trees are still significant to the social life of Bahrainis, 'they have the capacity to be urban', argues Doherty. To quote him: "they (date-palm trees) penetrate so many aspects of Bahraini life, providing food, shelter, building materials, social spaces, and social status as well as facilitating ancillary industries and produce, and a focus for poetry and folklore".

With the hope of impelling a more nuanced understanding of the notions of the society in transition, the chapters cover a range of issues that are discussed from various theoretical and political perspectives. And with different ways of looking at the effects of change this volume attempts to concentrate more on genealogical analyses of the process of transition.

2

The Change of Society in the Arab Gulf

David B. Roberts

Introduction

It would be hard not to be aware of the current rate of change in the Arab Gulf, for it has palpably visible manifestations. The skyline of many (if not most of the) cities in the region is peppered with cranes and buildings ascending ever upwards. Dubai is arguably the single best encapsulation of this phenomenon leading to a plethora of seemingly exaggerated statistics stating that a preposterously large percentage of the world's cranes are in fact in operation in the Emirate.[1] Furthermore, it is not just the skyline that is affected, but the coastline too. New particularly shaped islands are being and have already been created as the latest craze in property development. This particular phenomenon is not only confined to Dubai, as Doha and Bahrain boast their own similarly gaudy new islands too.

However, these types of engineering transformations are – need it be said – but one aspect of the overall transformation of the region. Every sector of society is beset by changes, yet, as Ramakrishnan and Ilias note in their introduction, there has been a surprising paucity of information examining such changes. The goal of this paper, therefore, is to attempt to broadly outline key factors that underlie some of the fundamental changes of Arab Gulf society itself.

In this context society will be broadly understood. It will follow the approach of the eminent philosopher Stephen Pepper who, in his essay *The Boundaries of Society*, sought only a working and not an over precise, philosophical definition.[2] Pepper asserts several characteristics of society:

> All are agreed that a society is some sort of unity constituted by some sort of activity by individuals of some sort...It is furthermore generally agreed that society is a vital phenomenon...All in all, it seems to be generally agreed that a society is a unity constituted by

> the purposeful activity of living organisms for the mutual benefit of one another.[3]

Society, therefore, will be understood as the aggregate result of actions undertaken by individuals. Thus, society can be affected by those with traditional power (i.e. Presidents, Kings etc.) and those without (i.e. ordinary people). It is understood that whilst it is easier for the ruler to make larger changes in an easier manner, this does not mean that ordinary people are totally powerless, especially if, for example, they act in a group.

This study will pay particular attention to the change of Arab Gulf society in the last two hundred years. There is, therefore, an implicit belief that there is a change to study. This would seem to be a reasonable supposition, given the time frame and general rate of Arab development, but it will still need to be proven. The impact of the numerous factors in the last two centuries will be evaluated in terms of the effects that the supposed changes have had on some of the underlying features of society, which will be delineated as the study progresses. This timeframe is advantageous as it is both manageable and encompasses the most profoundly affecting phenomena in the recent history of the Arab Gulf: their colonial experience and the impact of oil and subsequent development. This study has the further advantage that during the exploration of the central question, many other areas of societal change will be discussed providing a broader sketch of some of the literal changes *in* society.

This paper will follow the example of loosely analogous studies examining society by Balfour-Paul[4] and Stoakes[5] which do not conduct a massive statistical trawl of data looking for patterns. Statistical approaches can most certainly prove useful by, for example, empirically showing signs of educational development. [6] Overall, however, this paper prefers to endeavor to discern the central theme(s) responsible for the presumed change of society.

Breaking the Cycle

In the fourteenth century the great Islamic thinker Ibn Khaldun posited that the Arab world was subject to a cycle of dynastic rule. Families would rise to prominence, take power and last for no more than three generations before the cycle would begin again.[7] Khaldun suggests a logic for why dynasties mostly fail and disintegrate after the third generation.

> The first generation retains the desert qualities, desert toughness, and desert savagery…they are brave and rapacious…the strength of group feeling continues to be preserved among them. They are sharp and greatly feared. People submit to them...Under the influence of royal authority and a life of ease, the second generation changes from the desert attitude to a sedentary culture, from privation to luxury and plenty, from a state in which everybody shared in the glory to one in which one man claims all the glory…others are [in]…humble subservience…the vigour of the group feeling is broken…But many of the old virtues remain…because they [the people] had had direct personal contact with the first generation…The third generation, then, has (completely) forgotten the period of desert life and toughness…Luxury reaches its peak among them…Group feeling disappears completely…People forget to protect and defend themselves…In the course of these three generations, the dynasty grows senile and is worn out.[8]

In addition to Khaldun's immutable adage there have also been two primary checks on the power of a ruler, theoretically arresting or at least mitigating his potential descent into uncontrolled tyranny. Firstly, an imprudent leader could find himself deposed by a family member, a notable upstart or indeed the people could attempt to overthrow him in the typical sense of the word.[9] Secondly, a tribe or other conglomeration of people could simply vote with their feet and relocate *en masse* to another territory looking for better conditions.[10] Both of these options were pursued at various times and on various occasions throughout the Arab Gulf.

Both of these features and facets of society were, however, altered by colonial actions generally and British policies specifically. The Pax Britannica which pervaded the Arab Gulf and beyond during this period was maintained in a different way as compared to British rule in, for example, India. There were no garrisons deployed in each territory, nor was the British presence concentrated in strategic fortifications. Moreover, as Zahlan points out, "there were never more than four or five British residents [i.e. political overseers] living on both the Arab and Persian coasts at any one time."[11] Instead, Britain used a series of agreements and treaties with local rulers to keep control backed up by naval pre-eminence.[12] Al Naqeeb, for example, suggests that from the start of the 19th century until 1928 Britain signed over 200 protectorate treaties and agreements.[13] Balfour-Paul neatly sums up the crux of the issue.

> By signing individual treaties with whatever shaykhly figures were dominant at the time along the route through the Gulf to the Indian Empire...Britain's policy had the effect, wittingly or not, of 'legitimising' and perpetuating the fragmented political system which happened then to prevail.[14]

Instead, therefore, of the waxing and waning of various families as the rulers of a territory, Britain's intervention preserved the various families of the Gulf in power in perpetuity. British policy did this in several ways.

Explicitly, if and indeed when there was a real challenge to the leader or his chosen progeny, Britain intervened to reinstall or defend him at the point of a gun. For example, Britain intervened to protect the Sultan of Muscat from the Saudis in 1913 and rescue the Al Khalifah in Bahrain three times (1871, 1895 and 1905).[15] They also pursued policies that fostered the notion that each statelet was a separate entity. The policy of mandating ships to fly their own statelet's flag is a case in point.

Implicitly, the very fact that the British negotiated with each Sheikhdom independently contributed to these growing notions of separateness and along with their policies amounted to, according to Zahlan, the "the genesis of the Gulf states as separate political units, and of their sheikhs as independent rulers."[16] Furthermore, the British boosted the status of their chosen leader and family by association, their legitimacy by recognition and – most importantly – their coffers through trade agreements and extra freedom of action. Somewhat along Ibn Khaldun's lines, the new generation of leaders, backed, protected and cemented in power, were less constrained in their actions. This, Al Naqeeb maintains, had negative effects such as the raising of taxation levels and the expansion of the ruling family's power.[17] Traditionally, at this point, i.e. the raising of taxes or other bad treatment, tribes or merchants controlling groups of people had the ability to remove their labour and move to a different place seeking a better deal. This, therefore, would cut the tax-raising Sheikh's income and thus acted as a deterrent for pursuing such policies. Yet this too was to get more difficult to do as time wore on;

in no small part due to the creation of separate political consciousness across the region.[18] The increasing demarcation of borders hampered this as did the ever more pervasive power of the leader who could either attempt to force the groups to stay or do his best to make sure that they were not allowed to settle elsewhere.

British policies, therefore, began to eat away at some of the checks and balances that kept a reasonable equilibrium between the ruler and the ruled in the Arab Gulf. As time wore on, these checks faced further stresses and strains. The drawing and later solidification of borders in the region was the next step in this process.

The Changing Nature of Land

There was no pressing need for the strict delineation of borders in the Arab Gulf before the discovery of oil. Brauer, for example, conducted an exhaustive and authoritative study into medieval Muslim geography and boundaries and concluded as follows:

> It is not unjust to conclude that geographers...recognized the existence of political boundaries in the sense that as one progressed in a direction away from the center of a state, one would sooner or later pass from one sovereignty to another or that one's taxes would flow to different places on either side of such a division. Yet, clearly in the minds of these cartographers such boundaries were constituted not as sharply defined boundary lines but rather as transition zones of uncertain sovereignty between two states.[19]

Indeed, this is not surprising. Whilst it is sensible to conclude that some notion of a border would be needed for, as Brauer suggests, taxation purposes, the land in and of itself was not the issue. There were no Western-like notions of land being intrinsically important. For example, Roosens puts forward a thesis highlighting the importance in Western culture of "own soil" and "blood and soil" as being constituent parts of a "primordial autochthony...a social category or group of people, based on being born on a well-defined territory from parents and ancestors who are and have been "first occupants."[20] Yet this is far and away from the traditional view of land of those on the Arabian Peninsula who for centuries believed in notions of traditional nomadic rights, as Wilkinson explains.

> The fundamental Islamic injunction concerning nomadic rights, and one which clearly derives from traditions going back into pre-Islamic times and is still the basis of the legal philosophy of nomadic societies in our area today, is the reputed *hadith* (saying of the Prophet) 'Man holds three things in common, water, vegetation (*kala*), and fire.'[21]

Thus, as Wilkinson suggests, those rare pockets of land that were useful and potentially valuable for having water or being able to sustain vegetation were demarcated and respected as common land. Indeed, this fits in perfectly with Brauer's assessment which insinuates no intrinsic value or psychological importance of land in the Arabian Peninsula.

With the discovery of oil, however, the intrinsic value of the land skyrocketed. No longer did it just give vegetation and water, which were to be shared in any case, but now there was potentially untold wealth lying beneath the desert. The need, therefore, to demarcate one's land to the last inch became pressing in case oil or gas was present. This, therefore, negatively affected the possibilities of a tribe removing their labour from the market, as has been described. Overall, therefore, British policies instigating the creation of a separate political consciousness, British actions afforded leaders a firmer grip on power, and there was a growing need to define borders. The confluence of these factors militated, some argue, in a shift from *jus sanguinis* to *jus soli.*

A Shift from *jus sanguinis* to *jus soli*?

Jus sanguinis and *jus soli* are legal terms referring to questions of nationality and citizenship. Safran explains these complex terms.

> Originally, when states were defined in terms of the sovereignty of feudal lords or monarchs, citizenship...applied, according to jus soli, to those who were born on the estate or in the realm; later, when "nation-states" came into being, and the legitimacy of a state was based on the sovereignty of the national (or ethnic) community, jus sanguinis, or the criterion of inherited "blood" connections, became the common operative principle...Generally, jus sanguinis dominates in "historic" states, that is, those which arose out of a preexistent, or pre-political, ethnic or

> "primordial" community, whereas jus soli has been the preferred principle in settler societies, in which the state played a crucial role in forming the nation.[22]

Out-with Safran's legal framework *jus sanguinis* not only applies to the inheritance of nationality through blood connections (i.e. through family and the tribe) but it must also be understood that it suggests that one defines one's self through one's family and that that is where meaning and belonging are found. *Jus soli* implies that aside from obtaining citizenship through being born in a country, the nation state itself is the prime referent for a given person. They think of themselves as being, for example, French, before of their family or of another grouping, such as European, to continue the example.

Wilkinson, however, seeks something of a more nuanced middle-ground and suggests that in any case, "social organization is largely based around notions of territoriality."[23] Thus a clear-cut distinction between the two is not, in fact, realistic. He concludes his thoughts by suggesting that:

> [p]erhaps it…is as dangerous to assume that a notion of *jus soli* has only developed with the modernization of the Gulf as it is to assume that it is more strongly developed among settled peoples because nomadism is an earlier, more primitive state.[24]

The last sentence of Safran's definitions captures the change in the Arab Gulf perfectly. For it is quite clear that these states did indeed rise "out of a preexistent, or ethnic or "primordial" community." The tribal organization of society on the Peninsula goes back to pre-Islamic days and was based on "a lineage type of social organization."[25] This, therefore, insinuates the importance of *jus sanguinis*. Spencer continues and maintains that kin based and kin descendant relationships were, if not present across the entirety of the Peninsula, they were at least present in the form of local loyalties. Quoting O'Leary, Spencer continues to conclude that "It follows that the tribe was conceptually a basic relationship group, tracing its descent from a common ancestor, whether real or fictional, and recognizing close ties of kinship on the basis of this descent."[26]

However, the various actions and actors discussed earlier that fostered the creation of distinct states have led to a shift in this relationship, which fits in perfectly with Safran's definition: "*jus soli* has been the preferred principle in settler societies, in which the state played a crucial role in forming the nation."[27] Indeed, this was exactly what the statelets in the region were trying to do: form a nation. To do this, however, they needed to foster popular legitimacy: if you are going to build a state you need people to look up to it, indentify with it and believe in it. Therefore, thanks to the British 'fossilization' of the political system, the initial demarcation of borders and the initial development of individual political consciousness, the state *begins* to compete with the tribe[28] for loyalty and acquiescence. People *begin* to invest their energies and emotional attachment to and in the state; they enter a continuum where they can see themselves as, for example, Kuwaiti as opposed to of the Al Ghanim tribe. The state, therefore, in these circumstances, *begins* to gain loyalty, legitimacy, and thus power. This is not to say that people 'switched allegiances' overnight; of course this is not the case, as Wilkinson sagely cautions the reader.

> Even today the formal state divisions, which are largely the heritage of the British presence, are still permeated by tribal, clan and family relations, whilst membership and affiliation to commercial, linguistic, religious and ethnic groupings and networks cut across borders and are often still of greater significance than state citizenship.[29]

Nevertheless, around the start of the twentieth century, there was the very beginning of a key change in society itself. There was a challenge to the traditional conception of society as being mediated, ran and thought of as largely kin and tribally based. Another way of conceptualizing and indeed running a society came about. The germination of this idea was further strengthened and exacerbated by subsequent events, especially the dissolution of one of the key relationships in Arab society and the disappearance of its key industry.

All Change

Agriculture was, for obvious reasons, not pervasive in the Arab Gulf. Instead it was the sea that was the focus of economy and employment. Fishing and trading were important activities yet it was pearling that constituted "the main base of the economy in the nineteenth and early twentieth centuries."[30] This industry's effect on society was immense. It employed and took away nearly all able-bodied men for months at a time.[31] It had what amounted to endemic semi-slavery[32] built into it where the workers at the lowest end of the scales (the divers and pullers) had to take a loan off the captain or the local merchant to take care of his family whilst he was away and to cover him and his family for the off season. He paid this loan off by working long hours in dangerous conditions but this was often (90 percent of the time) not enough and, as Al Naqeeb puts it, "a relationship of perpetual indebtedness"[33] ensued. The similarities to slavery continue as this debt was not cancelled on death but had to be paid off by the son of the diver "along with any interest which had accrued from delay in payment."[34] Overall, therefore, Rumaihi concludes by saying that "[T]he running and financing of the pearl industry throughout its history proved to be disastrous socially to various sections of the community."[35] However, as a result of the First World War and the Great Depression which caused a massive drop in demand for the luxury product and the introduction of the cheaper cultured pearl from Japan in the 1930s, the industry was finished. This was a devastating blow for many countries, where the vast majority of men were connected to the pearling industry.

Thus when oil receipts finally arrived (mostly after World War Two) they rescued a region desperate for investment. The filling of the state's coffers to unheard of levels instigated massive changes, which, as will be described, supports the notion of a change from *jus sanguinis* to *jus soli*.

Oil and the Merchants

Oil proved itself to be something of a strange commodity for society in the Arab Gulf as it broke the traditional bond between merchants and the ruling elite. One of the foremost experts on the Gulf in recent years, Jill Crystal, encapsulates the dynamic perfectly.

> These merchant families were the link connecting the monarch to the money he needed...Merchants extracted revenues from pearl divers...and gave a portion of these extracted revenues to the amir through customs dues, pearl boat taxes, and personal loans. Their political power grew from their economic strength. Their ordinary input into decision making derived from the social institutions of marriage and majlis which gave them informal but daily access to the rulers. Their independent strength lay in their control of the mobile pearling and...nomadic work force. In a dispute the merchants would simply leave for friendlier nearby

> ports, taking with them their pearl divers, a sizable segment of the population. Until into the twentieth century, this kind of temporary exit was a powerful check on the amirs.[36]

Crystal continues to differentiate between the situations in different parts of the Gulf. These arguments get distilled into a comparison between Kuwait and Qatar.

Kuwait was a relatively culturally, politically and economically advanced state, indeed it has even been described as the "Marseilles" of the region.[37] This is because it found itself at the cross-roads of international travel and trade where Armenian, Jewish, Russian, Iraqi, Iranian, Syrian, Transjordanian, Indian and other traders from the Far East would come for business. Hence, Kuwait was often referred to as an êntrepot market. In short, the Kuwaiti merchants were successful, relatively rich and, following Crystal's impeccable logic, powerful.

This is in stark comparison to Qatar, which before oil had "never been a mercantile centre of any importance."[38] A generally weaker class of merchants, solely dependent on pearl fishing did not provide its leaders with a large enough tax revenue to warrant a significant say in affairs. Additionally, just before the advent of oil revenues, the country was nearly totally bankrupted with the demise of the pearling industry.[39] Many merchants left the country looking for new pastures and those that stayed had little to no influence over the ruling elite there. Thus, in contrast to the merchants in Kuwait, they could not drive a hard power sharing bargain with the elite when it came to the division of oil wealth.

Even in Kuwait, however, as a rule the merchants could not muscle their way into the oil industry and this is why oil was and is something of a strange business. The traditional middle-men class, the merchants, who had all been so crucial to the leaders and indeed the country in the past, as a whole were now nearly totally cut adrift because of the unique nature of oil extraction. Crystal explains that just about any other industry would require at some stage, "some accommodation between the rulers and the elite who control the work force and extract surplus revenues. Oil does not."[40] Therefore, Crystal concludes:

> The new revenues snapped the link binding the rulers to the merchants. The external nature of oil rents, the enclave nature of the industry, and the size of the boom

> spared rulers the need to extract, through taxation and repression, economic and social resources allocated through other (tribal, religious, but especially mercantile) networks of obligation, freeing the rulers from their historical, economically based dependence on the merchants.[41]

The merchants were further emasculated because of the near collapse of any remaining indigenous handicraft-type industries. Such industries had been suffering for a long time because of the hike in taxes by the ever more sure-footed leaders. Issawi, for example maintains that their decline began as early as the beginnings of the 19th century.[42] Thus with the state coffers filling nicely from oil, when extra European competition put paid to much indigenous industry, the ruling elite did nothing to protect it. Indeed, why would they? After all, they did not need the tax revenues. Socially, this further weakened the merchants as they lost the ability to pressure leaders with a walkout.[43]

Nevertheless, the disappearance of the merchant class must not be over exaggerated. They still – especially in a country like Kuwait – carried some sway. Crystal, for example, suggests that in Kuwait they were the only group "capable of sustained, organized, and possibly successful political opposition to the amir."[44] Thus, rather than seek a confrontation the governments of the region, to greater and lesser degrees, simply bought them off. The merchants swapped varying degrees of historical political oversight power for tacit guarantees of a share in the oil wealth, depending on their previous levels of influence.[45] This meant, therefore, that no longer was the dialogue and interaction only between the merchant class and the elite, as was the case pre-oil, for now with the merchants sidelined, the elite and the ordinary people struck up a relationship to tacitly continue the *jus soli* project.

As a part of creating this new relationship, the ruling families began to emphasize certain aspects of their history. Indeed, they used the very narratives of tribal loyalty to their advantage. The histories of the states became inextricably linked with the ruling families. Crystal sums up some of the measures taken and the reasons behind them.

> [Another] response to the problems of loyalty and control has been a renewed stress on normative socialization...the development of new civic

> myths...cultural heritage, in order to restrict or monopolize the loyalty options of the citizen population. These myths aim at legitimizing the regime through a writing or rewriting of national identity into a form more compatible with the ruler's public image. These histories aim to reconcile the monarchist and tribalist ideologies (of the ruler) with capitalize ideologies (for the merchants) and with welfarist ideologies (for the people).[46]

The naming of Saudi Arabia after the family of the rulers and the famous Kuwaiti adage of 'Kuwait is Al Sabah and Al Sabah is Kuwait' are further examples of the pervasiveness and, it could be argued, effectiveness of these policies.[47]

The Consequences of Fiscal Largesse

In order to attract peoples' loyalties, to further their transition from a tribal society based on *jus sanguinis* to a true modern Westphalian state, the governments of the region engaged in massive sets of distributive policies. The effects of these policies were numerous but the results have been neatly summed up by Crystal: "They [citizens on the Peninsula generally] are today healthier and better housed, educated, and fed than ever before, and they know that the state is directly responsible."[48]

Continuing her excellent summation, Crystal breaks up the effects into two broad categories: state action in social services and employment. As for the former, schools, colleges, universities, hospitals and recreation facilities were all built at quite a rate in the states of the Arab Gulf after the discovery of oil.[49] This must have been nothing short of astounding for a population not even a generation away from the hardships of the pre-oil life and the collapse of pearling. One must not forget too, the literal distribution of land, money and pay rises to citizens on special occasions such as Emir's birthdays, on the ascent to power of a new Emir, on getting married to another citizen, on the birth of your 'pure' child and so on. In terms of employment, the new apparatus of governing that the states were building (i.e. Ministries of Education, Health etc) all needed to be staffed. Thus began the truism that all Gulf nationals are guaranteed a job for life in 'a Ministry' with high wages, a good pension, and preferential treatment.[50] This, however, over time has created graduate expectations of a job for life somewhere in the state apparatus. It is, therefore, a challenge for some governments in the region (notably in Saudi Arabia) to combat this gap between expectation and reality or so called *anomie*.[51] Last but certainly not least is that fact that the citizens of the oil and gas rich states are not taxed by their governments. They get these services and opportunities for free. This is, therefore, the reverse of previous relationships where the citizens were taxed – at times – harshly. Indeed, the situation is about as different and as much of a wholesale change from the state of affairs in the hay-day of pearl fishing as is it possible to imagine.

What do the rulers get in return? Legitimacy and control. None of the countries in the Arab Gulf can be classified as democratic. Therefore, they operate under the principle of no taxation, no representation. As long as the government can keep that particular bargain going the citizens do not show much sign of complaint.[52] These policies are undertaken to tacitly encourage the shift from *jus sanguinis* to *jus soli*: now the state is the provider and bread-winner, not the tribe. Thus, whilst it is important to keep Wilkinson's cautionary note in mind, it is clear that there are numerous methods afoot which engender a shift towards *jus soli*. Indeed, Melikian & Al Easa[53] and Duke Antony[54] are but a few authors who believe that the cumulative effects mentioned throughout this paper have indeed weakened tribal loyalties.

It is worth examining further two aspects making up society which have had and will continue to have a profound affect on this debate.

Education and Ideas

The impact of modernisation thanks to the impetus of oil money has had, as has been demonstrated, numerous effects. Another interesting aspect of the modernisation issue arises when one considers the numbers of Arab nationals being educated abroad and then returning home. Balfour-Paul sums the essence of the problem.

> Can the intellectual elites of the Gulf countries dispatched as so many of them are for higher education in the West, where liberalism, individualism and personal pushfulness are the dominant social motif, accommodate themselves in large numbers on their return to the disciplines of a society which dominant motif is so different, where structure, hierarchies and

> group loyalties are the tradition and nepotism is almost a virtue?[55]

One must be careful not to exaggerate the necessary differences between Western culture and Arab culture and assume an intrinsic incompatibility. Indeed, perhaps it is instructive to look at the recent example of the Qatari government. Since Hamad Al Thani took over from his father in 1995, Qatar has pursued various policies designed to make the country more generally democratic, open and–essentially–different. Elections have been held, the media has been largely freed, they host a huge US Military base, they held the Asian Games, they invited top Universities from America to Doha and embarked upon a new foreign policy of international mediation. In short, these are a truly remarkable set of changes. Indeed, imbued within these changes, one can see what might be described as typically Western traits: democracy, free speech, even marketing. Yet why have they changed to such a course? In short, Qatar wants to distinguish itself from its neighbours, most of whom are culturally, geographically, historically, physically, industrially economically, linguistically, religiously and hereditarily similar.[56] Additionally, it is pursuing these policies to elicit a new form of public legitimacy[57] by – essentially – making Qataris proud to be Qataris; seeing their tiny little state opening up and making a positive impact on the world stage. All of these factors reinforce the shift towards *jus soli* by creating more and more of a different and positive national sense of identity.

Housing

Many authors have discussed the nature of urbanisation on the Arabian Peninsula as well as the changing nature of housing as potentially contributing to social change.[58] Balfour-Paul comes up with a pithy but perfect anecdote which encapsulates the crux of this particular issue. He describes, in 1967 the construction of a new Western style housing complex in Bahrain, built by the Wimpey construction firm. It was a typical (Western) housing development, with the "homogenized 3 bed, 1 sit'" housing unit. These arrangements, however, did not incorporate crucial elements of traditional Arab dwellings into their design. They were thus without "provision for the householder's immemorial *mejlis*, for the accommodation of granny, the widowed aunts and goats, for the open life-style of popular tradition."[59] He finished by commenting that the houses lay ready but empty for some time as presumably people did not want to move to such a relatively alien and culturally incompatible abode.

Indeed, the structure of cities and the rate at which they were populated militates against older, more traditional ways of living. Grill comments that in terms of space, Kuwait did in 10 years what Europe took 150 years to do, all because of the motor that was oil fuelled modernisation.[60] Crucially, however, he quotes Stephens and Hill who describe the changes that urbanisation like this had on society.

> Although there was little historic sentiment...attached to the old city, its destruction and replacement by a new motorised city covering twenty times the former area meant also a blow at the traditional way of life of a close-knit community which had been like that of a medieval town.[61]

Hill Continues,

> A traditional society, organised on the basis of kin grouping but without any pronounced ranking of its sub-groups, has been transformed into a highly structured community based on the economic and political positions occupied by the Kuwaitis.[62]

Such examples of the results of modernisation with a pinch of westernisation clearly actively impede the pursuit of traditional life and thus contribute to a weakening of *jus sanguinis*. For if one can not meet, connect and live with one's family in the traditional setting, considering the vast amount of other weakening forces that have been discussed, there seems to be little chance that *jus sanguinis* can be fostered to the same degree. Moreover, at times it was actually government policy to pursue just this goal. Crystal, for example, discusses the Kuwaiti government and their policies of "weakening the tribes' historical internal social and political cohesion."[63] They did this by mixing clans in housing blocks, giving out housing plots on an individual basis and not to tribes as a group and offering resettlement bonuses if families would resettle in Wimpy-esque 'nuclear family' housing. They did this to boost the Kuwaiti population and gain political patronage from the tribes in the face of the growing Iraqi threat.

Al Naqeeb, writing from an Arab nationalist point of view decries policies such as these and indeed the whole notion of resettling tribes as a way of breaking their traditional bonds. He eloquently but harshly describes these newly co-opted tribes as being "transformed into something resembling a decrepit lumpen proletariat in air-conditioned ghettos on the fringes of the 'metropolitan petroleum cities."[64]

Balfour-Paul too fears the same kind of social disconnection as Al Naqeeb.

> How does the countryman, whether of peasant of bedouin origin, bred to the communal loyalties and personal sense of identity that went with his previous life-style, react to life in a breeze-block cantonment in the suburbs of the depersonalized city to which he has drifted under the lure of industrial wage-scales?"[65]

He cites an example in Abu Dhabi where members of the same tribal grouping were allowed or even encouraged to move e*n masse* to a housing development, but he suggests that this is nothing more than a "minor palliative" that will, in the end, not be able to arrest the decay of traditional values.[66]

Conclusion

Before the advent of the British Empire society appeared to be based on what can most closely be described as *jus sanguinis*. Blood lines, family, kin and the tribe were the most important reference points for people in terms of how they saw each other, how they identified and how they lived more generally. Society was fundamentally based on loyalty to people. British policies, such as the initial demarcation of borders and the creation of notions of political separateness led to the strengthening of the ruling family. All of this combined with the discovery of oil, its pressure to fully solidify borders and the subsequent spurt of development to create the state as a challenger for loyalty and people's suzerainty. Broadly put, people had the option of defining themselves as of their family or of their state. This constitutes a fundamental change in one of the key relationships in society, which has been the same for scores of generations. It can, therefore, be classified as a change of society.

The true depth of this change is difficult to tell and has not been strictly within the remit of this paper, whose goal was confined to identifying such a change. However, examples such as the Qatari case where legitimacy is shifting more and more explicitly onto the government and its actions suggest that in parts of the Arab Gulf, the change is heartfelt. Nevertheless, one must recall Wilkinson and his sage, cautionary advice throughout this paper. He consistently suggests that there is a middle ground. That these two concepts of *jus sanguinis* and *jus soli* are not mutually exclusive and that it is perfectly possible and practical to have the two 'competing' identities side by side. Indeed, this is, as Crystal pointed out, one of the key features of state propaganda; to fit the traditional tribal values into a modern, capitalistic framework.

It appears, therefore, that there is a clear trajectory for Arab society. There are, of course, dissenting voices who seek a return to traditional ways, but they are on the fringes of society and largely in the vast minority. Indeed, there appears to be an ever strengthening confluence of the ruler and the ruled agreeing and tacitly and sometimes explicitly to edge towards *jus soli.*

Notes

1. See, for example, Emmanuelle Landais, "Burj Cranes of Dubai," *Gulf News*, 13th May 2006. Or Oxford Business Report, "Dubai: 2007" *Oxford Business Group,* 1st September 2008 (v. 3, No.1) p. 155.
2. Stephen C. Pepper, "The Boundaries of Society," *International Journal of Ethics* 32, No. 4 (1922): p. 420.
3. Ibid., p. 421.
4. Glen Balfour-Paul, "The Impact of Development on Gulf Society," in *The Impact of Oil Revenues on Arab Gulf Development*, ed. M. S. El Azhary (London: Croom Helm, 1984), p. 187.
5. See Frank Stoakes, "The Arabian Peninsula : Society and Politics," in *The Arabian Peninsula : Society and Politics*, ed. Derek Hopwood (London: Allen and Unwin 1972), p. 189.
6. Muhammad T. Sadiq and William P. Snavely, *Bahrain, Qatar, and the United Arab Emirates: Colonial Past, Present Problems, and Future Prospects* (Lexington, Mass.: Lexington Books, 1972), p. 103.
7. Ibn Khaldun, *The Muqaddimah, an Introduction to History*, trans. Franz Rosenthal, Bollingen Series ([Princeton, N.J.]: Princeton University Press, 1969), pp. 134-138.
8. Ibid., p. 137.
9. Khaldoun Hasan Naqeeb, *Society and State in the Gulf and Arab Peninsula: A Different Perspective* (London: Routledge, and the Centre for Arab Unity Studies, 1990), p. 59. Ibn Khaldun also

discusses how injustice such as the "unjustified imposition of tasks and the use of the subjects for forced labour" can lead to the ruin of civilization. Khaldun, *The Muqaddimah, an Introduction to History*, pp. 238-42.

10. Jill Crystal, "Coalitions in Oil Monarchies: Kuwait and Qatar," *Comparative Politics* 21, No. 4 (1989): p. 429.
11. Rosemarie Said Zahlan, *The Making of the Modern Gulf States: Kuwait, Bahrain, Qatar, the United Arab Emirates and Oman*, Updated ed. (Reading: Ithaca Press, 1998), p. 22.
12. For example, two of the most important treaties were the treaty of Perpetual Peace signed in 1853 and the Trucial States agreement in 1869 and 1892.
13. Naqeeb, *Society and State in the Gulf and Arab Peninsula: A Different Perspective*, p. 59.
14. Glen Balfour-Paul, "Kuwait, Qatar and the United Arab Emirates: Political and Social Evolution," in *Arabia and the Gulf : From Traditional Society to Modern States : Essays in Honour of M.A. Shaban's 60th Birthday (16th November 1986)*, ed. Ian Richard Netton and M. A. Shaban (London: Croom Helm, 1986), p. 157.
15. Naqeeb, *Society and State in the Gulf and Arab Peninsula: A Different Perspective*, p.59.
16. Zahlan, *The Making of the Modern Gulf States: Kuwait, Bahrain, Qatar, the United Arab Emirates and Oman*, p.14.
17. Naqeeb, *Society and State in the Gulf and Arab Peninsula: A Different Perspective*, p. 60.
18. See Crystal, "Coalitions in Oil Monarchies: Kuwait and Qatar," p. 434. For a more detailed discussion of this.
19. Ralph W. Brauer, "Boundaries and Frontiers in Medieval Muslim Geography," *Transactions of the American Philosophical Society* 85, No. 6 (1995): p. 5.
20. Eugeen Roosens, "National Identity, Social Order and Political System in Western Europe: Primordial Autochthony," in *Societies, Corporations and the Nation State*, ed. Erwin K Scheuch and David Sciulli (Brill Academic Publishers, 1990), p. 162.
21. John C. Wilkinson, "Traditional Concepts of Territory in South East Arabia," *The Geographical Journal* 149, no. 3 (1983): p. 303.
22. William Safran, "Citizenship and Nationality in Democratic

Systems: Approaches to Defining and Acquiring Membership in the Political Community," *International Political Science Review/Revue internationale de science politique* 18, No. 3 (1997): p. 314.

23. Wilkinson, "Traditional Concepts of Territory in South East Arabia," p. 301.
24. Ibid.: p. 302.
25. Robert F. Spencer, "The Arabian Matriarchate: An Old Controversy," *Southwestern Journal of Anthropology* 8, No. 4 (1952): p. 481.
26. Ibid.: p.483.
27. Safran, "Citizenship and Nationality in Democratic Systems: Approaches to Defining and Acquiring Membership in the Political Community," p. 314.
28. Or, indeed, any other form of supra-individual group to which people may belong.
29. John C. Wilkinson, *Arabia's Frontiers: The Story of Britain's Blue and Violet Lines* (London: Tauris, 1991), p. 29.
30. Mohamed G Rumaihi, "The Mode of Production in the Arab Gulf before the Discovery of Oil," in *Social and Economic Development in the Arab Gulf*, ed. Tim Niblock (London: Croom Helm, 1980), p. 52.
31. Zahlan, *The Making of the Modern Gulf States: Kuwait, Bahrain, Qatar, the United Arab Emirates and Oman*, p. 5.
32. Rumaihi quotes Harrison as testifying to the slave like nature of pearling. See M.G. Harrison *The Arabs at Home* (Thomas T Crowell Co., New York, 1924), p.80 in Mohamed G Rumaihi 'The Mode of Production in the Arab Gulf Before the Discovery of Oil' in Tim Niblock, *Social and Economic Development in the Arab Gulf* (London: Croom Helm, 1980), p. 60.
33. Naqeeb, *Society and State in the Gulf and Arab Peninsula: A Different Perspective*, p. 57.
34. Ibid.
35. Rumaihi, "The Mode of Production in the Arab Gulf before the Discovery of Oil," p. 54.
36. Crystal, "Coalitions in Oil Monarchies: Kuwait and Qatar," p. 429.
37. Jacob Goldberg, *The Foreign Policy of Saudi Arabia: The Formative Years, 1902-1918*, Harvard Middle Eastern Studies (Cambridge, Mass: Harvard University Press, 1986), p. 31.

38. John Duke Anthony, *Arab States of the Lower Gulf: People, Politics, Petroleum*, The James Terry Duce Memorial Series (Washington: Middle East Institute, 1975), p. 80.
39. Crystal, "Coalitions in Oil Monarchies: Kuwait and Qatar," p. 429. And Saif Marzooq Shamlan, *Pearling in the Arabian Gulf : A Kuwaiti Memoir* (London: London Center for Arabic Studies, 2000). For an excellent account of pearling generally and in Kuwait specifically.
40. Crystal, "Coalitions in Oil Monarchies: Kuwait and Qatar," p. 433.
41. Ibid., p. 430.
42. Although Issawi is specifically referring to Egypt in this example, similar changes were afoot in the Peninsula and thus a comparison is applicable. Charles Philip Issawi, *An Economic History of the Middle East and North Africa*, The Columbia Economic History of the Modern World. (New York: Columbia University Press, 1982), p. 2.
43. Crystal, "Coalitions in Oil Monarchies: Kuwait and Qatar," p. 434.
44. Ibid., p. 433.
45. Ibid, Issawi, *An Economic History of the Middle East and North Africa.*
46. Jill Crystal, *Oil and Politics in the Gulf: Rulers and Merchants in Kuwait and Qatar*, Cambridge Middle East Library (Cambridge: Cambridge University Press, 1995), p. 193.
47. Zahlan, *The Making of the Modern Gulf States: Kuwait, Bahrain, Qatar, the United Arab Emirates and Oman*, p. 95.
48. Crystal, "Coalitions in Oil Monarchies: Kuwait and Qatar."
49. See, for example, Sadiq and Snavely, *Bahrain, Qatar, and the United Arab Emirates : Colonial Past, Present Problems, and Future Prospects*, pp. 62-111. For a through recap of statistics relating to many facets of society.
50. Crystal, "Coalitions in Oil Monarchies: Kuwait and Qatar," p. 434.
51. Balfour-Paul, "The Impact of Development on Gulf Society," p. 189.
52. Crystal, *Oil and Politics in the Gulf: Rulers and Merchants in Kuwait and Qatar*, p. 191.
53. Levon H Melikian and Juhaina S Al-Easa, "Oil and Social Change in the Gulf," *Journal of Arab Affairs* 1, No. 1 (1980):

p. 82.

54. Anthony, *Arab States of the Lower Gulf: People, Politics, Petroleum*, p. 11.
55 Balfour-Paul, "The Impact of Development on Gulf Society," p. 189.
56. Andrew Rathmell and Kirsten Schulze, "Political Reform in the Gulf: The Case of Qatar," *Middle Eastern Studies* 36, No. 4 (2000): p. 53.
57. See J. E. Peterson, "Qatar and the World: Branding for a Micro-State," *The Middle East Journal* 60 (2006). For an excellent discussion of the reasons behind Qatar's recent foreign policy changes.
58. See N. C. Grill, *Urbanisation in the Arabian Peninsula*, Occasional Papers Series (University of Durham. Centre for Middle Eastern and Islamic Studies) (Durham: Univ. of Durham, 1984). For a thorough discussion of urbanization on the peninsula and, for example, Balfour-Paul, "The Impact of Development on Gulf Society," pp. 187-88.Or, Crystal, *Oil and Politics in the Gulf : Rulers and Merchants in Kuwait and Qatar*, pp.88-89. For a discussion of housing as a means to threaten traditional tribal unity.
59. Balfour-Paul, "The Impact of Development on Gulf Society," p. 188.
60. Grill, *Urbanization in the Arabian Peninsula*, p. 41.
61. R Stephens *The Arabs New Frontier*, London (1976) in Ibid.
62. A.G. Hill 'Segregation in Kuwait' 123-142 in Clark, B and Gleave, M (ed) *Social Patterns in Cities*, IBG Special Publication No.5 in Ibid., pp. 45-47.
63. Crystal, *Oil and Politics in the Gulf: Rulers and Merchants in Kuwait and Qatar*, pp. 88-89.
64. Naqeeb, *Society and State in the Gulf and Arab Peninsula: A Different Perspective*, p. 91.
65. Balfour-Paul, "The Impact of Development on Gulf Society," p. 188.
66. Ibid.

References

Anthony, John Duke. *Arab States of the Lower Gulf: People, Politics, Petroleum*, The James Terry Duce Memorial Series. Washington: Middle East Institute, 1975.

Balfour-Paul, Glen. "The Impact of Development on Gulf Society." In *The Impact of Oil Revenues on Arab Gulf Development*, edited by M. S. El Azhary. London: Croom Helm, 1984.

——. "Kuwait, Qatar and the United Arab Emirates: Political and Social Evolution." In *Arabia and the Gulf: From Traditional Society to Modern States: Essays in Honour of M.A. Shaban's 60th Birthday (16th November 1986)*, edited by Ian Richard Netton and M. A. Shaban. London: Croom Helm, 1986.

Brauer, Ralph W. "Boundaries and Frontiers in Medieval Muslim Geography." *Transactions of the American Philosophical Society* 85, No. 6 (1995): 1-73.

Crystal, Jill. "Coalitions in Oil Monarchies: Kuwait and Qatar." *Comparative Politics* 21, no. 4 (1989): 427-43.

——. *Oil and Politics in the Gulf: Rulers and Merchants in Kuwait and Qatar*, Cambridge Middle East Library. Cambridge: Cambridge University Press, 1995.

Goldberg, Jacob. *The Foreign Policy of Saudi Arabia: The Formative Years, 1902-1918*, Harvard Middle Eastern Studies. Cambridge, Mass: Harvard University Press, 1986.

Grill, N. C. *Urbanisation in the Arabian Peninsula*, Occasional Papers Series (University of Durham. Centre for Middle Eastern and Islamic Studies). Durham: Univ. of Durham, 1984.

Issawi, Charles Philip. *An Economic History of the Middle East and North Africa*, The Columbia Economic History of the Modern World. New York: Columbia University Press, 1982.

Khaldun, Ibn. *The Muqaddimah, an Introduction to History*. Translated by Franz Rosenthal, Bollingen Series. [Princeton, N.J.]: Princeton University Press, 1969.

Landais, Emmanuelle "Burj Cranes of Dubai." *Gulf News*, 13th May 2006.

Melikian, Levon H , and Juhaina S Al-Easa. "Oil and Social Change in the Gulf." *Journal of Arab Affairs* 1, no. 1 (1980): 79-98.

Naqeeb, Khaldoun Hasan. *Society and State in the Gulf and Arab Peninsula : A Different Perspective*. London: Routledge, and the Centre for Arab Unity Studies, 1990.

Niblock, Tim. *Social and Economic Development in the Arab Gulf.* London: Croom Helm, 1980.

Pepper, Stephen C. "The Boundaries of Society." *International Journal of Ethics* 32, No. 4 (1922): 420-41.

Peterson, J. E. "Qatar and the World: Branding for a Micro-State." *The Middle East Journal* 60 (2006): 732-48.

Rathmell, Andrew, and Kirsten Schulze. "Political Reform in the Gulf: The Case of Qatar." *Middle Eastern Studies* 36, No. 4 (2000): 47-62.

Roosens, Eugeen. "National Identity, Social Order and Political System in Western Europe: Primordial Autochthony." In *Societies, Corporations and the Nation State*, edited by Erwin K Scheuch and David Sciulli: Brill Academic Publishers, 1990.

Rumaihi, Mohamed G. "The Mode of Production in the Arab Gulf before the Discovery of Oil." In *Social and Economic Development in the Arab Gulf*, edited by Tim Niblock. London: Croom Helm, 1980.

Sadiq, Muhammad T., and William P. Snavely. *Bahrain, Qatar, and the United Arab Emirates : Colonial Past, Present Problems, and Future Prospects*. Lexington, Mass.: Lexington Books, 1972.

Safran, William. "Citizenship and Nationality in Democratic Systems: Approaches to Defining and Acquiring Membership in the Political Community." *International Political Science Review / Revue internationale de science politique* 18, No. 3 (1997): 313-35.

Shamlan, Saif Marzooq. *Pearling in the Arabian Gulf: A Kuwaiti Memoir*. London: London Center for Arabic Studies, 2000.

Spencer, Robert F. "The Arabian Matriarchate: An Old Controversy." *Southwestern Journal of Anthropology* 8, No. 4 (1952): 478-502.

Stoakes, Frank. "The Arabian Peninsula : Society and Politics." In *The Arabian Peninsula: Society and Politics*, edited by Derek Hopwood. London: Allen and Unwin, 1972.

Wilkinson, John C. *Arabia's Frontiers: The Story of Britain's Blue and Violet Lines*. London: Tauris, 1991.

——. "Traditional Concepts of Territory in South East Arabia." *The Geographical Journal* 149, No. 3 (1983): 301-15.

Zahlan, Rosemarie Said. *The Making of the Modern Gulf States: Kuwait, Bahrain, Qatar, the United Arab Emirates and Oman*. Updated ed. Reading: Ithaca Press, 1998.

3

A Note on Transformations of Gulf Societies in the Neoliberal Context

A.K. Ramakrishnan

The directions of change in the Gulf need to be understood not only in specific realms of society and state as separate entities, but also in the state-society linkages and dynamics. The purpose of this piece is to situate the changes that the Gulf societies are undergoing particularly within the terrains of such linkages in the context of neoliberal globalisation.

Neoliberal Transformations

If neoliberal ideology in general envisages the predominance of non-state actors like markets in everyday life while viewing the role of the state as intrinsically parasitical, it has not been successful in sidelining the state from various domains of Gulf life. Fox and others even suggest that "values clearly contrary to maximizing profit guide the normative behaviors in society and governmental policy and practice".[1] The attempt at claiming state resources has not gone down in any substantial manner. Rather, intermediaries enabling the realization of such resource seeking have prospered. An interesting study by Hertog points out that

> rentier states...tend to be characterized by an imbalance of resources between state and society. The relative abundance of state resources gives societal actors strong incentives to seek access to them. Because rentier state bureaucracies are relatively inaccessible through conventional administrative channels, societal actors seek alternative ways of tapping state resources. These are provided by "brokers," intermediaries who hold privileged positions and can make such resources available to nationals and foreigners who are not as well connected. Such brokers are a defining feature of state-society relations in rentier states.[2]

The very influence of brokers in Gulf societies denote the salient state function that obviously is not having a one-to-one relationship with its citizens as the region had before in a tribal setting. The distance of ruling sheikhs from the ruled and the continued invoking of tribal past in various legitimation exercises show new cleavages within the system. The rent-accumulating state grew both in its day-to-day functions and in its regulatory capacity. The neoliberal moment was captured by the state to optimize its provider role not by undermining traditional roles or market operations, but by avoiding a state-market disjuncture.

Studies about cities world over and the Gulf in particular throw new light on how contemporary globalization is engrained in and transacted through such nodes of capital, knowledge and cultural flows. The way cities like Dubai transformed itself with spectacular consumption inducements and showcasing of malls and exhibitions oriented to lure than to belong creates innumerable contradictions for those who live in these cities and for those who spent some time there.

The migrant worker, the local population and the visitor confront the spectacle of cities like Dubai in different perspectives that imagine the city-space as if one is taking part in an obsessive contestation, where some involve with huge resources and some others just as spectators. The transformation of Dubai is well captured in the two relevant chapters of this book, where both the historical and the contemporary changes are discussed. The contrasting nature of cities in the Gulf with other world cities is also important to note. If most world cities are constituted around advanced producer services, the Gulf cities are mostly based on migrant flows.[3] Yet, there are many claims of success of the Dubai model, in spite of all the tensions between the old and the new, the national and the expatriate, abundance and deprivation, the worker and the consumer, and above all tension between an economy of single resource and the requirement of diversification. As Kanna observes,

> More specifically, neoliberal is the *mithal* [model]. The fusion of neoliberalism with Dubai's unique national character emancipates the city-state from its "mere" Arabness, creating in the process an emergent Dubai identity both Arab and post-Arab or multinational.[4]

Thus, Dubai emerges as a global city in its economy of resource and labour flows as well as in its politico-cultural projection -- an endeavour many other Gulf cities wish to emulate. Kanna speaks about how "notions such as national or Arab identity became a space of ambivalence".[5] In a city like Dubai, "neoliberal ideology has come to play a central role in mediating ambivalences many locals...feel in relations to Arab identity".[6]

Diasporic Transformations

Most studies on migration to the Gulf have been concentrating on the economic aspect of the phenomenon. It is also important to note the social, cultural and political significance of the migration process. One of the studies on migration to the Gulf reaches the following conclusions on the emerging trends:

> In the years to come, in all the GCC states the employment of the nationals and the labor migration will remain politically a very sensitive issue as it will cause further tensions between the profit-driven concerns of the private sector, the indigenization efforts of the states and the national security considerations. Moreover, a large number of foreigners residing in these countries will bring new social and cultural challenges of consequences difficult to estimate, especially as the naturalization of many foreigners will take place. Asians will continue to dominate the foreign workforce at the expense of the non-Gulf Arab labor.[7]

A few Gulf migrants from Kerala publish a journal named "Moonnamidam" (Third Space) in the Malayalam language. This sort of cultural endeavour in the Gulf seeks to engage the migrant worker with the literary and intellectual production of both the home and host societies. This new space is not only of migration per se, but also of new creativity. The new cultural interface between the Gulf and the migrants seeks to capture contemporary realities of pain and pleasure and imaginative possibilities in the place of one's work. This sort of third space is about a reimagination of everyday life in the diasporic environment.

At the level of religious life, both the migrant and the local communities are compelled to recognise the multicultural character of one's own religion. As a study of transnational Islam puts it, "in the migratory or global city, Islam is forced to contend not only with a vast array of non-Islamic others but also with an enormous diversity of Muslim opinion as to the nature and meaning of Islam." Such a space also creates opportunities for interrogating authenticity that one ascribed to one's own received notions and provide "forums in which complex negotiations of Muslim identity take place today".[8] The implications of multiple encounters of diversely lived religion impact not only the migratory space, but also the home societies of the migrant community. In short, transnational religious practices are being localised in Gulf social spaces as well as in places of migrant's origin.

Civil Society, State and Citizenship

There obviously is an urge for democratisation of the Gulf in the civil society. The new media including the Internet, satellite channels like Al-Jazeera, and the social networking sites paved the way for the evolving of a transnational Arab public sphere that enables citizens to engage in critical discussions irrespective of the nature of regimes under which they live. It also means the very concept of citizenship and the notions of rights are undergoing some significant re-visioning. Such a recapturing of citizenship means a realisation of the deeply contrasting political situation wherein there is a consciousness about democracy but there is a clear lack of the very conditions and infrastructure of democratic transformation. There is also the international and regional environment that pulls things in different directions as far as civil society-state interaction is concerned. The emergence of a transnational sphere of politico-cultural engagement redraws a major realm of traditional political articulation with newly infused critical content. The direction this would lead the society is not yet clear. Some schisms in the state-society linkages of the old kind are visible, but a full-throated claim for change has not emerged yet wherein a redrawing of the political terrain in terms of a new social contract would be imagined.

This quest for democratic transformation in the immediate future from the society on the one hand and the Gulf regimes' interest and inclination for a slow and calibrated evolutionary change on the other are not merely a matter of temporal inconsistency between the rulers and the ruled. It involves a social push for change and a regime pull that refuses to alter the fundamentals of monarchic political order.

The notion of civil society is integrally linked with conceptions of identity and citizenship. This author has argued elsewhere that the diverse and layered identities that contemporary societies enable citizens to possess have not been fully asserted in most West Asian cases as there are still arenas of citizenship that are not allowed to be legitimately expressed. The limitations imposed on the articulation of multiplicity of identities denote the restricted terrain within which civil societies operate in West Asia.[9] The citizens of the Gulf face new dilemmas of identity and cultural values in the sense of coping tradition with fast changing dynamics of neoliberal globalization. Fox and others note that "globalization in the Gulf meshes with traditionalism rather than being an imported package of lifestyle and values".[10]

Politically, the Gulf states are not only ruled by a monarchical system in the temporal sense but also led by a ruling family value system. This politico-cultural mix of governance is a significant marker of the Gulf polity. As Dresch explains, each dynastic ruler of GCC countries makes "the principle of family rule explicit and the people of these states share a place in the world system that intersects with conceptions of moral order, which rulers in turn claim always to uphold".[11] The way such a genealogical moral world now enacts itself with neoliberal transformations is an interesting phenomenon to look into.

The monarchies have moved from personalised rule to complex web of state-citizen interaction. The production of hegemonic values that reproduces the system has to come from newer sources. A provider state with enough entrepreneurial freedom and an offer of paternalist security in place of democratic citizenship with full secular rights might serve the legitimation requirements of the ruling apparatus for a given period of time. What cannot be assured is the way citizens can respond politically given the unsettling of traditional moral order in the context of new technologies of everyday interaction that radically alter the nature of citizens' engagement among themselves and their interaction with migrant communities and the rest of the world.

Notes

1. John W. Fox, Nada Mourtada-Sabbah, and Mohammed Al-Mutawa, "The Arab Gulf Region: Traditionalism Globalized or Globalization Traditionalized?" in John W. Fox, Nada

Mourtada-Sabbah, and Mohammed Al-Mutawa, (eds.) *Globalization and the Gulf,* (London: Routledge, 2006), p. 9.
2. Steffen Hertog, "The Sociology of the Gulf Rentier Systems: Societies of Intermediaries", *Comparative Studies in Society and History* 52(2), 2010, pp. 282-83.
3. Edward J. Malecki and Michael C. Ewers, "Labor Migration to World Cities: With a Research Agenda for the Arab Gulf", *Progress in Human Geography* 31(4), 2007, p. 479.
4. Ahamd Kanna, "Making Cadres of the "City-Corporation": Cultural and Identity Politics in Neoliberal Dubai", *Review of Middle East Studies* 43(2), 2009, p. 211.
5. Ibid., p. 208.
6. Ibid.
7. Andrzej Kapiszewski, "Arab versus Asian Migrant Workers in the GCC Countries", Paper presented at the United Nations Expert Group Meeting on International Migration and Development in the Arab Region, Population Division, Department of Economic and Social Affairs, United Nations Secretariat, Beirut, 15-17 May 2006.
8. Peter Mandaville, *Transnational Muslim Politics: Reimagining the Umma* (London: Routledge, 2004), p. 107.
9. A.K. Ramakrishnan, "Politics of Civil Society in West Asia" in Sujata Aishwarya Cheema (ed.), *West Asia: Civil Society, Democracy and State* (New Delhi: New Century Publications, 2010).
10. Fox and others, note:1, p. 9.
11. Paul Dresch, "Introduction: Societies, Identities and Global Issues", in Paul Dresch and James Piscatori (eds.), *Monarchies and Nations: Globalisation and Identity in the Arab States of the Gulf* (London: I.B.Tauris, 2005), p. 4.

4

Responding to the Challenge of Change

Rushda A. Siddiqui

A wave of change has engulfed the Arab states of the Persian Gulf since the 1960s, when oil first started giving the states a break from poverty and socio-political marginalization. Since then, the variables of change for the region increased and changed in dimensions to include religion, the political, economic and military involvement of external powers in fostering socio-political change in the region, and the change in the domestic socio-economic situation that seeks political change. If the society has turned to the concepts of democratization, religion or political liberalisation to respond to the changes they face, the state in each case has faced a bigger challenge and its responses have matched the magnitude of each challenge. For the state the challenges included managing domestic socio-political and economic changes, along with coping with the emerging challenges of the regional and international dynamics.

There are two levels at which the oil wealth changed the dynamics of change in the Arab Gulf. Firstly, with the first flush of the power of the petro-dollar, in the 1973 Arab-Israeli conflict, the Arab-Arab, and Muslim-Muslim equations in the region underwent a sea-change. The regional centre of power and the pivots of change shifted from Egypt, Lebanon, Syria and Turkey to the Arab Gulf. The regional power dynamics shifted to the Arab Gulf. And as the Arab Gulf was now seen as the new financer of the Arab Israeli conflict, as well as the local aid giver to the underprivileged populations in the region. The external powers re-designed their foreign policies according to the shift in the power equations. Their priorities changed from securing the Suez, to ensuring that they do not suffer an oil blockade again. This reflected in the non-state movements too. Due to the official backing of the House of Saud, the Wahhabis grew to becoming the most influential school of sunni thought. While on the one hand the Muslim Brotherhood was suppressed and was undergoing a transformation under pressure to be more pliant, the Wahhabis were getting a free hand to expand and grow.

The second level of change in the Arab Gulf lay in the domestic socio-political dynamics of change. The rentier economy was instrumental in re-moulding the state society equations. As the state stopped taxing, and started maintaining its citizens, it was easy for the ruling elite to buy the society into conforming to its ideals, expectations and ethos. The result was the closer bonding between the Western political elites and the elites of the Arab Gulf. This helped the Gulf elites to retain the feudal political and social hierarchy, with an external support that was not coercive. The governments in the region could readily buy an opposition rather than crush it as the other governments in the region do.

The rentier economy is also responsible for the difference in the level of state formations in the region. While in the other societies, colonisation had smashed the existing political and economic equations of feudalism and replaced them with partly western models of polities, the Arab Gulf states were allowed to retain their feudal polities, structures and systems. While the other states were changing from colonial to post-colonial, and later attempting to either imitate socialist governments or experiment with partly liberal ideologies, the Arab Gulf was strengthening its own feudal structures. It fomented the asymmetries within the polities of the region.

As a result, the challenges of change for the governments of the Arab Gulf states have been as diverse and plenty. They had to counter the sunni society from turning into an Islamist inspired movement that would seek a welfare state like the societies of Egypt and others who were getting inspired by the social welfare model of the Muslim Brotherhood. They had to guard against the changes, which a country like Iraq could undergo. After the discovery and exploitation of oil as a resource, Iraq underwent a series of socio-political transformation that led to it developing into a socialist, one party, authoritarian, military dictatorship. It had started incorporating elements of democracy as a feature of governance, which however was a one party democracy. Iraq incorporated elements of suppression and co-option to not allow a religion based movement to emerge within the country. After the centralization of power in one place in Iraq, it became imperative for the other countries to drive a socio-political wedge between the Gulf region and the rest of West Asia.

The second time the region had to guard against change was with the success of the Iranian revolution. It was an eye opener for a typical rentier economy with a social welfare agenda, that it could be overthrown and replaced by an alternative state formation with ease. For the governments to stay in power they needed to condition the society into complacency and establish mechanisms that would separate their society from the rest of the world.

However, it is the tense Israel-Palestinian relations that till the turn of the millennium were the key element in defining the dynamics of change in the region. For the rentier governments in the Arab Gulf, despite their ability to provide economic security to their own people, the creation of Israel and the subsequent regional conflicts changed the dynamics of socio-political equations within their countries. At one level, they needed to take on the leadership role in the fight against Israel. At the second level, they needed to keep power equations between the Islamists from the rest of the region (particularly the Ikhwan al-Muslimin) and themselves, tilted in their favour.

Though oil, the presence of western military forces and the dominance of western financial institutions have been important external challenges in the region, it is the management of the Israeli-Palestinian dispute that has been the most important of all. With the declaration of a war on terror, and the subsequent occupation of Afghanistan and Iraq by the US and allied forces, the focus of attention of the Islamists, the governments and societies shifted momentarily, it is the Israel-Palestine conflict that has been the testing point for relations between the Arab Gulf governments and the United States.

The Arab Gulf States

For purposes of analysis it is useful to view the Arab states of the Persian Gulf as a group because they share similar economies and a similar culture. The social formation of the Arab Gulf, prior to the discovery of oil wealth, has been described variously as 'pre-modern', 'patriarchal feudal', 'nomadic tribal or Bedouin'. Like the rest of the region, these states too faced a political and economic transition from the decline of the Ottoman Empire to the rise and decline of the European powers in the region. The Arabs of the Persian Gulf have strong ethnic affinity to the Arabs in the rest of West Asia and North Africa. The affinities have spread from race to religion to language to culture and finally to history. Though Iraq too is an Arab state that can be put within the ambit of being an Arab state within the Persian Gulf, it has not managed to make it to the club of the Gulf Co-operation Council, despite strong historical and social similarities. For a start, Iraq does not have a government by hereditary monarchy. Also, the linkages between Iraq and the rest of West Asia and North Africa does not allow for its inclusion in this category for the purposes of this article.

The region has known to be oil rich, it was after the shift of the European industries to oil as a fuel, that the economic dynamics of the region changed. Till the end of the Second World War, coal had been the primary source of energy that fueled economic modernization. With the global shift in focus from coal to oil as the major source of energy, the dynamics of political equations between the ruling elites and the societies within the boundaries of a nation state underwent major transformation. The equation between the Arabs of the Persian Gulf and the states and societies in the region of West Asia and North Africa also changed in tune with this development. Most importantly, it released a new dynamics of socio-political equations between the Arabs of the Persian Gulf and the rest of the world.

A study of the society within the parameters of socio-economic and political shows uniqueness, that sets it apart from even its neighbours in the rest of West Asia and North Africa. In the last several decades, since the end of the Second World War, and the discovery of the use of oil as an economic resource, have these states been confronted with the enormous challenge of developing economically while preserving social integrity, and with balancing quasi-traditional political systems with greatly enhanced regional and international responsibilities. Oil and pearls are the two main economic resources in the region. The increase in the global demand for oil as a source of energy transformed the economic character of the region in the 1950s and the 1960s, and by the 1970s, it was in a position to give the region significant global political and economic clout.

State Formation in the Arab Gulf

To study the changes that the Arab Gulf faces today, one needs to go back in history. However, the history would need to be limited to the policies of the Europeans in the region from the fall of the

Ottoman Empire. The Arab Gulf that we see today, as well as West Asia and North Africa, are still reconciling to the legacy and policies of Western imperialism. On the basis of improved technology in agriculture and industry, the Europeans were able to build up enough military capability, along with economic strength, to challenge the Ottomans in the eighteenth century. By 1800, France, England, Holland, Spain and Austria, all had managed to wring benefits and privileges through treaties with the Ottomans. The ascendancy of European economic penetration leading to later political interference was the crucial factor that altered the relations between the Ottomans and its provinces in the region.

• The uniqueness of European colonialism lay in the fact that it changed the entire fabric of society, polity and economy. As a result, the region did not see a transition from feudalism to capitalism in the stages that the West underwent. The sequence did not follow the pattern of an economic development or modernization, followed by a gradual political and social transition to liberalism. As the critics of the theory of Modernization would point out, colonization thrust the concept of socio-political and economic liberalism on the region.

Colonial legacies refer to the impact or the aftermath of the economic, political, social and legal structures and management techniques the countries inherited at the time of their independence. The importance of these legacies lies in the fact that the structures and systems that the colonisers created remained with the governments that succeeded them. The colony was getting re-integrated with global systems, but on the same terms and conditions, as the colonisers had wanted it. In the 1980s, the Marxist school came up with a new term for the process and called it neo-colonialism. Through this framework they have been able to explain the reason for the regressive economic and political growth in the region, which subsequently led to a skewed social growth.

Colonization took place at different levels of society, economy and polity affecting the peasants, the urban masses and the local elites. It changed their essential character and redefined their roles in society and state. It also created its own class of administrators, and urban and rural sections which would assist it in enforcing the colonial legacies. It gave the region artificial boundaries, and made them into nation states, each with a national identity of its own. In many cases, the borders of the colonies had been set by colonial powers with little regard for ethnicity and history. The old structures and systems were completely destroyed, and those that survived the destruction fell into the trap of marginalization and neglect to the extent that they were unable to cope with the changing systems without adapting to them.

> Invariably, the colonial mechanism was a centralized bureaucracy in alliance with wealthy merchants, large land owners and tribal sheikhs (chiefs), and linked the economies of the occupied countries to their own. To realize the linkage, the European powers monopolized foreign trade as well as the supply and management of public utilities. They also tied the local currencies and foreign trade earnings to their central banking system.[1]

Halim Barakat argues that Western intervention in the domestic politics of the region was a process started by the British in the 1800s, has now reached a peak whereby the United States is able to become the largest domestic player. With the passage of time the Western interventional has become the single most dominant variable for change in the region.

> Meddling in Arab affairs by European powers, and later by the United States accelerated after Britain dishonoured her World War I pledges. Instead of permitting Arab unity, Britain issued the Balfour Declaration, which promised a homeland for the Jews in Palestine, and the Sykes-Picot Agreement, which led to the partitioning of geographical Syria into British and French spheres of control. The subsequent period saw further attempts to establish fragmented pieces of Arab world as separate states. These states were based on the Western Orientalist "mosaic" perception: they define as "national" constituents a few subgroups in Arab society. For example, states were proposed for Alawites and Druze in Syria, Berbers in North Africa and Kurds in Iraq. New states, such as Israel were created. Parts of one country were annexed to another (for example, Iskenderun to Turkey). Certain communities were imposed on others within the same country (for example, the Maronites in Lebanon).[2]

Western scholarship till date is accused to support and propagate the concept of mosaic states and mosaic societies. It is understood by analysts as a tool to fragment the region politically and socially. The ideas of conflicts within society are understood as in-built and inherent. As a result, most policy makers from the West seek solution to the political and social problems in the region, in the tools of management.

The Regional Challenges

The biggest challenge of change that the region faces, that is largely a carryover of its history, is the challenge of the changing West. Western scholarship and understanding of the region has been in terms of grouping various aspects of society, history, geography, and polity of the region, and being selective in the understanding of the subject. The broader prism within which the region is evaluated is economic, whereby the Arab Gulf, becomes a rentier economy. Rentierism is supposed to be the primary reason why the region has failed to develop foundations for democracy, or reasonable civil society institutions. The lack of accountability of government expenditure and the lack of demand for it are supposed to be the two major indicators of an economy dominating the socio-political developments in the region.

Another framework within which the events and the state and social formations of the region is analysed is using the dynamics of religion. Islam, being the dominant religion, and since the time of European colonization, the only vent for socio-political and economic grievances in the region, is understood as a fission causing variable. The Wahhabi variant of Sunni Islam, Shiism and Sufiism in the region, are all understood to have a potential for being radical, regressive, and with little tolerance either for each other or for any other religion. With the built-in fundamentalism within Wahhabism and the rise of Osama bin Laden, the focus has been on the built in violence in the preachings of Wahhabism, and by extension, Sunni Islam.

The Arab Gulf has had to face the challenge of religion based states in the region. The states of Pakistan, Iran and Israel use religion to give them an identity. Though they are not theocratic states in the classic sense of the term, they represent three important challenges to all states where Muslims form a significant part of the population. Between Pakistan and the Arab Gulf, the clash of leadership for guiding Sunni Muslims has been a challenge that both state actors and non-state actors have had to contend with at different platforms. The governments had to deal with the influence of the fundamentalist ideology of the Pakistani state in forums like the Organization of Islamic Countries. While the Wahhabis and the Sufis have had to work towards containment of the fundamentalist ideas of the Baerlvis.

The Pakistani Islamist variant of understanding of Islam, their idea of an Islamic state, their philosophy and political activeness have always been a challenge to the Wahhabi leadership, particularly in the global context. Also, unlike other ideological states, Pakistan had little opportunity to develop as a mere nation state, based on territory, institutions and citizenship: it always stuck to its ideological and transnational claim of being the vanguard for all Muslims, across the globe.

The second challenge that the Arab Gulf face from Pakistan came with the US decision to use Pakistan to implement a policy of spreading Islam through madarsas, particularly the concept of violence and jihad, creating the *Mujahedeen* in Afghanistan to resist Soviet expansion, in the 1970s and 1980s.[3] The year 1979 was a landmark in the history of the state society relations between states and Muslims across the globe. Three major events changed the manner in which Islamists and states dealt with each other. The first was the Soviet invasion of Afghanistan in January 1979 and the ensuing mobilization of Muslims from across the region for a *jihad.* The role of the United States in interpreting the term *jihad*, teaching *Jihadi* ideas through the system of madarsas across the globe[4], propagating the idea of holy warfare, grooming and arming the populations to wage the holy war and free the land of the defiling communists, have been responsible for creating a legacy of fanatics that is at war with the West today.[5]

As Pakistan integrated the US foreign policy into its own foreign policy, the challenge for the Arab Gulf states became a quagmire that threatens to engulf its own polity. The US and British use of the petro-dollars to fund the exercise of using the ISI to create a force of non-traditional soldiers, spreading the concept of *jihad* through madarsas, created a force that after successfully containing the Soviets became a loose cannon that threatens to destabilise the existing political regimes and structures across West Asia. If the creation of the non-traditional forces and movements was the first challenge that the Arab Gulf governments had to address, the second challenge that they had to address was the containment of the movements within their own territories. The contingent of Arab Gulf volunteers who joined the *Mujahedeen* and later the Taliban or Osama's network, work on the goal of removing the US troops from the Holy Land and their own homelands.[6]

The challenge thrown up by the successful revolution of the Iranians has only increased with time. The first challenge that the revolution threw up was in the form of having an organised Islamist movement. Ayatollah Khomeini's success lay in the organisation using his formulation of an ideal Islamic State, organising the followers in a manner that could overthrow the existing government, along with all its structures of governance, and replace it with their own. The similarities between the pre-revolutionary government under the Shah and the monarchies of the Arab Gulf were strong. Traditionally, a fundamentalist movement creates a yardstick by which it measures the performance of the other states and societies. States, societies and individuals who fall short of the ideals are seen as the 'Other', who need to be either reformed or liquidated.

A success of a mass movement of this nature, was a challenge the Arab Gulf contained within its own borders by either buying out the Islamist leaders within their countries. To stop the spill of fervour and leadership, the Arab Gulf states have extensively taken the assistance of external military forces. Stationing of the US troops is one such measure. It is a move that has ensured that opponents of the government are identified, tracked and controlled before they could become a threat to the stability of the government.

The third and the most important regional challenge to the Arab Gulf states comes in the form of Israel. The creation of a Jewish state, in the middle of the Muslim Arab world, with no clear international mandate offered a new source of challenge to the states in the Gulf. Compounding the problems were the embargo on Israel in the 1948 war.

There has been hostility between Israel and the region, from the time of its creation. Israel has harboured the ambition of establishing a 'Greater Israel'. Greater Israel is an irredentist term that denotes historical and Biblical boundaries of the Land of Israel. Though the borders of Greater Israel are not clearly defined tentatively it would comprise of modern-day Israel, Jordan, Lebanon, much of Egypt, Syria, Iraq, Saudi Arabia, as well as parts of Turkey and Kuwait, though the exact definition of Greater Israel is open to interpretation. The expansionist ambitions of the Israel are a challenge to the Arab Gulf.

After its creation, Israeli rhetoric became staunchly anticommunist, skillfully mobilizing friends in Washington by presenting Israel as a bulwark against communism and a strategic asset. When this appeal became anachronistic, some Israelis developed a new rhetorical basis for strategic cooperation with the United States on the basis of cooperation against fundamentalist Islam. The realpolitik assumption that yesterday's enemy is tomorrow's potential friend flies in the face of the Jewish image of an implacable enmity between Israel and its eternal foes. The normalization of Israel's relations with the rest of the world, however, has made it increasingly imperative over time for Israel to modify this doctrine.[7]

The issue of survival and security is a question that besieges all three states of Pakistan, Iran and Israel. The need to protect their identity in a hostile world, safeguard their uniqueness and to ensure that they are not swallowed up in the new secular world, has shaped the focus of the primary role of the state in these societies. The basic insecurity of their existence has led to the states being dependent on the armed forces to be the biggest player in these societies. Their leaders are aware of the responsibility of making and projecting a strong religion[8], both in terms of religious discourse, and in terms of being the ideal state. The ideal state would be able to militarily and ideologically counter enemies that are perceived as strong and potentially overwhelming.

The acquiring of nuclear weapons and technology has therefore been a top priority for the three states. Though only Pakistan has till date declared its nuclear arms potential, the other two states have been working towards acquiring nuclear weapons. Israel also has access to the US weapons and technology, in case of a crisis. Iran, does not have known or proven nuclear weapons. However, it has managed to acquire the capability to assemble the technology.

Being surrounded by nuclear capable states, who could turn hostile at any time, has been a challenge for the Arab Gulf governments, both in terms of diplomacy as well as military capability.

Economic Challenge

Though the original intention of Western colonization of the region was to set themselves up as role models to be emulated, over a period of time, the West has emerged, more as a challenge, than as a role model that can be imitated or followed. Their military and economic dominance has been the primary variable for change in West Asia and North Africa. Depending on their interests in the region, the polities, geographies and societies have been re-structured. From creating Israel, to helping it wage wars in the region, to militarily opposing any move towards nationalisation of its domestic resources, the West has only increased its military presence, social hostility and economic domination in the region.

For the Arab Gulf today, this has translated into a peculiar contradiction of state formation whereby its increasing income has become a resource curse. The states though rentier, cannot be called rentier economies as the Western powers are the ones in charge of oil exploration, refining and sale. The management of the economies too is external. The governments follow the structural adjustment programs. The IMF has been working towards including structural adjustments within the administrative and economic policies of the Arab Gulf.

The period from the 1950s to the 1970s was marked by a wave of nationalization of economy. It was a process of de-colonization that was strongly inspired by communism. The governments from Egypt to Kuwait wanted control over the revenue that was accruing from their economies. Nationalization, as a concept ran counter to the European logic of free trade, and a process of integration of the global economy.

With the growing strength of oil as a source for revenue, the concept of rentier states started being applied to the entire region of West Asia and North Africa. The theory was originally developed in relation to Iran's mid-20th century economy, when Iran was able to amass major income from the nationalization of the oil revenue. Hussein Mahdavy, the economist who first popularized rentier state theory, believed that the 1951-1956 period represents a landmark in the economic history of the Middle East: an historical era when radical nationalizations transformed ex-colonial models of petroleum exploitation into what he termed 'fortuitous etatism'. Massive amounts of foreign currency and credit generated by petroleum development, flooded into the state coffers and, Mahdavy argued, turned at least some oil-producing countries into rentier states. Kuwait and Qatar are extreme examples of the phenomenon, with limited capabilities for industrialization and few alternatives to rentierism. The case of Iran was very important to Mahdavy because, given its size and potential, it had alternatives that the extreme cases lacked. Indeed, Mossadegh had fought for diversifying Iran's economy at the same time it nationalized its oil industry.[9]

There is a strong moral string attached to the unearned aspect of the rentierism. In the Arab Gulf, once the economy of oil became the primary economy, the states became free of any social contracts with their citizens that come when a government taxes its citizens for its existence. The concept of surrendering political rights by citizens in return for social services and goods provided by the government came to a head. The accountability from the state now needed new parameters. Since the state is not dependent on taxation, the only way its society can seek accountability from its government is by seeking an accountability of its process of expenditure, particularly on the manner in which it spent it on the welfare of its citizens.

The unearned aspect of the rentier income of the states has been a major cause for the Western scholarship's disdain for the Arab Gulf. There is a very strong moral blinker attached to the Western understanding of the Arab Gulf's economic, social and political priorities. For them, the government has become an allocation state. As a result its priorities do not match with those of nation states around it, be they democracies or authoritarian regimes.

According to Yates, the rentier mentality is a psychological condition with profound consequences for productivity: contracts are given as an expression of gratitude rather than as a reflection of economic rationale; civil servants see their principal duty as being available in their offices during working hours; businessmen abandon industry and enter into real estate speculation or other special situations associated with a booming oil sector; the best and brightest abandon business and seek out lucrative government employment; manual labour and other work considered demeaning by the rentier is farmed out to foreign workers, whose remittances flood out of the rentier economy; and so on.[10]

What is important in the case of the Arab Gulf, is the manner in which the revenue has been spent. The external variable as a factor in determining the manner of expenditure is unique in the case of the Arab Gulf. From the 1950s, when the oil income started coming to the region, the external players have been the most important in the socio-political and economic development of the states. The rentier income of the Gulf comes not from a simple sale of its oil, but from the sale of the developed products. The state needed and still needs to invest in technology for extraction of oil, refining it, packing it and selling it in the global market. None of these technologies are present in the region. The states depend on external players for the technology.

Economists like John Waterbury have classified the post-WWII economies of West Asia and North Africa as ISI (Import-Substituting-Industrialization) economies. These economies are characterized by investing capital in the industrial development projects and importing other goods that would fill the lacunae in sectors like agriculture or consumer products. The industrialization experiment was also not an indigenous development. Machines, etc. were imported on a large scale to substitute for the lack of domestic production of the same. The finished product of these was then marketed as domestic produce. The main drawback with this kind of industrialization was the life of the industry itself. Since neither the technology nor the capital were indigenous, any loss suffered on them (either wear and tear or the need for investment in higher and better technology), demanded a great price and the need for further importation of technology, skills and capital. This inevitably led to a shortage of capital and a later dependence on foreign capital to bail out the domestic deficit.[11]

Most advocates of the 'resource curse theory' contend that after the discovery of oil, many Arab Gulf states failed to diversify and expand their economies beyond the oil sector. There are two aspects to the debate about rentierism in the Arab gulf. The first is regarding the role of religion in shaping the challenges of change and the state responses to it, and the second would need to deal with the changing political power equations in the strategic environment of the region. Though the two are inter-related changes, a distinction needs to be made with regard to the role of the state and the role of the external forces in the situation.

The oil blockade by the Arabs during the 1973 Arab-Israeli conflict brought home the economic strength of the region. Within days, the Arabs were able to hold economies of the industrialized nations to ransom. It was to counter the power of bargain based on the oil that the United States in particular, and the Western world in general re-designed their foreign policies. Regimes were cultivated as political allies and an external legitimacy was given to governments so that they could crush any opposition they would face within their populations. It was ensured that after the 1980s, any foreign movement in the region, be it from Israel, or direct military intervention by the Western powers, would not face a regional reaction – social, political or economic, of a magnitude that they faced in the 1970s.

External power apart, the oil wealth brought abundant resources to the region that had been witnessing chronic poverty. The 1970s saw massive infrastructural development in the region. External interventions in the region grew, but not as military interventions that would seek direct occupation or indirect colonization. A large part of the income of the region once again went to consultants, advisors and developers from the West. The most important part of the external investments from the Arab Gulf, till date, lies in the investments made in the military sector. The Arab Gulf governments, over a period of time, have outsourced a major part of their defence duties. For example, Saudi Arabia pays over 18 billion dollars to the United States to protect Saudi sovereignty, apart from giving it bases within its territory.

Works by John Anderson[12], among others, point out the mechanism of US functioning in the field of socio-political change in the Arab Gulf. They point out that the US partially funds but works towards a complete control over the Arab educational system. This has been marked, particularly since the occupation of Iraq after 2001. The basic idea of the Bush administration came from the logic that if a society is democratic, it would be an ideal ally of other democracies in the region, as well as of the US. The Kantian logic that democracies won't fight wars with each other has been the bedrock of US foreign policy in the Arab Gulf.

As the Council for Foreign Policy study on Arab democracy pointed out that with the assistance of Arab partners such as Egypt, Saudi Arabia, Jordan, Bahrain, Kuwait, and Morocco, the United States built a remarkably good record of achieving its objectives—notably, protecting the free flow of oil from the Persian Gulf, ensuring Israel's security, confronting rogue states, battling terrorism, and during the Cold War, containing Soviet influence in the region. Yet the terrorist attacks on New York and Washington, DC, on September 11, 2001, challenged the underlying assumption of U.S. Middle East policy. The Bush administration clearly believes the best way to "drain the swamp" that produces terrorists is to promote democracy and reform more broadly in the region.[13]

Socio-Political Challenge

The challenge of the ownership and control of the oil wealth of the Arab Gulf region is also linked with the US and Western foreign policy in the region. The three key elements that form the basis of their policies towards the region remain un-interrupted access to the oil, countering religionists who may oppose the Western value systems and Israel, and thirdly the establishment of democracy in the region.

The role of religion in the process of state or social formation cannot be undermined. The development of a specific state and social system cannot, however, be studied in isolation. With the passage of time, as the world has shrunk due to more economic, social, cultural, political interactions, so has the development of the two systems.

Though Wahabbism is not a sect, but as a variant of Sunni Islam, it remains one of the richest forms of Sunni Islam that the world sees today. Sunni Islam does not have sects. However, there is a tradition for a re-interpretation of the Quran and the ideals of the religion in Sunni Islam and Wahabbism represents one such strain of re-interpretation. Abd-al-Wahhab advocated a return to the practices of the first three generations of Islamic history. His preaching and interpretation of Islam found favour with the House of Saud, as a result of which Wahhabism has grown to be the dominant form of Sunni Islam in Saudi Arabia, Kuwait and the United Arab Emirates. The British support to the Wahhabis and later the American support to the House of Saud has had long term implications for the socio-political developments both in the Arab Gulf and the region of West and South Asia.

Theoretically, the moot question in a state-society interface is that of power. Different state responses to social demands and vice versa yield different results. How much of the dominant social groups or the social customs and bindings are able to guide and mould the government, and from the other end, to what extent the state is able to influence the making of the social setup, indicates their power over the other. The nature of the state-society interface is decided by the interaction between the two forces, at whatever level and at whatever point of time, whether complimentary or hostile, or a combination of both. There are multiple layers of both state and society, and both interact at different levels in different fashions. Neither of the two actors, state or society can be taken as a homogenous unit or a single identity on its own. It is important to understand how the state used the idea of religion to establish its hold over its society, give itself a legitimacy and most importantly be part of the international interplay of politics of religion, oil and military might.

Under the post 9/11 campaign for promotion of democracy, Western and international organizations funded hundreds of projects intended to help democratize Arab politics, applying a strategy conceived largely to influence post-communist transitions and political liberalization around the globe. Democracy promotion projects — broadly, those designed to enhance legislative, judicial, and civic responsibility — differed from most traditional services-delivery aid programs in their high grant component, the channeling of funds around the executive branch of government, and the output of ideas and information.[14] This has led to both the Western, particularly the US following a policy and the governments in the region that are struggling to make a balance with their society and the socio-political aspirations of their Western allies. It has led to a situation where the US supports democracy, the governments it calls 'authoritarian regimes', Wahabis and counter Islamist movements at the same time.[15]

Conclusion

Though the region has known to be oil rich for several decades, the radical change has largely been a result of economic transformation, with massive infrastructure development, wealth creation and exposure to international economy. A study of the society within the socio-economic and political the parameters shows uniqueness that sets it apart from even its neighbours in the rest of West Asia and North Africa.

With the petroleum boom-bust cycle, which culminated in a thorough social and economic transformation, Arab Gulf states have been confronted with the enormous challenge of developing economically while preserving social integrity, and with balancing quasi-traditional political systems with greatly enhanced regional and international interactions. The increase in the global demand for oil as a source of energy transformed the economic character of the region in the 1950s and the 1960s, and by the 1970s, it was in a position to give the region significant global political and economic clout. The economic growth along with unique geo-political position gave a strategic significance to the region. The oil blockade by the

Arabs during the 1973 Arab-Israeli conflict, for the first time, provided the Gulf regimes with an opportunity for showing their newfound economic might. This particular event itself brought a situation in which the United States in particular and the Western powers in general had to redesign their policies towards the region. With the shift in policy provided an external legitimacy for the monarchic regimes to crush any opposition they would face from within. Quite interestingly, after the 1980s, any foreign movement in the region, be it from Israel, or direct military intervention by the Western powers, would not face a regional reaction – social, political or economic, of a magnitude that they faced in the 1970s.

Domestically, oil wealth offered a relief to the otherwise poverty-stricken region. The economic growth in the 1970s resulted in massive infrastructural development. A large part of the income of the region went to consultants, advisors and developers from the West. On the security front, as the external intervention in the region grew (not essentially in the form of military intervention that would seek direct occupation or indirect colonization), the Governments in the GCC States spent most important part of their foreign expenditure in the military sector.

With the increasing emphasis on the social welfare sector, the Arab Gulf governments, over a period of time, have outsourced a major part of their defence duties. For example, Saudi Arabia pays over 18 billion dollars to the United States to protect Saudi sovereignty. It has allowed the US to develop a naval base within its boundaries. In addition, the acquisition of a land base in the region, allows it the ability to project power in West and South Asia. It formally enlists Saudi Arabia as an ally of the US, which has immense political and economic connotations in the changing political, military and economic dynamics of the region.

The external variables that have been responsible for change, though most powerful and important, cannot be studied in isolation. The inter-linked internal movements of change also need to be evaluated within the larger context. Most of what is dubbed as a reaction to the West, like the religio-political movements of the fundamentalist Muslims, or the Shia-Sunni strife that threatens to overthrow the existing socio-political equilibrium, or the movement of establishing and funding madarsas across the globe, are changes that have implications not only within each country but regionally and globally as well.

Notes

1. El-Ghonemy, Riad, *Affluence and Poverty in the Middle East*, Routledge, London and New York, 1998, p. 30.
2. Barakat, Halim, *The Arab World: Society, Culture, and State*, University of California Press, 1993, p. 6.
3. The idea was incorporated in the school syllabi, and taught through schools and *madarsas* across Afghanistan. Today the education ministry of Afghanistan is attempting to reverse the literature taught in schools. It is working to erase the imageries of violence and interpretation of the terms of jihad in textbooks. The literature that was used to create the forces of *mujahedeen* in Afghanistan in the 1980s, is the literature that is used by the non-state forces today to mobilize forces against the US and its allies. This literature is at the root of the teachings that are used by movements like the Taliban and also by network leaders like Osama Bin Laden or Abu Sayyaf. See "The ABC'S of Jihad in Afghanistan Courtesy, USA", By Joe Stephens and David B. Ottaway, Washington Post, 23 March 2002, Posted online on 3 April 2002, http://emperors-clothes.com/news/abc.htm; and also see the news report at: http:// www. cbc.ca/news/background/ afghanistan/schools.html.
4. Ibid.
5. The Pakistani Inter-Services Intelligence (ISI) was the interagent used in the majority of these activities to disguise the sources of support for the resistance. Under Reagan, U.S. support for the mujahedeen evolved into an official U.S. foreign policy, known as the Reagan Doctrine, which included U.S. support for anti-Soviet resistance movements in Afghanistan, Angola, Nicaragua, and elsewhere, according to the Wikipedia online.
6. One of the most comprehensive readings on the rise of the mujahedeen, the Taliban and bin Laden is John Cooley, *Unholy Wars: Afghanistan, America and International Terrorism*, Pluto Press, 2002. He discusses the role of the combined secret service agencies from Europe to the US, Saudi and Pakistani in creating forces have in the long term contributed to creating a force that is destabilising South Asia and is posing a serious challenge to the security of Asia and the United States.

   Also see, Afghanistan Crisis of Impunity: The Role of Pakistan, Russia, and Iran in Fueling the Civil War, *Human Rights Watch Report*, July 2001 Vol. 13, No. 3 (C), http://www.hrw.org/reports/2001/afghan2/index.htm#TopOfPage (accessed on November 22, 2008), and The Afghan quagmire by M B Naqvi, *The News International*, http://www. thenews. com.pk/ print1.asp?id=33642 (accessed November 22, 2009).

7. See Cohen, Raymond, *Israel's Starry-Eyed Foreign Policy*, Middle East Quarterly, Vol.1, No. 2, June 1994.
8. I am borrowing the term from the book, *Strong Religion: The Rise of Fundamentalisms Around the World*, Gariel Almond, et.al, ed., The University of Chicago Press, Chicago, 2003.
9. What is a Rentier State?, *Biot Report #227*, June 23, 2005, http://www.semp.us/publications/biot_reader.php?BiotID=227 (accessed on 20 December 2008).
10. Yates, Douglas A., *The Rentier State in Africa: Oil rent Dependency and Neo-Colonialism in the Republic of Gabon.* Trenton, NJ, Africa World Press, 1996, p. 22.
11. See the works of John Waterbury, Tim Niblock and Rodney Wilson in this regard. The *WORLD ECONOMIC OUTLOOK: Globalization and Inequality*, October 2007, is also a good indicator of the assessment of the Arab economy from the perspective of the financial institutions.
12. See Religion, democracy and democratization, Ed. by John Anderson, Routledge, 2006.
13. http://www.cfr.org/content/publications/attachments/Arab_Democracy_TF.pdf also see (http://news.bbc.co.uk/2/shared/bsp/hi/pdfs/04_02_08_world_bank_arab_education2.pdf accessed on January 24, 2009).
14. Sheila Carapico, Foreign Aid for Promoting Democracy in the Arab World, *Middle East Journal* Vol. 56, No. 3, Summer 2002, p. 379.
15. http://www.saudi-us-relations.org/articles/2008/ioi/080228-khouri-respect.html.

5

Economic Diversification in the Gulf Co-operation Council (GCC) States

Mohamed Al-Thani

Introduction

Despite the enormous quantities of capital that have flowed into the Gulf region over the past decade as a result of the sale of oil and other hydrocarbons, an internationally competitive industrial base has not yet materialised in the GCC. Given the deepening downturn in the global economy, demand for energy is likely to weaken, bringing hydrocarbon revenues down from their recent peaks. Facing the combination of uncertainty over the rate at which oil reserves are being depleted, and a rapidly growing population, economic diversification in the Gulf region is becoming an ever more urgent issue. This paper discusses the mechanisms by which external hydrocarbon revenues have acted to dampen incentives towards productive investment and assesses the prospects for diversification in the future.

'The Natural Curse': The Case of the Rentier State

The term 'Rentier State' was coined in 1970 by Hossein Mahdavy in reference to Iran.[1] A number of different definitions of the term have been proposed, but broadly speaking a rentier state can be defined as one in which a significant proportion of the income of the state arises not as a result of direct productive activity, but in the form of an externally originating rent.[2]

States which derive a significant proportion of their income in the form of rents, usually in the form of revenues that accrue due to the existence of some externally scarce natural endowment, have historically exhibited a number of structural, political and developmental patterns.

Firstly, these rents primarily accrue to the government of the state rather than to the private sector. The government then acts to distribute this revenue throughout the rest of the economy. The specific mechanisms through which this allocation occurs dependent on the form of government, the structure of the economy, and the levels of political influence of the actors within the economy.

The rentier state is therefore unique in that the government derives the majority of its income from sources external to the economy over which legislative power is exercised. The state allocates this income within the local economy. The role of the state as an intermediary between—in the case of the GCC countries—the hydrocarbon sector and the rest of the economy gives rise to an economic structure in which public expenditure is of primary importance, and the public sector dominates the economic system, even in liberal economic regimes.

It is sometimes claimed that a key characteristic of 'rentier economies' is that the usual link between productive effort and pecuniary reward is weakened.[3] Because household incomes are derived mainly through the allocation of external revenue flows by the state, the primary focus of effort on the part of agents in the economy is to obtain a share in these revenues, whether through employment in the public sector, distribution via the welfare state or—for entrepreneurs—through preferential treatment in the form of subsidies or grants. Moreover, the effort required to maintain these external rents, for example through maintaining pipelines, servicing machinery and so on, is expended by a small, often expatriate, minority of the population. The remainder of the population largely engages in efforts to secure a share of these rent flows.

The relationship between state and citizen is thus qualitatively different to that observed in advanced liberal democracies. Public consent is maintained via a set of mechanisms quite different to those that operate when the primary function of the state is to provide the basic legal and institutional framework under which business can be conducted: private property, the rule of law and monetary administration.

In contrast, much of the allocation decisions made by governments of 'rentier states' are informed by the exigencies of maintaining the consent of the population. This gives rise to a specific set of tendencies in government spending programmes. Firstly, present consumption is often preferred to investment, with large amounts of resources channelled to the population in the form of welfare spending. Secondly, where investment does occur—other than that which is required to maintain revenues—it tends to be directed towards highly visible projects such as large-scale infrastructure, prestige projects and military spending. Long-term investment projects aimed at initiating self-sustaining productive output have less immediate benefits, require the diversion of resources away from current consumption, and are therefore politically more difficult.[4]

These structural features often give rise to patterns of capital formation in which the standard concerns of economic development are overlooked. These include the existence of 'linkages' between different sectors of the economy, the importance of economies of scale, coordination to avoid duplication of projects and a consideration of the position of industries in the global economy. Further, there is some evidence that even in profitable export sectors of the economy, efficiency is lower than in similar sectors in other parts of the world.

The problem of low rates of capital formation is compounded by what is commonly referred to as 'Dutch Disease'. This refers to the tendency of the real exchange rate to rise during oil booms, as strong demand for oil gives rise to a shift in the terms of trade. This in turn reduces the competitiveness of other industries, reinforcing dependence on oil revenues.[5]

The direct link between external rents and government expenditure gives rise to fact that the causal relationship between economic actions and the effect of those actions on aggregate incomes is of a different nature to that in advanced capitalist economies. Changes in the rate of growth occur less as outcomes of the investment decisions of entrepreneurs and policies of the state than as a function of the levels of supply and demand in global commodities markets. Levels of government expenditure are thus largely determined by conditions outside the country. Whilst this implies that in times such as the present—when energy prices are at historically high levels—governments enjoy high revenues and are able to undertake large-scale investment projects, the converse is also the case. When commodity prices fall, leading to a reduction in export revenues, the corresponding reduction in spending has to be implemented largely in the government sector. Often it is politically more convenient to reduce expenditure on capital investment than current consumption, so in times of falling energy prices, rentier states tend to cut back on productive investment.

It can therefore be seen that one important aspect of the transformation from rentier state to an economy based on capitalist production is the creation of a stable fiscal base. This is necessary so that government revenues are protected from changes in international commodity prices, thus reducing the liquidity risk associated with longer term public investment projects. This fiscal base must largely arise through the taxation of corporations and individuals. This is problematic in polities where states have traditionally assumed an allocative role, and taxes have been very low. As a rule, populations that don't pay taxes are less likely than those that do to try and hold their government to account. The question of fiscal stability is therefore linked to issues over the pressures towards democratic representation.

Another feature of the 'rentier state' is that the usual sequence of economic development is reversed. The commonly observed pattern of development is for agriculture to be augmented over time by industrial production, with a service sector occurring last. In states dominated by natural endowments, a large service sector often springs up to cope with the requirements of—in the case of the Gulf—the energy export sector. Thus a transition occurs directly from an agricultural economic system to a services based system, with industrialisation occurring only later, often as part of a strategy of 'diversification'. The existence of this service sector, funded through the revenues of external rents, has lead some authors to point to the existence of a 'rent multiplier' effect, similar to the familiar Keynesian multiplier mechanism. As hydrocarbon rents are directed into the economy in the form of salaries for public servants, investment in infrastructure and the like, these flows represent income for agents in the system. This income is spent on consumption, housing and other services, increasing demand in these markets and thus generating further income. The full effect on the economy of changes in levels of external rents is thus not fully captured in the raw export figures, but will generally be of a higher level.[6]

One final feature of the rentier state is the problem of statistics. A number of related issues with respect to standard national accounting practices can be raised. The first is that the published nominal figures for GDP, government revenue and exports are problematic in the case of rentier states. Because such a large proportion of these figures are made up of external rents, they are strongly affected by changes in international commodity prices. In the case of the GCC countries, these figures therefore reflect the supply and demand for hydrocarbons more than any real measure of domestic productivity.

Another issue related to the measurement of GDP figures for large-scale exporters of finite natural wealth is that there is no balance-sheet counterpart to the sale price of that wealth. To illustrate this problem, consider the example of another finite commodity—foreign exchange. In the case of a country running down its foreign exchange reserves to purchase imports, or to pay off its national debt, the foreign exchange expended in the transaction is deducted from the national accounts, and inverse adjustments—e.g. a reduction of the national debt—are also made accordingly. This is not the case with mineral wealth. The export proceeds are added to the asset side of the balance sheet without a corresponding deduction for mineral reserves. Thus oil and gas deposits are treated as 'manna from heaven', and are accounted for in value added terms, in the same way as, for example, commodities that are renewable on an annual basis such as agricultural produce.

Overview of the GCC: Oil Dependency

In the Gulf region we observe a unique case in international economic development. Nowhere else in the world has the transition from tradition to modernity occurred so rapidly and so dramatically. In only a few generations the countries of the GCC have undergone a transition from agrarian society to a system based around hydrocarbon extraction, and increasingly a modern service sector.

The rapidity with which this economic transformation has taken place goes some way towards explaining the fact that an equivalent social transformation has not taken place. Systems of government, power structures and relationships, and patterns of distribution and consumption within the resident population have in many respects remained largely unchanged during the last few decades. This despite the enormous magnitude of the changes to the economic base upon which the society rests.

From an external perspective, the countries of the GCC are in many ways exemplars of modern western-style capitalism and consumerism. Nowhere is this more immediately pertinent than in the ultra modern city-state of Dubai, with it's burgeoning financial services sector, record-breaking skyscrapers and artificial palm-tree holiday islands. Beneath this 21st-century surface however, a deeply conservative, tribal society remains very much in control of all aspects of social, political and economic life.

The polities of the GCC thus represent a unique synthesis of the modern and the traditional. While skilled Western 'guest labour' drinks in the bars, and shops in air-conditioned malls, the political structure of the GCC countries remains based around traditional patterns of kinship and tribal allegiance. These familial power bases were the primary beneficiaries of the enormous revenues that arose from the exploitation of the region's oil wealth. These revenues have served to strengthen the traditional ruling classes in these states and have allowed them to consolidate their position in the face of the travails of globalisation.

Through the allocation of oil revenues via traditional systems of patrilineage, the ruling elites were able to maintain the consent of the local population and thus arrived in a position where they were able to make selective decisions about which aspects of western consumerism and culture they would accept as concomitants of integration in the wider global economic system, and which they would reject.[7]

The Gulf states now find themselves in a position in which they have access to the latest Western technological innovations and lifestyle choices, without having passed through the upheaval of social transformation that is the usual inevitable side-effect of the transition from agrarian society to advanced industrial nation. The power of 'big capital' to weaken political structures and to leave national systems of legislature beholden to it in globalised capitalist nations is held at bay in the Gulf states. The revenues arising from private enterprise are dwarfed by the rents controlled and allocated by the ruling class. Furthermore, much of the non-hydrocarbon economic activity that occurs in these economies is undertaken not by foreign multi-national firms, but by local businesses, often controlled by or in some way attached to members of the ruling classes.[8]

We can see then how the confluence of a traditional tribal society and the existence of enormous externally-arising rents gives rise to a largely stable political structure in which the centralisation of power remains implicit. The question of economic diversification in the Gulf is thus not simply a technical exercise of adjusting structural macroeconomic policy variables. It is more fundamentally a question of how to modify the structure of incentives such that it is in the interests of the population to enter into productive effort, and to what extent these adjustments will require associated changes to the political system.

An important characteristic of the Gulf economies is the existence of a two-tier social system. We have sketched out the structural features of an economic and political system based around the allocation of rents within the native population, but to complete the picture we need to add to it the large numbers of expatriate workers that undertake the majority of the physical labour required to maintain the status quo. This group constitutes the wage-labour required by the Gulf states for the upkeep of oil extraction machinery, construction projects, and all the other unskilled and semi-skilled manual work necessary to sustain the economic system. For the most part this labour is drawn from the South Asian sub-continent, and while receiving relatively high wages in comparison to what is available at home, is poorly paid and generally lives in conditions of poverty. This army of cheap foreign labour is segregated from the mainstream of Gulf society, often housed in camps outside or on the outskirts of cities.[9]

The final social class that exists in the Gulf is that of skilled professional 'guest labour'. These workers fill technical and managerial roles in sectors such as hydrocarbons, construction and financial services. In return they receive a share of the rents controlled by the native elites in the form of generous tax-free salaries and incentives.

In summary, the economic system that characterises the Gulf region is one in which huge external rents are distributed via traditional tribal and kinship based hierarchical systems, while being maintained by a large (in some countries majority) expatriate workforce, which is itself divided into a skilled, largely Western, sector which receives a share of the economic rents, and a much larger, unskilled, low-wage, largely South-Asian sector which does not.

This picture is complicated by a rapidly growing local population. This is problematic for several reasons. Firstly, the general level of education of the native population is not sufficient that they are able to fill professional or managerial business positions. This implies that this segment of the labour force will have to remain 'imported' for the foreseeable future. Secondly, the levels of remuneration in the public sector, and the segmentation of the labour force give rise to significant obstacles to absorbing the increasing local population into the private sector of the economy. This problem is exacerbated by the fact that the public sector is reaching the limits of its ability to absorb new employees.

Economic Diversification in the GCC states

Over the past few years, the Gulf region has consistently reported figures for GDP growth above the 5 percent mark, has made—and to continues to make—significant progress towards the liberalisation of the ownership of capital, and in recent years has reported growth figures in the non-hydrocarbon sectors that have been above the overall rate of GDP growth. On the surface this would give the impression that economic growth, development, and diversification are proceeding successfully.

This is largely the view of international organisations such as the IMF, which in 2003 reported that 'the GCC countries are implementing policy reforms to accelerate non-oil growth and create employment opportunities for a rapidly increasing labour force in a sustained fashion, while reducing vulnerability to oil price shocks'.[10]

Beneath the surface of these statistics, a different picture emerges however. Among the non-oil sectors of the economy that are currently experiencing significant expansion are the following: natural gas, real estate and construction, financial services and tourism.

In the case of the expansion of production of natural gas, as is the case in Qatar, dependence is shifted from oil revenues to natural gas revenues. One revenue stream based on rents for a non-renewable resource is simply augmented with another. It is therefore impossible to regard a shift in production from oil into natural gas as 'economic diversification' in any real sense.

In the case of construction and real estate, the current activity is underpinned by the needs of an expanding local population combined with the pressures of inflows of large numbers of foreign workers. The rise of states such as UAE as international tourist destinations has further fuelled the boom in construction of hotels, shopping malls and so on. These factors have exerted upward pressure on rents and real estate prices and given rise to the enormous expansion of construction activity that has occurred over the past few years.

This sector must therefore be regarded as secondary in the scheme of economic diversification. A booming real estate sector may well be a symptom of a dynamic and flourishing economic system. If, however the demand is largely from highly paid guest labour living on oil rents, or from an expanding local population that receives significant revenue flows via the government, there exists a risk that demand for property will diminish as oil rents decrease.

Finally, it should be noted that the Gulf region is not immune from speculation in real estate, as the experience of the Soukh-al-Manakh bubble shows. Even if fundamentals indicate that the conditions are right for a protracted increase in activity in the real estate and construction sectors with the associated asset price rises that occur as this activity expands, this does not preclude the existence of speculative buying. This is illustrated by the extent to which current demand is augmented by foreign investors looking for safe havens for 'parked money', and seeking investment returns as property comes to be viewed as an asset class in its own right. Moreover, much of the current real estate and construction boom has been financed by credit. As the effects of the fallout from the recent financial crisis begin to make themselves felt, sources of this credit will dry up, resulting in reduced activity and a reduction in confidence in the sector.

Another sector that has seen significant growth over the past decade is that of financial services. Dubai in particular has begun to market itself as the financial hub of the Middle East. Related to this development is the existence of the Gulf's sovereign wealth funds, through which the GCC governments recycle their hydrocarbon revenues back into foreign financial assets. Taking the example of the sovereign funds first, it can be argued that the transfer of oil revenues into external financial assets is a way of transforming the yield of one form of external rent into an asset from which another external rent is derived. There is one key difference in that the rents from these financial assets are potentially sustainable—they have the advantage that, unlike hydrocarbon revenues, they are not directly linked to a finite resource. Nonetheless, by switching resources into external financial assets, the government serves to perpetuate the existing structure of the rentier state.

The expansion of financial services in the Gulf can be viewed in a somewhat more optimistic light. The financial sector provides an essential service to the real economy via the allocation of surplus capital to deficit economic units. Financial service is therefore at least theoretically, a sustainable economic sector into which significant numbers of employees can be drawn on the basis of wage labour. The emerging status of Dubai as a regional and international financial centre can therefore be seen as a positive development. In light of the recent global economic crisis however, it seems that a retrenchment of finance is now inevitable internationally, with activity being scaled down across the world. It seems increasingly unlikely that the Gulf can remain immune to the problems faced by other financial centres around the world.

Other potential problems exist with respect to the creation of successful financial services industries. The lack of education in the local workforce remains a significant obstacle to fully realising the potential of the sector. While expert knowledge is largely imported in the form of guest workers, the benefits of expanded employment opportunities will not be available to local citizens.

Finally, what promise does tourism hold as a potential route out of oil-dependency? In its favour, it is relatively labour intensive, and consequently offers potential to provide private sector employment to the growing population. However, much of the work is low-paid, menial and considered demeaning to the native population. Further, incomes from tourism can in some ways be regarded as quasi-rents: foreign revenue received in exchange for the use of hotel rooms and beaches. Thus the structure of the tourist industry in many ways resembles that of the wider economy. Low-paid South Asian workers provide the manual labour, while profits and rents accrue to the native population.

Considerations for the Future

It should be clear from the previous section that substituting one form of rental income for another, as is largely the case with the sectors that have seen the greatest expansion in recent years in the Gulf, does little to further the goal of economic diversification. Encouraging the growth of these sectors may be politically convenient, both because it does not require significant social restructuring, and because it largely serves to reinforce existing power structures through the maintenance of rental incomes for the ruling elites.

In the longer term however, the creation of a viable industrial manufacturing base must be viewed as a crucial element in any programme of economic diversification. One 'stylised fact' that has emerged from recent economic history is that almost without exception, the countries that have achieved self-sustaining capital accumulation are those that have been able to create successful industrial manufacturing sectors, and subsequently integrate these sectors successfully into the global economy via competitively priced exports.

The route by which this transition has taken place has varied across countries, and debates still continue about the extent to which governments should offer protection from overseas competition to nascent industries. In almost all of the recently industrialised nations however, the transition to manufactured goods exports started from a largely agricultural system. Much of the classical literature on the subject is an analysis of the mechanisms by which the transition from pre-capitalist agrarian socio-economic systems to modern industrial manufacturing takes place.[11]

These models are therefore not directly applicable to the GCC states. Agriculture in the Gulf has suffered since the discovery of oil. Locally produced items have been replaced by imports, leading to the contraction of the agricultural sector. Instead, any analysis of the route that Gulf states should take out of oil dependency must consider the mechanisms by which oil rents can be productively invested in the economy in such a way as to give rise to industries that will provide employment for the increasing population and have the potential to compete in global markets.

One important prerequisite for self-sustaining growth under a market system that the Gulf does have in place is that of infrastructure. Much of the seminal literature on development economics had a focus on the question of how to finance and undertake the large-scale infrastructure which is necessary for a modern market system to take root: utilities, communications, transport and power. Much of this is in already in place in the Gulf region, as successive generations of ruling elites have found it in their interests to invest heavily in these popular and publicly visible projects.

With respect to the direction of investment to productive sectors in the economy, the record of most governments of the GCC region is poor. Putting aside the enormous expenditures on largely unnecessary military programmes and the lavish lifestyles of the ruling elites themselves, much of the rents that have accrued from hydrocarbon revenues have been redirected to external portfolio-type investment. Concurrently, the availability of credit for local business has been decreasing, leading to difficulties in financing private projects.

Private enterprise itself in much of the Gulf region is largely subordinated to the ruling classes. Strong rules apply on the foreign ownership of businesses and capital, and in many cases local entrepreneurs are required to obtain permits from the government to set up in business. Often businesses cannot be set up without a 'patron' in the ruling family who may provide nothing to the business other than his name.

In light of the previous discussion, it can be seen that the process of diversification in the GCC states cannot be looked upon as purely economic, but must also be seen as a process of political diversification. In order for industrialisation to progress, a transfer of power from the ruling families to owners and managers of business must inevitably occur. The role taken by the ruling classes must shift from the control and allocation of rents, to a position closer to that of governments in more advanced economies.

The creation of a fiscal base through which government can reduce its reliance on external revenues is one essential part of this process. This can only come about through the introduction of taxation on incomes and businesses. This in turn alters the relationship between ruler and subject: as the slogan goes, 'no taxation without representation'. It therefore seems inevitable that the grip of power held by the ruling elite in the Gulf nations will have to diminish as a necessary condition for successful diversification. Instead of buying legitimacy through bestowing favours, and the provision of jobs and services to the native population, the governments will face the difficult task of levying taxes, and compromises will have to be sought in order to retain popular consent.

The process by which the transition occurs from tribal or familial based patronage systems to broader industry-driven systems of allocation and distribution has been the subject of strong debate, particularly with respect to the path taken by the recently industrialised East Asian countries. One school of thought holds that the existence of 'crony capitalism' and a failure to adhere to liberal market-based norms in these countries necessarily retards economic development and prevents a successful transition to industrialism.

This view is supported by empirical evidence showing a correlation between measures of 'good governance' and national income.[12] These approaches have recently been taken up by the international development institutions, with the brief leadership of Paul Wolfowitz at the World Bank giving rise to a strong emphasis on 'good governance' reforms.

The problem with the statistical correlation between 'good governance' and income levels is that of causation: the existence of a correlation tells us nothing about the sequence of events. A more balanced view holds that as economic development progresses and income rises, pressures arise that may lead to greater democratic representation.[13] The path taken by the Gulf states in terms of the political reforms that take place as an integral part of the social and economic transformation involved in economic diversification, cannot therefore be determined in advance as some pre-formed set of 'good governance reforms'. Nonetheless, with states like Qatar and Saudi Arabia consistently scoring poorly on such measures[14], it is hard to see how economic diversification can occur to any significant extent in these economies without simultaneous 'political diversification'.

Reforms will also be necessary in the labour markets of the Gulf states. The current segmentation of the market gives rise to a number of significant problems. Firstly, the division between the poorly paid expatriate workforce, and the wealthy local population results in corresponding segmentation of local markets for consumption goods. With the bulk of hydrocarbon rents allocated among the native population, a large proportion is spent on imported goods such as luxury items. This gives rise to a low level of demand for locally produced consumption goods, in turn causing problems for the development of industry based on local markets—a key factor in the early stages of development of the East Asian states. A rationalisation of the labour market is therefore necessary in the Gulf region as part of any diversification strategy. The differentials between private and public sector pay need to be reduced and labour market legislation introduced to increase the rights of workers and reduce the legal discrimination between local and foreign workers.

Conclusion

It is argued here that much of the recent development and investment that has come under the heading of 'economic diversification' in the Gulf states, can more realistically be viewed as a form of 'portfolio diversification', in that much of the income that will arise as a result of these investments will be in the form of rents or quasi-rents. It is also argued that any significant reduction in dependence on hydrocarbon rents in the Gulf states must arise through a process of industrialisation, and eventually integration into international markets for manufactured goods.

It is possible to point to positive developments on this front. For example, the planned aluminium smelter at Taweelah, a joint development between Abu Dhabi and Dubai, will be the worlds largest when it gets commissioned. Plans are also underway for developments in other heavy industries such as steel and petrochemicals, as well as sectors such as aerospace and renewable energy research.[15] If successful, these large-scale heavy industry investments should reduce the need for imports of materials such as steel and aluminium for example in the construction industry, in turn reducing foreign exchange requirements.

Significant risks are being faced by the economies of the Gulf as the world economy contracts. A weakening demand for oil as global activity slows is likely to lead to a fall in energy prices, reducing revenue flows to governments in the region. Investments by sovereign funds in Western financial institutions and instruments are likely to have suffered significant losses, although estimates are difficult due to the lack of transparency surrounding these funds. With credit markets likely to remain tight for the foreseeable future, external investment in the Gulf is likely to drop, leading to pressure on real estate and property prices.

It is critical that, given the challenges that face the economies of the Gulf region, priority must be given to long term investment projects, even if this requires politically difficult reductions in state spending elsewhere. Taking the easy route of reducing expenditure on capital formation when faced with a reduction in oil revenues will only serve to compound current problems for the future.

Notes

1. Beblawi, H. The Rentier State in the Arab World. in *The Rentier State*, H. Beblawi, Ed. London: Croom Helm Ltd, 1987, ch. 2.
2. In economics, the term 'rent' is used to refer not just to the income derived from ownership of land or property—as is the case in popular usage—but also includes any incomes derived as

a result of prices being in excess of production costs. Revenues from hydrocarbon extraction are therefore, in economic terms, regarded as rent.

3. Beblawi, H. The Rentier State in the Arab World. In *The Rentier State*, H. Beblawi, Ed. London: Croom Helm Ltd, 1987, ch. 2.
4. Fasano, U., and Wang, Q. Fiscal Expenditure Policy and Non-Oil Economic Growth: Evidence from the GCC Countries. IMF Working Paper, December 2001.
5. Stevens, P. Resource Impact: Curse or Blessing? A Literature Survey. *Journal of Energy Literature 9*, 1 (2003), 1-42.
6. Stauffer, T. Income Measurement in Arab States. In *The Rentier State*, H. Beblawi, Ed. London: Croom Helm Ltd, 1987, ch. 1.
7. Noreng, O. The Predicament of the Gulf Rentier State. In *Oil In the Gulf*, D. Heradstveit and H. Hveem, Eds. Aldershot: Ashgate Publishing Ltd., 2004, ch. 1.
8. John W. Fox, N. M.-S., and al Mutawa, M. Traditionalism globalized or globalization traditionalized? In *Globalization and the Gulf*, N. M.-S. John W. Fox and M. al Mutawa, Eds. Oxon: Routledge, 2006, ch. 1.
9. See e.g. http://www. guardian.co.uk/ world/ 2008/oct/08/ middleeast.construction.
10. Fasano, U., and Iqbal, Z. *GCC Countries: From Oil Dependence to Diversification*. International Monetary Fund, 2003.
11. See e.g. LEWIS, W. A. Economic Development with Unlimited Supplies of Labour. *The Manchester School 232* (1954), 139–91 for the classic model of this type.
12. Christopher Clague, Philip Keefer, S. K., and Olsen., M. Democracy, Autocracy, and the Institutions Supportive of Economic Growth. In *Institutions and Economic Development: Growth and Governance in Less-Developed and Post-Socialist Countries*, C. Clague, Ed. Baltimore: John Hopkins University Press, 1997, pp. 91-120.
13. Khan, M. What Is a 'Good Investment Climate'? *Investment Climate, Growth and Poverty* (2005).
14. Noland, M., and Pack, H. *The Arab Economies in a Changing World*. Washington DC: Peterson Institute for International Economics, 2007, p. 31.
15. Financial Times, March 18 2008.

6

Gulf Arab Women between Cultural Resistance and Knowledge Economy

Elena Maestri

Habits, customs, traditions and beliefs are the terms normally used to define resistance of informal bonds; the interaction of these aspects with formal rules within a certain community affects daily life by directing its members' activities and way of life; it is a concept well expressed by Douglass North, which seems to be quite apt even when referring to cultural resistance in the process of the economic empowerment of women in the Gulf Arab States.[1]

This article presents a brief outline of the evolving role of women in the economy of the Gulf Arab countries, in the light of transformations and changes generated by the oil era, and in the light of cultural resistance factors still affecting these societies, in which the development of women's full economic potential is still restricted by certain cultural limitations.

Women between the Traditional Environment and the Advent of the Oil Era

Oil and the subsequent development process had a strong and clear impact on the traditional societies as well as on their peculiar economic structure and traditional activities. Boat-building, pearling, fishing, land and sea trading, oasis agriculture among sedentary people, breeding and herding among Bedouins were the most common activities of Gulf Arabs in the pre-oil era. When and where men were often absent, such as during the pearling season, women had to take upon themselves the responsibility to manage the various activities within their community, in the harsh environment they lived in; moreover the "cruel sea" did not always give them back their dear ones and left them alone, as well described in the well-known Kuwaiti film *Bass Ya Bahr* by Khalid al-Siddiq.[2] Amongst Bedouins, women would normally contribute very actively to the well-being of the group, by watering camels, spinning camel and goat wool and making both clothes and tents. Fishing, by the typical fish traps of the Gulf, like *qarqūr* and *hadhrah*, was another economic activity in which women played their own part, by collecting fish at the low tide time and selling it directly after the catch at the nearest *suq*.[3]

Within the traditional sedentary framework, the role of women was strictly linked to the interactions of the extended family (*hamulah*) with the rest of the community, and exclusively conceived within the women's domain in their neighbourhood (*fereej*); the latter within the urban tribal model was the physical and social expression of family and clanic ties, represented by a well-defined group of dwellings close to one another, forming connected units, and binding its members to one internal frame, in which women had their own duties and played their own economic role. They used to sew and provided with clothes the whole family: within the *fereej* "they [would] visit each other through the roof routes and spend the whole morning working together..."[4] That was a reality shared in traditional settlements both in Central Arabia and along the coast of the Gulf. Within the traditional home environment rules were strictly determined and defined by the eldest woman, who established very precise norms of behaviour for all the other female family members living in the same house, and quite frequently for the whole household.[5]

Every woman had a very precise task in the house, as decided by the eldest, but some women were also engaged in trade within their neighbourhood, carving out their own specific role in the traditional economy of the community and in the economic well-being of the family. Widows, who were in need, dedicated themselves in particular to some trade activities in their homes, but this habit was also shared by other women, who just considered it a way to socialise with their female neighbours: they would sell perfumes, cloth and other wares at the end of the traditional female gatherings (*ziyārāt*, sing. *ziyārah*), a practise which has survived till most recent times even in the most prosperous households in the region. Some enterprising women would also invest their inherited money in a shop or business, which, nonetheless, they would not run directly, as they would charge an agent (*wakīl*), either a slave or a male subordinate.

The oil era in the Gulf soon started to modernise the commercial sector as well, by making the old merchant families—the so-called *tujjār*—the only agents for those foreign companies exporting to the countries of the region modern goods and luxury, fashionable items.[6] Women were not excluded by this wind of change and, within the commercial sector, some of them even expanded the traditional involvement in trade as previously practised by their mothers and grandmothers, by selling rare imported goods within their expanded family and friends' circles, while, at one and the same time, some female members of ruling families and of the *tujjār* group also started investing either their inheritance or their *mahr* (dowry) in real estates and, in particular, in compounds for foreigners, which they would let; returns were profitable and started being quite often re-invested.[7] Male secretaries, or agents, belonging to subordinate tribes often used and still use to assist these businesswomen in managing their activities: that is a very clear case in which it is not gender, but the tribal affiliation that makes the difference.

Modern Education and the Economic Role of Women

It is obvious that the link between economic growth and the task to build an enabling environment that empowers females, by ensuring them new and wider economic opportunities in their countries, is not automatic. Education and civic clubs, involving both males and females, certainly acted as crucial modernising agents during the second half of the last century in all the Gulf Arab states; they enhanced female self-consciousness as well as female willingness to gain a dynamic public role in their societies. And yet, cultural resistance factors, trying to reduce women's economic empowerment cannot be neglected: the family still has a very strong influence on girls' attitudes and choices, and even if the legal guardianship of a woman is not everywhere as strict as under the Hanbali *fiqh*, such as in Saudi Arabia, no doubt in most cases women are strongly influenced in their decisions by the family and, more specifically, by their fathers or, after marriage, by their husbands, with reference in particular to education, employment and travelling abroad; all that certainly leads also to less economic opportunities for women.

The *iltizam* factor, which means the financial responsibility of men for the female members of the family, can represent a strong cultural restriction. It tends to prevent women, in Saudi Arabia in particular, from looking for a job after graduation, but, at the same time, it can also favour women who, well aware of their rights, are willing and able to work: they are not legally obliged to contribute financially to their family and, under the Hanbali *fiqh*, which clearly recognises women, since the age of sixteen, full economic capacity and equal financial rights, they are formally free to keep and invest/re-invest their money.[8]

The formal legal aspect is nevertheless often contradicted by the prevailing practice in the Gulf Arab region, as the male control over women often prevents them from managing their financial resources, coming either from inheritance, dowry or work. The gap between the Law (*Shari'ah*) and the general prevailing custom (*'urf*), resulting from the cultural limitations still imposed by tribal practices in the area, re-emerges clearly even with reference to the need to enhance the employment of local human resources in the labour market and to a more effective and positive role of local women within the economic realities of their countries. It is true that a rising number of them leaves the domestic circle and obtains jobs, but only the ones recognised by local culture as the most suitable for them; besides, women work primarily as teachers, and their salaries often go to their fathers, brothers and finally their husbands.[9]

Within the framework of the often unthinkable adaptations worked out in the region between tradition, custom, religion and modernity, it is not negligible to notice, on the one hand, that the financial benefits some legal guardians obtain by collecting the salary of their female family members are indicated among the causes of the increasingly widespread non-standard marriages in the region: as a matter of fact, under the provisions of a non-standard marriage contract, the woman's financial contribution to her guardian does not stop, as her legal guardianship does not change. On the other hand, it is not less impressive to consider that, within such a patriarchal conservative context, trying at the one and the same time to absorb modernity on the basis of self-referential solutions, a certain number of single Saudi businesswomen, willing to bypass the legal prohibition for them to travel alone abroad, is sometimes prone to use a non-standard marriage contract as an "employment contract" of a male, who, becoming relative (*mahram*), can accompany them wherever they need to go for work.[10]

The progressive establishment of female schools in the region (Table 6.1), during the last century, was certainly a first important agent of modernisation of the female role in traditional Arab Gulf societies. It contributed to opening up new public roles for women outside the domestic space, and the extremely high level of illiteracy even among them was progressively and quite rapidly reduced throughout the second half of the century.

The majority of local population, in general, never opposed modern education for both genders since its beginnings, provided segregation was respected and education would not divert girls from their traditional role in society as future wives and mothers. Thence, a clash became quite natural and unavoidable with the access of women to higher education institutions and with their successive demand to enter the labour market. Since the 1980s, cultural resistance factors tried to curb what was increasingly perceived as a threat to traditional values, by influencing school curricula, which started putting more emphasis on "the necessary respect of local culture". The cultural discourse was certainly influenced by the regional and international situation, such as the Islamic revolution in Iran in 1979, but, locally, it ended up affecting deeply women's position within their societies; it acted as a regressive factor also with reference to the expansion of their role in the economy, which, on the contrary, should have been enhanced by the rising number of educated young women willing to enter the labour market and, in theory, ready to be more empowered.

Table 6.1: Year of Establishment of the First State Schools for Girls in the Gulf Arab Countries

Country	Year
Bahrain	1928
Kuwait	1937
Oman	1975
Qatar	1955
Saudi Arabia	1961
UAE	1953 (Sharjah) and 1966 (Abu Dhabi)

Source: ECSSR, Abu Dhabi.

On the basis of this trend, in the last decades of the 20th century, the educational systems played a clear role in gender stereotyping and cultural resistance, which was even more evident in the most liberal contexts, which seemed to go back about twenty years. That was particularly plain in Bahrain and in Kuwait, where, since the 1970s, female societies and clubs, though to a different degree, according to their composition, had supported women's rights and the idea to enhance their involvement in their countries' development.[11] The step back of the 1990s emerges from the analysis of the language used in many textbooks of basic education (primary and intermediate), showing a kind of terminology which depicts and favours male role and work in most public spheres (national, political, religious, economic and scientific), while highlighting the positive role of mothers and wives, committed to charitable activities and, when coming to professions, employed only as teachers and medical doctors.

At the beginning of the new century, the Arab Gulf governments seem to be more and more determined to expand women's education and to unblock their potential, by integrating them progressively in the labour market and in the economy of their countries, and yet the governments' political willingness and efforts keep being hindered by cultural resistance factors deriving from custom and tradition. The topical issue of "tradition and identity" comes to the fore within the new doctrinal debate in the Gulf. It is a controversial debate centred around the equation "identity and tribalism versus modernity"; it highlights the present social complexity of the Arab Gulf countries and those inherent contradictions and fragilities, that the positive energies aim to overcome. Avoiding superficial adaptations to modernity is a challenge for human development as a whole in the region and, more specifically, for women and their contribution to development.[12] In this sense, the confrontation with cultural resistance factors sometimes re-emerges in the most unexpected ways; it is not uncommon, for instance that, in some very conservative tribal families, the attainment of a diploma abroad by their young female family members, even in branches of learning quite unusual for girls, is simply considered as "a property for show" within the tribal group and the community.

The only objective of the family is to give their daughters more chances to attract the attention of a future husband, who, in any case, is not supposed to give them the opportunity to practice and integrate in their country's workforce. Distortions of this kind are a quite negative factor breaking in a drastic way the natural link between education and social development that the Gulf Arab states, on the contrary, need to strengthen. The Gulf Cooperation Council (GCC) member states are called to preserve the positive and most authentic values of the past while pursuing, at one and the same time, a kind of modernity which, going beyond the surface, can be the constructive expression of a promising human development they can successfully drive. Employing women's energies in a constructive way for a real modernisation process is a challenge these countries are more and more confronted with, and in which women have their own role to play and their responsibility.

The key is to develop an educational curriculum at all levels of the educational experience that instils knowledge and skills in the mix of technical, analytic and behavioural skills required to support a modern economy. Knowledge economy values teamwork, creativity, invention, problem-solving and communication skills[13]; one cannot forget that education, work and family are always highly interdependent and moral and character development is integral to education. Economic and social developments are overlapping domains: avoiding innovation means avoiding change and progress. The self-mobilised efforts of some female pioneers, supported by their families on the basis of self-referential models, are extremely valuable along the way to engineer new forms of social behaviour in the transitional environment of the Arab Gulf region: the evolutionary process from tribe to state[14] provides the appropriate conditions to re-shape local societies in the light of the challenges and opportunities of the present time.

Behind any highly educated and motivated woman in the Arab Gulf States you always find an enlightened father and family. If the prevailing inertia is overcome, social evolution giving women a new role and space in different spheres, from business to politics, can become an inevitable outcome even in the traditionally conservative environment of the Arab Gulf states; in the last few years the more assertive governments' support in this direction and their massive investments in education are likely to make the difference; they can really steer the region towards that knowledge-based economy more and more looked at as a major priority by the leaderships in our global era. That is definitely the only way these countries have to take in order not to be marginalised and to grow in an integrated and constructive way with their major economic partners.

Knowledge is the cornerstone which the whole process of human development depends on; at the dawn of the new century it is more and more conceived as the most effective driving force of productivity and enhancement of human capital's potential. Local debates in the Gulf often emphasise that creating and spreading knowledge is an essential prerequisite to confront one of those shortcomings often complained of by Gulf Arab academics concerning a local schooling system still too focused on rote learning; the latter is clearly seen by the majority as a method which does not help the adoption of that necessary critical approach to the issues leading to creativity and intellectual curiosity, and thus it does not prevent young people from falling into that general inertia that affects negatively a real shift towards knowledge-based societies.

Such a shift is conditional upon the ability of all the countries of the Gulf region to take a series of steps forward, by actively involving the female members of society, while providing, at the one and the same time, successful models for human development within the wider Islamic and global context. The success of the process would finally be a major result within a network of cooperation efforts for enhanced human security between the Gulf, the Mediterranean basin, the EU and Asia. The final objective is to provide local human resources—males and females—with the necessary skills to operate in diversified economies. The general perception is that this phase seems bound to enhance that gradual change in the status of Gulf Arab women that began with the dawning of the oil era.

In spite of all the social and cultural hindrances, the rising role of women in regional economy is more and more evident nowadays; it is not at all conceived as a westernisation process, on the contrary, it is strictly linked to the re-evaluation of the positive attitudes of the past, as supported and legitimised by the beneficial values of tradition and Islam, and it is re-visited in the light of the new economic reality and of the rising number of educated women in professions, even in the most conservative societies such as Saudi Arabia, where some changes can be perceived, although women's participation in the labour market is still very low—around 8 percent of the total—compared, for instance, to Bahrain, where it reached approximately 35 percent.[15]

Between Slogans and Reality: Which Perspectives?

An ever wider involvement of women in projects aimed at developing knowledge-economy in the region seems to be a quite natural and inevitable trend. The success of the reforms of the schooling and university system currently under way, and the new initiatives aimed at improving the quality of education and training are essential prerequisites to strengthen this trend. The approach to education reforms vary from country to country: UAE and Qatar, for instance, seem to be much more interested in opening branches of prestigious foreign universities; Saudi Arabia is more committed to strengthen public universities, without neglecting, at the same time, the growth of private education institutions, of which the transformation of the female Effat College in University in 2009 and the involvement of Aramco in the project of the King Abdullah University for Science and Technology (KAUST), launched in 2007, are very telling expressions.

An innovation process is dawning, a new phase in which appealing to education as an agent of modernisation and development is much stronger than in the past. Involving local human capital in more diversified economies can effectively strengthen motivation and continuity at the management level, which is not negligible at all for the success of the projects in this direction. The rising presence of women in these projects is the result of the first significant initiatives, which are creating the required basis to strengthen the local female human capital in the labour market. There are some interesting regional examples one can mention. In the most recent years the United Arab Emirates, in spite of their demographic anomaly—the very low percentage of indigenous population—and their manpower needs, decided the establishment of training centres for women aimed to train them for leadership and management positions or, if they are already employed, aimed to enhance their expertise, allowing them to improve their positions and performance in various sectors and fields. "Women for leadership" seems to have become the slogan of an uneasy effort to identify the skills that women need to move into leadership positions in society and business, and to find out the most appropriate blend between formal and informal training, which will open up new career opportunities for them.[16]

In Saudi Arabia, in spite of the policy of strict gender segregation and the already mentioned cultural and social barriers hindering more than elsewhere the female component in the labour market, the most active university-educated women, if and when properly involved, are ready and willing to offer much more to some specific sectors, such as education, social services and medicine, which have already proved to challenge successfully the most conservative culture, and have already offered some enlightened local women the opportunity to contribute effectively to human development in their country. Favouring the access of women to professions traditionally considered a male preserve, such as, for instance, in administration, industry, business and the media, cannot be set apart from that process of improving education in society. Education must be conceived in its comprehensive meaning, so well expressed by the Arabic term *tarbiyyah*, and it involves the person as a whole, with his/her character and values.

In this sense, education can really contribute to social development by combining knowledge and authentic positive values; it is the precondition to development, and the responsibility of educators in every field is even greater in this delicate phase of transition. It is not by chance, for instance, that the section of "Research, Promotion and Education" at the King Abdulaziz Medical City in Riyadh, in which male and female healthcare personnel is together (without segregation) jointly committed to work, can assume particular importance with reference to medical genetics education in a region with an extremely high frequency of genetic disorders largely determined by cultural and legal limitations: the very high consanguinity rates, due to the traditional endogamic tribal marriages, as pointed out by some local medical doctors, make Saudi health authorities well aware of the enormous social and economic costs of a tribal practice affecting a healthier development of indigenous human resources. That is a very positive example of the necessary cooperation between female and male educators and medical doctors for the benefit of future generations against attitudinal and social problems.

Evolution in the female role in society is certainly dependent on a change in attitudes of both males and females, as the various restrictions women are subjected to are often supported by the majority of them and not only by men. The general segregation of female workers in Saudi Arabia is a major example, although, in Riyadh for instance, some professionals often complain of the impossibility to interact directly in conferences and seminars: speaking through a video is not like looking somebody in the face in front of you, some women argue, and the impression can be misleading. And yet, in spite of the stricter segregation in Saudi Arabia than in the other GCC countries, and, somehow, thanks to this gender segregation, the banking and financial sector in the economy is emerging and rising both in terms of female employment rate and investments. Many only for women banks were established in the country in the last few years and the total number of female employees in the sector rose from 972 in 2000 to 3,311 in 2007.[17]

The rising financial female power in the GCC region as a whole is not at all a negligible factor: that is a real power which seems to strengthen the influence of women in the public sphere and in the workplace, opening up to them new higher decision-making positions, which were unthinkable a few years ago within these societies. The number of women as major shareholders in local companies is growing, and strengthening the role of female models in the economy and business in particular tends to erode the entrenchments of tradition; the latter can also emerge quite clearly as contradictory with Islam, its most authentic precepts and its early history. Not surprisingly, Islam is more and more seen by Gulf Arab women as their best vehicle for change and improvement of their status.

The evolutionary process in this direction is confirmed by some facts and figures. In Bahrain, the appointment of a number of women in executive positions in private sectors industries, the appointment of the first Gulf Arab female director of a bank and the election of a businesswoman to the Board of Bahrain's Chamber of Commerce and Industry are considered important steps forward of this decade, and although in the most conservative context of Saudi Arabia women are still barred from the board of directors' meetings in the presence of men, their exercise of power through money in society is a reality fully legitimised by the historic Islamic model of the first wife of the Prophet, Khadijah, who was a successful businesswoman.

The figures in this direction are quite amazing, as Gulf Arab female citizens in our decade are progressively becoming much richer than their male counterparts and they are contributing to economic and social development in a quite effective way: Saudi women already control a very large part of their country's wealth and, according to some estimates, they keep between US$ 7 billion and US$ 10 billion in deposits, besides, between 25 and 40 percent of private businesses in the GCC region are owned by women, the number of businesswomen is rising at a high speed almost everywhere, considering that only in the Emirate of Abu Dhabi by the end of 2006 they had already exceeded 4,000 and that in the year 2007, 35 percent of the investors in the regional real estate sector and 60 percent of new investors in the GCC stock market were represented by women.[18]

In the light of this interesting phenomenon, local associations and councils of businesswomen seem to be quite active in supporting and promoting initiatives aimed at improving the entrepreneurial, managerial and leadership skills of businesswomen, through training and professional networking, in productive and knowledge-intensive sectors in particular. Within this encouraging framework, nonetheless, the growing female participation in the labour market, as it was supported by the development strategies started since the 1970s, is only one of the factors contributing to the rising female financial and economic power in the region, and it is certainly not the main one, as it is quite clear that, on the whole, it remains very modest. Inheritances and dowry certainly keep representing the main factors contributing to local women's wealth, and yet entrepreneurship emerges more and more as a new factor not to be neglected in the future and clearly challenging both cultural resistance forces linked to the local tribal tradition and Western stereotypes.

The development of the women's banking sector is another interesting phenomenon connected with the rising women's economic and financial power. The provision of special services and products for women is strictly linked with the rising importance of the services sector for women and, in particular, with the growth of Islamic banks in the region: new job opportunities emerge at the managerial level too, while, at the same time, within the new dynamic financial communities, gender-segregation can be easily respected, and it can even be reinforced.[19]

No doubt, greater involvement of women in the labour market and in the economy of the GCC states is an essential contribution to the building of social, economic and human capital in the region. Women's task and responsibility is to be promoters of a kind of modernity which, being consistent with the most positive values of Islam and tradition, will give them more opportunities to be empowered. And yet many steps forward are still needed. Some Islamic movements and conservative forces in society are there to hinder such a trend and they cannot be ignored, since they still affect female attitudes and choices, such as the preference for certain jobs and early retirement. The full integration of the female human capital in the regional labour market is still to come and new efforts are needed in this direction.

It is incontrovertible that some amendments to the existing laws regarding labour and personal status are supported by some authoritative women in the region and they could possibly oppose those discriminations strengthened by a mentality which is difficult to modify, and yet it is true that legal provisions do not always produce actual practices. It is a long way. It is made even harder by the very limited or non-existent presence of women in the region's representative organs, such as the *Shura* Councils, but it is also hindered by the fact that parliaments are rarely considered qualified to debate or decide on matters rooted in Islamic jurisprudence[20] and by the not less negligible fact that tribal traditions, custom and practices quite often outweigh legalism. The real question is whether women's rising economic activity and power can really produce major positive changes in the medium term. Some female associations, if managed efficiently, can certainly play a relevant role by coordinating the application of specific programmes aimed at enhancing the female participation rate in the labour market and in the economic growth of their countries: in this direction, for instance, some initiatives supported by Saudi associations promoted both specific training programmes and the issue of loans (micro credit) to women willing to start some private businesses.

Nevertheless, the most important structural changes, which can really enhance the female contribution to the region's development, are strictly linked to a shared responsibility of all the parties: males and females, the government and the private sector, private and public education, schools and universities. The objective of the intellectual *élites* in these countries is to identify and implement new strategies of economic, social and cultural growth founded on innovation in education and training, and thus on a transition towards that knowledge-based economy, which is more and more acknowledged as a priority to make the most of the local human resources of both males and females.

Within this framework, one can understand the reason for the numerous projects and investments in the domain of education, and more specifically, in university education in the last few years. The number of universities in Saudi Arabia rose from 8 to 20 between 2004 and 2008, a series of cooperation agreements were signed with American, European and Asian universities. The already mentioned King Abdullah University of Science and Technology (KAUST) was established at Thuwal, on the Red Sea, in 2007 as the first co-educational university in the Kingdom and, according to king Abdullah, it is there to act as a scientific base as well as a driving force for the national economy, to support knowledge-based industries and innovative economic projects and to serve as a cultural channel for the rest of the world, while integrating, at the same time, with the local reality and the King Abdullah Economic City (KAEC).

Qatar established its "Education City" aimed at educating and training "innovative" leaders of tomorrow, and, beyond any rhetorical declaration, it is supposed to involve with the "Qatar Science and Technology Park" a certain number of both males and females who should be able to benefit their country's economy by "exporting knowledge" as well. In the UAE, the National Authority for Scientific Research was established with the aim to fund research activities in the country. In Abu Dhabi, the Sorbonne and the New York University opened their local branches, while the Dubai School of Government, in collaboration with the National University of Singapore, started offering programmes of "executive education" and it was almost immediately followed by the Centre for Executive Education and Research of Abu Dhabi. The Mohammed bin Rashid Al Maktoum Foundation as well started emphasising its support to all those initiatives aimed at creating in the UAE a knowledge-based society, through grants, scholarships, leadership skills programme and online programmes specifically addressed to women who, otherwise, would not be allowed to continue their higher education.

No doubt, all these initiatives are very significant and they are expression of a trend, which, on the medium term, might have a clear impact on human development, and create new job opportunities for local women, and their wider empowerment in GCC countries' societies, and yet one cannot ignore some inconsistencies and shortcomings: financing research is very positive and important, but the number of local researchers is still very small, opening local branches of foreign universities cannot be disjoined by the abilities of local human resources to attend courses and programmes offered in those universities. Reforms in schooling, started a few years ago, do not generally seem to have given the much-awaited results yet, and a waste of energies and huge investments in higher education is a concrete risk. Educational investments and technological innovations can really lead to the optimal utilisation of human resources only when social attitudes are oriented towards the clear awareness of the importance of responsible and creative participation by all the people in the evolution of the socio-cultural environment. That is an acknowledged dynamic principle in an Islamic framework, since Islam often stresses the need to optimise the utilisation of resources with which God has endowed human beings and nature.[21]

Within this perspective, a more constructive and active involvement of women in the developmental efforts is needed, and the already well-educated and rich women are expected to use their knowledge and their economic and financial power to shape more effectively the context for an enlightened phase of sustainable growth. That is an evolutionary process, in which both females and males, while interacting more and more with their partners in the global economy, can really benefit future generations in the region on equal terms, and help them to develop their full potential and to share the fruits of development.[22]

Notes

1. D.C. North, *Istituzioni, cambiamento istituzionale, evoluzione dell'economia* [*Institutions, Institutional Change and Economic Performance*], Bologna, 1994, p. 123.
2. R. Said Zahlan, *The Making of the Modern Gulf States*, Reading, 1998, p. 83.
3. See R.B. Serjeant, *Customary Law Documents as Source of History*, in R.G. Smith (ed.), *Society and Trade in South Arabia*, London, 1996, p. 102.
4. With reference to the *fereej*, see M.A. Al-Naim, *The Home Environment in Saudi Arabia and Gulf States*, Vol. I, Milano, 2006, pp. 168-169, 176.
5. F. Heard-Bey, *From Trucial States to United Arab Emirates*, London, 1996, p. 144.
6. Cf. S.N. Khalaf, *Gulf Societies and the Image of Unlimited Good*, in *Dialectical Anthropology* 17: 53-84, 1992, p. 56.
7. Cf. F. Heard-Bey, *From Trucial States to United Arab Emirates*, *cit.*, p. 235.
8. See M. Yamani, *Some Observations on Women in Saudi Arabia*, in M. Yamani (ed.), *Feminism and Islam. Legal and Literary Perspectives*, Reading, 1996, pp. 276-277.
9. K. Al-Azri, *Gender, State and Culture in Oman*, in V. Fiorani Piacentini, E. Maestri (eds.), *From Tribe to State. Perspectives on Identity, Social and Cultural Dynamics in Eastern Arabia*, Milano, 2007, p. 56.

10. See Maha Yamani, *Modern Variations to the Standard Muslim Marriage Contract: The Saudi Experience*, paper presented at the conference on "The Global Gulf", University of Exeter, 4-6 July 2006, in particular pp. 2, 4. For a thorough analysis of the new trends in marriage contracts in Saudi Arabia see by the same Author, *Polygamy and Law in Contemporary Saudi Arabia*, Reading, 2008.
11. With reference to women's societies in Bahrain and their role in the country in the first half of the 1970s, see E.A. Nakhleh, *Bahrain: Political Development in a Modernizing Society*, London, 1976, pp. 52-55.
12. Cf. V. Fiorani Piacentini-E. Maestri, *The Gulf Region and Regional Historiography on Issues such as Modernity vs. Tradition/Identity*, in "Nuova Rivista Storica", September-December 2006, pp. 795-812.
13. T.A. Kochan, *Government Polices for a Knowledge-based Economy*, in ECSSR (Ed.), *Human Resource Development in a Knowledge-Based Economy*, Abu Dhabi, 2003, pp. 126-127.
14. On the subject see F. Heard-Bey, *From Tribe to State. The Transformation of Political Structure in Five States of the GCC*, Milano, 2008.
15. The approximate percentages of women's participation in the labour market of the other GCC countries vary between the low percentage of Saudi Arabia and the most encouraging percentage of Bahrain.
16. An interesting initiative in this direction is the project proposed and carried out by Dr. Amna Khalifa of the UAE University, Director of the Humaid ibn Rashid al-Nuaimi Institute for Human Development in Ajman. See G.H. Talami, *Women, Education and Development in the Arab Gulf Countries*, ECSSR, Abu Dhabi, 2004, p. 36.
17. See SAMA, *Annual Report*, Riyadh, 1429 H. (2008 A.D.), p. 230.
18. I am particularly grateful to the Saudi economist Dr. Hend Al-Sheikh for providing me with some of these data. See also N. Biberovic, *Women's Capital in the Gulf's Islamic Banking Sector*, in "The GRC Economic Research Bulletin", Issue no. 5, January 2008, pp. 22-26.
19. The reference is to the banks' branches for women in Saudi Arabia and to the so called "VIP Centres for Women" providing

several services (brokerage, car-hire, etc.). As for the Islamic banking sector, it is interesting to notice that it tends to raise in a very significant way the number of very qualified women in their staff.

20. The case of Bahrain, for instance, is quite indicative of this fact: in May 2009 Bahrain's *Majlis al-Nawab* (Lower House) endorsed the draft of a family law, aiming to improve the legal status of women, and yet such a draft law covers only Sunnis, after the Shiite parliamentary group al-Wefaq refused to endorse this law, considering it unacceptable from a religious point of view.
21. Cf. A. Khurshid, *Economic Development in an Islamic Framework*, Leicester (UK), 1979.
22. Cf. J.S. Al-Suwaidi, *Human Resource Development in a Knowledge-Based Economy*, in ECSSR (Ed.), *Human Resource Development in a Knowledge-Based Economy*, Abu Dhabi, 2003, pp. 3-15; N. Janardhan, *Economic Diversification and Knowledge Economy in the Gulf*, paper presented at the "Gulf Studies Conference", Exeter (UK), 1-4 July 2008; S. Wahab, *KAUST. A Dream Come True*, in "Diplomat", Issue 10 – Nov. 2007, pp. 17-20.

References

Al-Azri, K., "Gender, State and Culture in Oman," in V. Fiorani Piacentini, E. Maestri (eds.), *From Tribe to State. Perspectives on Identity, Social and Cultural Dynamics in Eastern Arabia*, Milano, 2007.

Al-Naim, M.A., *The Home Environment in Saudi Arabia and Gulf States*, vol. I, Milano, 2006.

Al-Suwaidi, J.S., "Human Resource Development in a Knowledge-Based Economy," in ECSSR (ed.), *Human Resource Development in a Knowledge-Based Economy*, Abu Dhabi, 2003.

Biberovic, N., "Women's Capital in the Gulf's Islamic Banking Sector," *The GRC Economic Research Bulletin*, Issue no. 5, January, 2008.

Fiorani Piacentini V.-Maestri, E., "The Gulf Region and Regional Historiography on Issues such as Modernity vs. Tradition/Identity," *Nuova Rivista Storica*, September-December, 2006.

Heard-Bey, F., *From Tribe to State. The Transformation of Political Structure in Five States of the GCC*, Milano, 2008.

Heard-Bey, F., *From Trucial States to United Arab Emirates*, London, 1996.

Janardhan, N., *Economic Diversification and Knowledge Economy in the Gulf*, paper presented at the "Gulf Studies Conference", Exeter (UK), 1-4 July, 2008.

Khalaf, S.N., *Gulf Societies and the Image of Unlimited Good*, in *Dialectical Anthropology*, New York, 1992.

Khurshid, A., *Economic Development in an Islamic Framework*, Leicester (UK), 1979.

Kochan, T.A., "Government Polices for a Knowledge-based Economy," in ECSSR (ed.), *Human Resource Development in a Knowledge-Based Economy*, Abu Dhabi, 2003.

Nakhleh, E.A., *Bahrain: Political Development in a Modernizing Society*, London, 1976.

North, D.C., *Istituzioni, cambiamento istituzionale, evoluzione dell'economia* [*Institutions, Institutional Change and Economic Performance*], Bologna, 1994.

Said Zahlan, R., *The Making of the Modern Gulf States*, Reading, 1998.

SAMA, *Annual Report*, Riyadh, 1429 H. (2008 A.D.).

Serjeant, R.B., "Customary Law Documents as Source of History," in R.G. Smith (ed.), *Society and Trade in South Arabia*, London, 1996.

Talami, G.H., *Women, Education and Development in the Arab Gulf Countries*, ECSSR, Abu Dhabi, 2004.

Wahab, S., *KAUST. "A Dream Come True," Diplomat*, Issue 10 – Nov, 2007.

Yamani, Maha, *Modern Variations to the Standard Muslim Marriage Contract: The Saudi Experience*, paper presented at the conference on "The Global Gulf", University of Exeter, 4-6 July, 2006.

Yamani, Maha, *Polygamy and Law in Contemporary Saudi Arabia*, Reading, 2008.

Yamani, Mai, "Some Observations on Women in Saudi Arabia," in M. Yamani (ed.), *Feminism and Islam. Legal and Literary Perspectives*, Reading, 1996.

7

"Only for Women": Women, the State, and Reform in Saudi Arabia

Amélie Le Renard

In Saudi Arabia, women have constituted a separate category, legally discriminated against and spatially segregated. This segregation often has been perceived as "traditional." However, reference to the "traditional" or "conservative" character of Saudi society does not help us understand the persistence and consolidation of sex segregation. It is not at all evident that the strict frontier separating men and women, inscribed in the law as necessary and compulsory, has been weakened following the development of the state, even if practices have varied according to regions and changing political contexts in the Kingdom. Both women's educational level and (daily) activities have completely changed over the last 50 years; at the same time, most of these activities have developed inside a "female sphere" consisting of a mosaic[1] of new female spaces where entry is forbidden to men. Indeed, a large majority of Saudi women do not at least officially frequent male spaces except to visit their male relatives (*mahram*, plur. *maharim*).[2] Thus, in this article I show how contemporary sex segregation is inseparable from the state's development and enrichment.

Moreover, segregation often has been approached in terms of bans and repression. In contrast, and without denying the limits of women's activities and mobility and more generally the relationships of power between Saudi men and women,[3] I will show what spatial segregation as a public policy has produced in terms of social categories, spaces, norms, and identifications.[4] Governmental discourses, including laws, measures, and policies, have served to perpetuate and consolidate the principle of sex segregation. The economic, political, and social context of Saudi Arabia must be taken into account in the analysis of sex segregation. This article will expose first how this specific spatial and ideological categorization of women has emerged together with discourses of national development, then how it has been both transformed and reinforced through the more recent discourse of reform. Sex segregation will be studied on different levels, as this organization is daily produced and reproduced by women. This is why it is important to highlight the ways in which Saudi women, targeted by this categorization, are practicing this category daily, justifying it, and using it to arrange an autonomous space for themselves — an increasingly widened and diversified space for female socialization.

The following observations are based on fieldwork in Saudi Arabia. My first field study, in April-May 2005, focused on female elites (university professors, journalists, businesswomen, and intellectuals with different orientations) who graduated in the 1980s and live in Riyadh or Jeddah. Some of them had been invited by the government to participate in national events and conferences organized under the slogan of reform and told me about their experiences. Then, in 2006 and 2007, I spent eight months in Riyadh studying young women's lifestyles, daily activities, aspirations, and the constraints they are subjected to in the city.[5]

Sex Segregation and the Production of "Saudi Women" as a Category

The position of women must be analyzed in the context of the political projects of contemporary states and of their historical transformations,[6] including their projects and discourses on "remaking women."[7] In a number of Muslim countries, a specific political discourse on women has tended to transform them into a symbol, to ascribe to them a uniform identity. In some states, they are supposed to represent the virtuous implementation of Islam by way of the obligation of being veiled in public space[8] (in the Islamic Republic of Iran, for instance), whereas in other countries, they embody a discourse of modernity, imposed by the state through a ban on veiling (Turkey, Tunisia, Pahlavi Iran),[9] among other measures. The formation of a national identity implies a specific discourse about women's place in society: it is not possible to understand the current situation of women in Saudi Arabia without taking into account the history of the formation of the state.

In contemporary Riyadh, women are rarely visible in "mixed" public places, which does not, however, mean that their activities are limited to the domestic sphere. In fact, the segmentation of Saudi society into different spaces, where access is restricted either to men or to women, should not be confused with a division between a male public sphere (for production) and a female private sphere (for reproduction). This paradigm does not correspond to contemporary Saudi society, given that exclusively female public spaces exist, such as schools, universities, charitable organizations, women's administrations, government offices, and shops. In fact, the strict segregation between women's and men's workplaces and socializing spaces has been instituted legally and perpetuated through a discourse on modernization, including specific laws, since the 1960s. This process differs from what has generally happened in other countries in the region, where the rise of paid work for women in the cities has engendered the entry of women into a pre-existing male public sphere and the gradual decline of the frontiers between a (female) private sphere and a (male) public sphere where women would have to prove themselves to be accepted. In Saudi Arabia, the barriers separating male and female spaces are solidifying while female spaces are becoming increasingly wide and diversified, ranging far beyond the private sphere.

The Institutionalization of Sex Segregation

This segregated social organization has been put in place in a specific context, or rather a double context: on the one hand the Islamic revival movement (*Sahwa*)[10] took hold within society and the state, while on the other hand the regime found itself financially capable of creating parallel female institutions by advocating development. The economic change has indeed been a *sine qua non* for the establishment of a specific discourse on the status of women and their place in Saudi society. The spread of the Saudi state's authority and bureaucracy over the peninsula,[11] followed by the oil boom, have materially enriched the population, further giving rise to greater urbanization and the decline of women's work. Even if women's staying at home is often presented as linked to "traditions and customs" (*'adat wa taqalid*) by Saudis, several academic works[12] have shown how large numbers of rural women previously used to work in the fields or earn money through crafts; Bedouin women also participated in family activities such as camel and sheep breeding. Once in the city, these tasks almost disappeared; men's salaries were enough to provide for the family's needs. Moreover, imported goods were cheaper than local craft products.[13]

With the improvement of standards of living, the fact that women did not have to work has been considered a marker of both richness and moral distinction in the context of the oil boom, a privilege protecting them from outside dangers, as opposed to foreign women who have to work. Oil rent has been an important precondition, first, for this decline of women's work within the city,[14] and second, for the development of a segregated female sphere, composed of parallel and exclusively female institutions, whose creation and maintenance have necessitated the expenditure of large sums of money.[15] My point is not to pretend that the Saudi state has invented spatial segregation between men and women, but rather to show how it has imposed and institutionalized this principle of organization in a specific manner, whereas previously customs, social conventions, and judicial principles were flexible, changing, and highly diversified across regions and social groups, each marked by a different history and diverse influences, and following different Islamic judicial schools. Spatial segregation and various state rules concerning women have contributed to defining Saudi women as a unified category encompassing their different origins and groups of belonging. Through these policies, influenced by Sahwist discourse, a model of the Saudi woman as pious and virtuous, modest, educated, financially comfortable, and devoted to her family has been promoted by the state.[16] At the same time, frontiers separate her from Saudi men and from the abounding foreign population, whose status is different.[17]

From the 1960s, free and non-compulsory education for boys and girls spread across the territory[18] as the *ulama* still controlled the public debate over the central values of society.[19] Through this process, the state, whether the government or the official *ulama*,[20] acquired more influence over the lives of the individuals and families who were to make up the "new" Saudi society. Education, organized on strictly segregated lines,[21] institutionalized the separation between the sexes at the same time as it opened a legitimate public space for women in which they would be able to carry on various kinds of activities. Instead of being dispersed in different houses, girls henceforth would be gathered in one place; instead of seeing only the members of their families, they would come face to face with women from other social groups, other backgrounds, and other ways of life. Other segregated places for women developed gradually, in accordance with laws imposing separation between men and women.

The 160th article of the work law, established in 1969, bans mixed workplaces.[22] It thus restrains women's choices concerning paid work - but at the same time, it legitimizes the fact that women work outside the home, a possibility which was henceforth officially mentioned.

Sex Segregation in a Global City

These principles mark social organization in a particular way: the economy of spaces shapes women's daily lives and activities, especially in Riyadh, where sex segregation is stricter than in Jeddah and the Eastern Province which nuances the uniformity of state policies. In a few decades, the city of Riyadh has exploded both in terms of population and spread, and has been transformed by the construction of new buildings, skyscrapers, and shopping malls. While Riyadh's socio-spatial configuration changed following economic and political transformations, sex segregation has not declined, but rather has been renewed and re-invented. In contemporary urban Saudi society, the principle of segregation between men and women has repercussions on spaces, attitudes, and bodies, which intensify women's constitution as a category distinct from the rest of the population. To some extent, space in Riyadh is sexualized. Each space involves specific interdictions. Sometimes, these codes are implicit, because they are considered obvious, such as in most cafés, where entry is forbidden to women. Bans that are not considered to be obvious are mentioned on the entrance door. The spaces dedicated to families are *implicit*, because they are obviously forbidden to single men, but *explicitly* forbidden to women unaccompanied by a man, through a sign: "unaccompanied women are not allowed."[23] However, this ban has not been respected for a few years now, and groups of female friends spend time together in restaurants and cafes without accompanying males.[24] A sign reading "only for women"[25] marks women's public spaces as forbidden to men, the number of which is increasing. These codes define frontiers between different spaces and categorize them. The basic public/private dichotomy turns out to be difficult to apply as such. For instance, the tinted windows of a car act as a sieve, a sort of airlock between private space and women's public space. In family restaurants, the boxes concealing one "family"[26] from another constitute a private space transplanted to public space. However, in the city,[27] no space (flat, hotel room, restaurant, or car) is inviolably private, since it is never entirely safe from the possible intervention of the religious police (the Committee for the Promotion of Virtue and the Repression of Vice, *Hay'a lil-amr bil-ma'ruf wa al-nahi 'an al-munkar*). However, this institution, which has been involved in several scandals[28] has lost a good deal of its previous prerogatives in the past few years.[29]

Such a division between male and female places is only possible because of modern means of communication: the phone, the Internet, and videoconferencing.[30] Without them, and without the economic means their intensive utilization requires, the development of a separate women's space for professional activities, however limited, could not be envisaged. At the university, classes through closed-circuit television have existed since the 1970s,[31] but according to a female professor at King Saud University (in Riyadh), some mixed PhD classes took place up to 1995; after which, they were replaced by videoconference.[32]

Nor should the spread of the *'abaya* (long black overcoat) across Saudi Arabia be understood as the simple conservation of a traditional dress. In many regions, it is a relatively recent phenomenon, a symbol of national identity based on a specific implementation of Islam, thus linked to the expansion and development of the Saudi state, rather than a symbol of custom; on the contrary, it is meant to transcend the fragmentation of customs. More precisely, this is the symbol of an urban Saudi identity which supplants other identities, such as the *Hijazi* one.[33]In other words, it could be described as an invented tradition,[34] linked to the state's growing influence on people's lives. In the southwestern province of 'Asir, women, who used to participate in agricultural activities until a few decades ago, mostly stopped working outside the home and began wearing the *'abaya.*[35] This phenomenon is not limited to women: men's dress also has been transformed, but not with such a religious connotation.[36] Nowadays, traditional dresses are relegated to exhibitions about heritage, but in the malls, one of the only accessible mixed places, women wear the black *'abaya.*

Let us be more specific on how the *'abaya* is used, because it permits a better understanding of the economy of space within urban society, which is quite different from the way the Islamic veil is worn in other countries. The *'abaya* is not worn the whole day; it works rather as a passage through the mixed public space, between the different women's spaces and the private space. It is not held with a pin unlike the Egyptian women's veil, for instance, which is worn all day long it is light, easy to put on, and easy to take off. For instance, in the girls' section of King Saud University, students arrive concealed under their *'abaya,* maintaining a correct covering because of the possible inspections at the entrance. As soon as they have gone through the entrance, a special room permits the removal of one's overcoat. Once beyond this point, the university girls' section looks like a vast luxuriant garden surrounded by walls. Except for the compulsory long skirt, students exhibit a keen awareness of the latest Western fashions.

Thus, women's current status is linked to the political and economic formation of the state, as state authority progressively spread and became inscribed in social relations and spatial organization, embedded in a particular way with familial relationships of power. The boundary between state and family as institutions and networks of power is ambivalent. On the one hand, the state has partially supplanted the family and domestic sphere in girls' education. On the other hand, state reforms regarding women are not compulsory, but rather depend on the family's choice: in the end, it is the legal guardian who decides to give or withhold consent to his daughter's education, work,[37] or, to mention a more recent example, to a woman's possession of a personal identity card.[38] In general, every initiative a woman might take is dependent upon her legal guardian's agreement. Thus, due to state policies, women have broken out of the domestic sphere and entered a public female sphere of activities, but only on condition of their families' agreement.

Making Women's Status a Public Problem: Saudi Women and the Government's Discourse of Reform

Beyond these measures implementing physical separation, a discourse of reform on Saudi women has progressively emerged: their status has become one of the thorniest problems in Saudi society, especially after the opening of debates between intellectuals under the aegis of the government consequent to September 11 and the bombings in Saudi Arabia in 2003. Since then, the government has been engaged in policies fighting against "deviants,"[39] "terrorism," and "extremism," and promoting "reformism," "moderation," "tolerance," and "the culture of dialogue," a discourse addressed both to the American ally and, above all, to the Saudi population. As the regime's legitimacy was put at stake by bombings and clashes on its territory, it was necessary to produce a discourse aimed at remaking the "nation," a word central in this rhetoric. In this framework, groups affected by particular problems in Saudi society-as defined by the government-have been solicited to participate in various state initiatives. Saudi women, as a category, were among them. Consequently, contrary to widespread opinion, the women's question in Saudi Arabia is not taboo-at least, not anymore. It has been discussed intensively by public personalities such as certain members of the government, some official and unofficial *ulama*, and a number of female and male intellectuals with different orientations. In this context, elite women have become more visible within national media and state institutions. I would like to show how the government's discourse of reform, while putting forward elite women and publicizing the debates about various problems Saudi women confront, contributes to strengthening the category of "Saudi women" as a necessary framework to which the latter are confined.

The National Dialogue on Women

In this respect, the third "national dialogue" on women's rights and duties in Saudi society among a cycle of "national" debates organized under the aegis of the government[40] - marks an important step, indicative of how the government's current initiatives tend to organize Saudi society through units represented by monopolistic institutions controlled by the state.[41] The third national dialogue was held in Medina and involved 70 participants, half of whom were female. The topics under discussion had been defined by the organizers: women's rights and duties; women and work; women and education; and women and society. The invited female participants were well-known women who had reached prominent positions in professional fields: university professors in sociology, psychology, education, Islamic sciences; physicians; or leaders of social or religious foundations and associations. Eighteen researchers and intellectuals had written papers on different subjects, such as the image of women in educational textbooks, the problems encountered by poor women in Saudi society, or the psychological consequences of domestic violence.[42] Generally speaking, the debates, which were not public and are therefore only accessible through the prism of the media, seem to have been limited to the antagonism between those who claim to be "with" women and for their increasing "participation in society" and those who oppose any change, including women's work outside the home.[43] Saudi newspapers published descriptions of this antagonism, which apparently culminated in one of the male participants affirming that Saudi women had more than they deserved, given that the "car driving" female demonstrators of 1990 were back in their posts at the university;[44] after these words, according to the press, one of the female participants appeared to have burst into tears.[45] At the end of the dialogue, the participants agreed on 19 final recommendations which the male participants then presented to the then-Crown Prince 'Abdullah, and the female participants to his spouse, thus respecting sex segregation. The recommendations were discussed with him before being published with his agreement.[46]

The recommendations reaffirm the first duty of women, their role "side by side with men" in the "conservation of the family as a unit," while specifying their right to work and to earn their living within the limits defined in the Qu'ran, Sunna, and consensus of religious scholars (*ijma'*). The recommendations also ask for the creation of a "national" organization aimed at treating "the subjects linked to women and family" in coordination with governmental and "civil" institutions. A common feature of these recommendations is that they do not question sex segregation but rather reinforce it by suggesting the creation of more specific institutions for women. It corresponds to the opinions expressed in the interviews with elite women: even if some of them envisage the end of sex segregation in the long term or are theoretically against this spatial organization, in the contemporary context, they would rather ask for the creation of more female institutions, such as tribunals within which women could defend their rights (especially in divorce cases), means of transport for women, and more segregated workplaces, etc.

Aside from the limited impact of the negotiations, the dialogue mainly has permitted the participants to complain or to give their suggestions for changing the state of affairs, without clear practical consequences. The female participants I interviewed appeared to appreciate the initiative for being new, despite its lack of results, as one interviewee, a participant in the dialogue, indicated: "I think that even if there are no clear results, the important thing is to open the dialogue, including in the media: I switch on television and I see that they are talking about Saudi women, not on a foreign channel, but on a Saudi channel. This is a change."[47] This might mark a step towards making women's problems public. Some of them explained that the government would take into account, from all the recommendations, those which fit its objectives, and then considered that the participants' grievances had been heard. However, most of them seemed disappointed, if not angry, concerning the dialogue and what they expected from it, though some of them explained they did not expect anything from it anyway. Most interviewees seemed to not take the dialogue seriously and did not see in it any hope of significant short-term change.

The dialogue appears to have been aimed at making public a debate under the aegis of the state, a process through which women are now recognized by the state as a specific category of the population with specific problems to be discussed within state institutions, rather than at launching new measures. Its effects have been to institutionalize this debate, to designate problems pertaining to a category, and to appoint female elites considered legitimate to symbolize the category. They are supposed to *represent* women as a category; but I would rather say that they *symbolize* women for two reasons. First, they are not elected, but designated as representative by state institutions, and second, they are not endowed with effective prerogatives. Through this event, some specialists in sociology, literature, or Islamic law, who are under the impression that they have a real opportunity to have their say, come to defend their opinions in debate with opponents. Through this confrontation, two camps, Islamist and liberal, to some extent appointed as such by the organizers, were supposed to represent Saudi women. In the end, such antagonisms only led to a weak, empty consensus. The main effect of the dialogue was to make the category of "women" exist, to the extent that women considered experts on women and on "women's problems" and experiences will have no other choice but to address the state as women, and in ways that the state has defined.

Integration of Some Elite Women into State Institutions

In the framework of this discourse of reforms, other initiatives have participated in the symbolization of Saudi women as a category, i.e. the appointment of some women supposed to represent all women within state institutions, without having real prerogatives. For instance, the government has appointed some women, generally with an academic background and coming from different regions in the Kingdom, as consultants of the *majlis al-Shura* (Consultative

Council).[48] This is a double strategy: the symbolization of "Saudi women" as a category of the population is coupled with the necessity of improving the Saudi image abroad. They have two types of prerogatives: first, they have to represent Saudi Arabia within international parliamentary meetings;[49] second, the council members can have recourse to them as advisers when they consider it necessary.[50] Their interventions in the *majlis* are apparently confined to subjects linked to their "category." According to Salwa Hazza', one of the three first female consultants for the *majlis al-Shura*, the council members only ask the female consultants about specific, so-called women's and family questions such as the inflation of dowries, the opening of consulting institutes for concluding marriages, and even breastfeeding.[51]

Given this limited role, some elite women solicited as consultants in the framework of this policy expressed their disappointment. A businesswoman, who was asked by the council members to give her opinion about the reform of workplace law, explained that her scope had been limited to "questions concerning women" and regrets not having been informed about the final decisions.[52] A female journalist, committed to making public women's problems through her articles, explained how the image of the participation of women was used for publicity in the newborn Committee of Journalists,[53] which would not have bothered her if women had an effective role in decisions: "Now, in the committee of journalists, there are two women. The presence of women in this place where decisions are taken is a good thing, even if their presence for the time being is a question of appearance. Anyway, the presence of women has been until now a question of appearance, it is not effective...The committee of journalists represents the educated, cultured stream in the country. They have to give a positive image. There are women, we vote, we are elected, it is a positive first step, but I am in a hurry. It does not go quickly."[54]

Because of women's symbolization within governmental institutions, all the women are supposed to feel that, through the process of reform, they are represented and heard. This formation of a category may seem natural in this context of segregated social organization; in fact, it is a consequence of this social organization and indeed contributes to its reinforcement. Through the recent discourse of reform, the government tries to make state institutions appear to be integrating diverse "groups" that used to be marginalized in order to renew the state's legitimacy. Concerned "groups," designated as such, are now consulted, in a strictly defined framework, before decisions are made. The integration of elite women as consultants and experts, who are supposed to symbolize Saudi women as a category and to be able to talk about their specific problems, is a change in the regime's organization. More precisely, it is indicative of a process of authoritarian consolidation, renewing the modalities of elites' integration and the regime's legitimization.[55]

This process of elite women's inclusion and promotion is ambivalent. Elite women's participation occurs in strictly defined frameworks, as has been shown previously, and was denounced by some interviewees as mere window dressing.[56] Many women do not pay attention to initiatives labeled as "new" in a context where change is promoted inside the country and abroad[57] while they do not perceive changes or just do not care about them. Women do not necessarily feel affected by these initiatives, as the failure of the women's list at the Eastern Region Chamber of Commerce has shown.[58] The presence of elite women in state institutions, their visibility in newspapers, and the way these women with brilliant careers in several fields (e.g. medicine, business, and academia) are publicly promoted as models engender the spread of new images of Saudi women, occupying unusual roles. However, a good deal of interviewed young women, while pursuing high professional objectives, said they did not identify with these women, who had often studied abroad, came from rich families, and were far from their own daily problems. This reflects the divisions and frontiers inside the female sphere, and the limits of Saudi women's identification with a category symbolized within state institutions.

Appropriating Female Spaces, Developing a Female Sphere of Activities

State institutions have designated women as a category for which they develop a particular discourse as well as policies adapted to the issues, as they view them, pertaining to this group. For its protagonists, the women's category has become the necessary and monopolistic framework for relations of solidarity as well as for initiatives of change. Women can only act as women and can only do so inside this visible and recognized framework erected by the state. Gender segregation deprives Saudi women and Saudi men of many outlets for their activities, but at the same time, it opens another, legitimate field of action up to them. This protected space works as a lever to develop all kinds of activities. The category of "women" eventually becomes the starting point of every action; subsequently, the expansion of women's activities, which brings about the expansion of segregated space, logically leads to the strengthening of the category.

As mentioned before, in the 1980s and 1990s, the strengthening of segregation laws together with the increase in educated women caused the emergence of a female sphere of activities. Education was the first segregated sector and has remained, until now, the premier employer of women. Since the 1960s, women also have been participating in charitable organizations, generally under the aegis of princesses, an activity easily accepted since it requires skills considered typically female, such as generosity and devotion to others. In the charitable sector, a female space first emerged through the creation of the female "association" *Nahda* (founded by Princess Sara al-Faysal in 1962), then the opening of female sections in the biggest charity foundations charged with taking care of poor women, handicapped children, orphans, etc. This field is closely controlled by the Ministry of Social Affairs, which has had a female branch since the 1960s; as associations and foundations have multiplied, they represent currently a broad space for women's socialization, as well as voluntary and paid work.

Women's Appropriation of Religious Discourses

The religious sphere stopped being a male monopoly after female faculties of religious sciences opened,[59] which led to the graduation of increasing numbers of female students in religious sciences and the creation of female sections within the religious foundations. It is worth pointing out that Saudi women do not follow custom and go to pray at the mosque, because most *ulama* advise female believers to stay at home for prayer, except for the period of Ramadan.[60] Women's religious practice used to be individual or familial, contrary to the practice of men, for whom the mosque is a space for socialization. With the opening of religious spaces for women, a religious discourse by women and for women emerged; through this process, women became enunciators and subjects of Sahwist discourse, which had had an important role in implementing sex segregation and defining Saudi women as a category of identification.

Female Islamic intellectuals have been writing in newspapers and publishing books most of them about women and Islam since the 1980s.[61] In this period, women involved in the religious field were unusual; among them, it is said that a few female preachers went to Afghanistan.[62] Islamic female institutions, or female sections within male institutions, opened at the beginning of the 1990s. As a young interviewee explained, women go to this type of institution both to be entertained and to learn [*tarfih wa tathqif*],[63] as well as to escape from the domestic space, filled as it is with sometimes suffocating obligations. The interviewee, a female student at the Imam Muhammad bin Saud (Islamic) University in Riyadh, who also was working on a business project with three of her female friends, went to the female section of an Islamic institution twice a week. In these spaces for women, various activities are proposed, such as conferences featuring invited female preachers, lessons to memorize the Qu'ran, and classes on religion, in addition to training courses in English, self-improvement, and even beauty care.

These spaces, autonomous from the family, have spread quickly, since participation in religious-based solidarity groups is easy and legitimate in the Saudi context. Lessons to learn the Qu'ran by heart are organized in all urban areas. Female preachers' conferences are frequent within universities, religious or charitable foundations, and on television. More recently, female preachers have been allowed to preach in some mosques, entry to which is reserved to women for the occasion, indicating the expansion of the phenomenon.[64] Through this female religious space, some female preachers have become well-known. For their female audience, religious activities allow them to achieve, to some extent, an emancipation from domestic duties and to have their own commitments in another field and another space beyond the domestic one. This kind of emancipation can be perceived in the words which a young interviewee, committed to these activities, used in describing a female preacher she particularly appreciated: according to her, this well-known preacher would appear to have "decided not to marry" to "devote herself to her cause" and "to be able to work from sunrise to sunset."[65] The interviewee perceived the preacher as both an exception and a model, because she was totally devoted to her religious activities.

Generally speaking, in the contemporary period, female preachers do not contest the official discourse about women, approximately the same as that of the Council of State *Ulama*, a discourse which according to them is more favorable to women than to custom. For example, they affirm girls' right not to be married against their will, the right to have a job, to inherit, to be educated, and the right to get a living allowance in case of a repudiation. Most of the time, they do not speak beyond their "specialty" (women in Islam, women's role in society, Muslim women and globalization, the family in Islam, children's upbringing in Islam, etc.), and do not deal with what are not specifically "female" subjects. Unlike their male counterparts, they are generally not committed to making particular political claims or protests, except in their criticism of the "Western" (American) way of life[66] and the supposed intention of the West to impose it on Saudi society. But although their discourse stays confined within the boundaries of the category of "women" and does not clearly contest the established order, their practices reveal their personal commitment and some emancipation vis-à-vis their families. With a deep knowledge of religious matters, women shape certain spaces of religiosity and sociability in their image, redefine the pious to assert themselves as subjects and to claim rights—even limited ones—in a context where religious language, to a great extent, monopolizes debates.

Women's Access to Workplaces

Religious spaces are part of the mosaic of female spaces where increasingly diversified activities are found. Non-constraining development plans, elaborated with the participation of foreign experts, have recommended the creation of workplaces for women since 1980.[67] In the 1990s, given the high rates of joblessness in the country, especially for the young who no longer could find opportunities in the saturated public sector, manpower has been designated as an important problem. In this context, the question of women's work has been linked to both nationalization of the labor force ("Saudization") and the development of the private sector. The nationalization of jobs in the private sector has been confronted by problems that have been attributed to double standards between Saudis and expatriate workers, given the absence of a constraining legislation on the expatriate workers' schedules and salaries. This made the cost of Saudi workers too exorbitant, or placed the salaries too low to attract them.[68]

As Saudi women are generally graduates from universities and have their own motivations to work which might not only be earning money, but also going out of one's home everyday and feeling "active" in life[69] they have been targeted as potentially good employees for the private sector, except for the necessity of respecting sex segregation rules. To go beyond this difficulty, some firms have opened female sections. The first female branch of a bank (Al Rajhi bank) was opened in Riyadh in 1980 and was aimed at serving female customers. In 1982, 13 female branches of banks existed in Riyadh and Jeddah.[70] More recently, this dynamic has been facilitated by the change of some laws concerning women's work in the context of reform. Some banks and firms have created female sections; some women, too, have created their own enterprises and have employed women.[71]

Women have been allowed to open a firm in their own name only since 2004, though previously they could do so by borrowing a male relative's name. However, this is far from being a mass phenomenon; in fact, it only touches a small minority. A woman willing to create a firm generally receives a license specifying that men's entry into the building is forbidden, as explained to me by a woman who founded a computer training center in Riyadh: "Here, this is a training center for women, men are not allowed to enter because I have a license for women only. The commission which gave me the license regularly comes to check how the center is working, and I do not have any means to make it a mixed place...The employees are women and the people who do the training sessions are women. In any case, there is another center for men."[72] Sometimes, this process of segregation gives rise to complications; for instance the entrance door has to be transferred to another place if it is judged to be too close to a men's entrance door, as explained to me by a woman who wanted to create a training center and eventually gave up after months spent changing the building's configuration and waiting for administrative permission.[73]

Given these restrictions, the expansion of the female sphere of activities is proceeding slower than the ambitions harbored by women are; permission to create more parallel female institutions takes a long time to be granted. Since 2004-2005,[74] in the framework of the discourse of reform previously described, the government has been promoting young women's work by recommending the creation of female sections and the hiring of Saudi women by public administrations and private firms, which development plans had recommended since the 1990s. In June 2005, the Minister of the Economy launched a measure aimed at replacing all the foreign shop assistants in lingerie outlets with Saudi women within one year, while at the same time forbidding entry into these shops to men.[75] The measure was presented as reinforcing sex segregation, as it would avoid contact between a male vendor and female customers. However, well-known unofficial *ulama* opposed the measure on the grounds that women would then be working as shop assistants in exclusively female shops, but in mixed malls, which is perceived as the beginning of a mixed public space, thereby threatening sex segregation. Thus, supporters as well as opponents of the measure referred to sex segregation, a quite consensual principle, to legitimize their position. Aside from this, for a lot of people it was difficult to imagine Saudi women, who are stereotyped as "privileged" persons compared to expatriate female workers, working as sellers of lingerie. The stronger opposition came from shop owners, who argued that it would be too expensive to employ Saudi women rather than immigrant workers, and to change the configuration of stores by closing the shop window in order to conform to sex segregation principles. Given these various objections, the government eventually declared that the measure was postponed, without giving any other deadline.[76]

While the principle of sex segregation is to some extent consensual, it engenders high costs: for this reason, there are few available jobs for women. Many qualified young women are looking for a job; their aspirations, developed in the context of widespread higher education[77] and the diverse media available via satellite television and the Internet, differ from those of their mothers' generation: the young want to be financially independent, to live an active professional life rather than "being bored" at home (according to their perceptions), and to be able to ask for divorce (*khul'*) if necessary.[78] Many of these young women have a financial need for a wage to help their parents or to complement their husbands' salary, which often no longer meets the family's expenses, including the employment of a maid and/or a driver. However, many young women prefer to work in segregated spaces, for various reasons: to feel more "comfortable" and "relaxed," according to their own words, as they are used to frequenting female spaces most of the time; not to have to wear their *'abaya and niqab* (face cover) all day long; for religious reasons; or because their family or husband prefers so.

On the whole, the separation between men and women has not been significantly weakened through women's paid work, even though in some firms women and men work in the same buildings in this case, women generally work in a separate office. However, the number of more or less mixed workplaces (mainly hospitals, the head offices of banks, which hire more and more young Saudi women, and some other firms that are often owned by princes) is increasing. This is not in contradiction with the increase in segregated workplaces, and indeed is indicative of the fact that women's participation in the workforce is rising globally.

Which Autonomy for Female Spaces and Activities?

This "female society" (*mujtama' nisa'i*) or "women's world" (*'alam al-nisa'*), as Saudi women sometimes call it, includes spaces for consumption as well. In Riyadh, there are more and more commercial centers and places for leisure activities designated for women, such as the exclusively female floor within the prestigious Kingdom Tower (*Burj al-Mamlaka*). A businesswoman has created a women-only center, called *al-multaqa* ("the appointment") where the generally well-off customers can have dinner, practice sports, shop, book a holiday, or invest in one of the flats in the new buildings which are being constructed in Mecca, from where the *Haram* (Holy Mosque's interior) can be seen. The center's manager enumerates the qualities of the place that she has created: "relaxation, freedom, and security." Indeed, at the entrance, women take off their *'abayas* and their veils (*tarha*) and leave them at the cloakroom, which enables them to wander comfortably.

Finally, the women's sphere includes cultural circles, conferences, newspapers, and magazines dealing with topics linked to women. Saudi women's magazines have existed for about 15 years[79] and most daily newspapers offer one or several pages specifically addressed to women. In these spaces, a discourse by women and for women is elaborated, as explained by a journalist from the magazine *Hayat*: "I have particular ideas to communicate to the female part of society. The aim is to gather girls in order to shape a unit. The magazine's message is to address young women, as a group, and to increase their level of culture. And to help them solve their religious and personal problems."[80] This kind of publication reinforces the existence of a category of belonging that encompasses Saudi women.

Female protected spaces work as a lever to develop all kinds of activities in different fields: religion, work, charity, media, and consumption. Subsequently, the expansion of women's activities, which brings about the expansion of segregated space, logically leads to the strengthening of the category. Thus, provided they accept, or inhabit, the boundaries that are imposed upon them, women can pursue their own activities within relatively autonomous spaces. This is expressed in the discourse and the representations of a number of women working in prestigious professions within universities and bureaucracies dedicated to women: they often assert the legitimacy of this spatially segregated organization, which has, to some extent, benefited them. At the beginning of their professional careers in the 1980s, women from this generation, few of whom were qualified and ready to work, have experienced a quick professional ascent within new female sectors. This might have been different if they had been obliged to fit into the pre-existing male institutions.

However, the level of autonomy attained by women's institutions should not be exaggerated. While women's institutions or sections to some extent constitute a space of autonomy vis-à-vis familial norms, they are generally subject to decisions coming from above, first of all from men's institutions in which they are only a section, then from state rules and laws that must be respected. Therefore, these women's institutions are at once spaces permitting to some extent emancipation vis-à-vis the family and relatives, but at the same time spaces where rules and orientations fixed elsewhere are implemented. For instance, at the university, although the pay scale for female teachers is the same as for their male counterparts, female professors have little power in decision-making during negotiations taking place on the phone, about which an interviewee complained: "The teachers from the female section have a limited authority in the department. Male teachers, leading the department, make the decisions for us in all circumstances. Their authority prevails over ours...They take the decisions concerning a female teacher, or a female student, without even consulting us."[81] Usually an institution's director is represented in the women's section by a female agent (*wakila*) whose role is to implement the decisions made outside the women's section.

In this context, most elite women who were interviewed (university teachers, businesswomen, etc.) were asking either for greater power in decision-making and more autonomy for female sections within mixed institutions (i.e. universities, chambers of commerce etc.), or for the creation of independent spaces and firms, only for women, where women constitute the whole hierarchy. These two desires have a common feature: they do not question the spatial organization based on sex segregation, but rather aim at its appropriation by women willing to take advantage of it.

Aside from these relationships of power between male-led institutions and female sections, the female sphere of activities should not be idealized as a space of autonomy and solidarity between women. It is structured by relationships of power among women, as in any social grouping. For instance, even if there were fewer legal and administrative obstacles to women doing business, firms owned by women and hiring only women would not necessarily hire young, qualified Saudi women. In a forum for businesswomen in Riyadh,[82] firm owners and managers were more concerned about how to get around Saudization laws while at the same time complaining about their problems with foreign workers, than about how to train and hire Saudi young women in search of jobs.

Conclusion

State measures vis-à-vis Saudi women have brought about their separation from the rest of the society namely, Saudi men and foreigners and their constitution as a particular category, through sex segregation and through the discourse of reform, which to some extent is a process of dividing society into categories while co-opting certain social elites.[83] What is original in the case of Saudi women lies in their physical separation, a quite well-respected rule which has led to the development of a female sphere, a mosaic of female spaces forbidden to men. Sex segregation has not been weakened, but rather reinforced in the context of economic transformations, Sahwist discourse, and the discourse of reform. Meanwhile, women's ways of life have been transformed as they become educated, employed (for some of them), and much more mobile within cities. Some women have tried tc re-appropriate this category and the space that was offered to them in order to widen their margin of autonomy. Now, paradoxically, to include and to divide go together: by trying to include women in the workforce, the government reinforces sex segregation within society, because the most socially acceptable way of creating jobs for women consists of the feminization of mixed places or the creation of women's sections within men's institutions.[84]

This policy engenders women's separation from the rest of the society and from the family, whereas the state is officially supposed to be the protector of family: the Basic Law (*al-nizam al-asasi lil-hukm*) mentions that "family is the heart of Saudi society" (Ninth article), an often repeated principle. By developing spatial segregation between the genders (though aimed at protecting the family unit and honor), by disseminating a discourse on women, by establishing policies addressed specifically to women, and by considering "women's problems" as they pertain to its policies, the government takes possession of a field which used to belong to the domain of the family, and thereby enters the domestic sphere. Measures affecting the spatial organization of society, as well as the discourse on women, contribute to the institutionalization of a female identity.

This identity is combined in specific ways with distinctions between women of different backgrounds and generations, as all women do not necessarily identify with the ones who are promoted through the discourse of reform. On the one hand, there is a gap between elite women participating in state institutions, who often come from well-off families and some of whom have studied abroad, and most women of their generation, who have received a much briefer education. On the other hand, there is a gap between this generation and the young generation of women, among whom a large proportion are educated and want to have their own activities beyond their families whether they are religious activities, informal business, writing, shopping, or work since many of them need a salary in order to be able to enjoy the lifestyles to which they aspire.[85] While sharing the same spaces and belonging to the same category as defined through state policies, women have different aspirations and go beyond the models that are supposed to determine their ways of life.

Notes

1. Even if they did not intend physical spaces, but rather the public sphere in their book, I borrow this expression from Erik Neveu and Bastien François (dir.), *Espaces publics mosaïques: acteurs, arènes et rhétoriques des débats publics contemporains* [A

Mosaic of Public Spaces: Actors, Arenas and Rhetorics of Contemporary Public Debates] (Rennes: PUR, 1999).

2. This word more precisely designates the father, brother, son, uncle, or husband.
3. Of course, this should be nuanced, as these relationships are not equivocal and must be analyzed along with other distinctions such as the level of revenue and family status and origin.
4. This article follows Foucault's conception of power as relational and productive. See Michel Foucault, "The Subject and Power," in Michel Foucault, *Power,* James D. Faubion, ed., translated by Robert Hurley and others (New York: The New Press, 2000).
5. My first field study on female elites included more than 30 semi-directive interviews with Saudi women holding prominent positions. My criteria was to meet well-known women who had participated in the general debate on women, either through their writing in newspapers or books, by participating in one of the national dialogues, or by speaking at conferences on the subject. The interviews dealt with both their own experience and their general opinion of the government's policy toward women. My second field study, which is not developed in this article, is based on ethnographic observations and interviews with young women working or studying in the city of Riyadh. Altogether, I stayed about nine months in Saudi Arabia over the course of four stays between 2005 and 2007.
6. Deniz Kandiyoti, ed., *Women, Islam and the State* (Basingstoke: Macmillan, 1991).
7. Lila Abu Lughod, ed., *Remaking Women: Feminism and Modernity in the Middle East* (Princeton: Princeton University Press, 1998).
8. Cf. Fariba Adelkhah, *La Révolution sous le voile: femmes islamiques d'Iran* [Revolution under the Veil: Islamic Women of Iran] (Paris: Karthala, 1991).
9. On Turkey, see Nilüfer Göle, *The Forbidden Modern: Civilization and Veiling* (Ann Arbor: University of Michigan Press, 1996). On Tunisia, see Ilhem Marzouki, *"La modernité, pour ou contre les femmes?"* ["Modernity: For or against Women?"], in Ephesia, *La place des femmes: les enjeux de l'identité et de l'égalité au regard des sciences sociales* [Women's Place: Identity and Equality from the Point of View of the Social Sciences] (Paris: La découverte, 1995).

10. Beginning in the 1960s-1970s, what is called the Islamic awakening (*Sahwa*) has spread in Saudi society and official institutions; it includes several branches, resulting from variable hybridizations between the official quietist doctrine of state *ulama's* and the Muslim Brotherhood's political Islamism.
11. On how the new Saudi power became a state and how its authority progressively spread over the peninsula, see Ghassan Salame, "Political Power and the Saudi State," *MERIP Reports*, No. 91. (October 1980), pp. 5-22 and Christine Moss-Helms, *The Cohesion of Saudi Arabia: Evolution of Political Identity* (London: Croom Helm, 1981), p. 313.
12. On women's work in the Arabian Peninsula before the oil boom, see Center of Research in Human Sciences, *Masirat al-mar'a al-su'udiyya wal-tanmiyya fi ma'at 'am* [Saudi Women's Journey and Development in a Hundred Years] (Riyadh: King Saud University, 2002); Fawziyya Abu Khalid, *"Athar al-naft fi mas'alat al-mar'a fi-l-mujtama' al-su'udi"* ["Oil Influence on the Question of Women in Saudi Society"], in Maryam Salim et al, *Al-mar'a al-'arabiyya bayn thaql al-waqi' wa tatallu'at al-taharrur* [The Arabian Woman between the Weight of Reality and Aspirations to Liberation] (Beirut: Markaz dirasat al-wahda al-'arabiyya, 1999), pp. 197-220; Motoko Katakura and Jacob C. Hurewitz, *Bedouin Village: A Study of a Saudi Arabian People in Transition* (Tokyo: University of Tokyo Press, 1977); Aisha Almana, Economic Development and Its Impact on the Status of Woman in Saudi Arabia (Unpublished Ph.D. Thesis, University of Colorado, 1981); Mai Yamani, *Cradle of Islam: The Hijaz and the Quest for an Arabian Identity* (London and New York: I.B. Tauris, 2004); Soraya Altorki and Donald Cole, *Arabian Oasis City: The Transformation of 'Unaiza* (Austin: University of Texas Press, 1989).
13. Almana, *Economic Development and Its Impact on the Status of Woman in Saudi Arabia.*
14. Even if it did not prevent women from having an influence on some public affairs, at least in elite families, where marriages are political matters. See Soraya Altorki, *Women in Saudi Arabia: Ideology and Behavior among Elite Women* (New York: Columbia University Press, 1986). The author demonstrates women's almost exclusive power over marriages, which have

important consequences on public relations within the big elite families in Jeddah.

15. Altorki and Cole, *Arabian Oasis City: The Transformation of 'Unaiza*; Eleanor A. Doumato, *Getting God's Ear: Women, Islam, and Healing in Saudi Arabia and the Gulf* (New York: Columbia University Press, 1999).
16. On this subject see also Eleanor A. Doumato, "Gender, Monarchy and National Identity in Saudi Arabia," *British Journal of Middle Eastern Studies,* Vol. 19, No. 1 (1992), pp. 31-47.
17. Gender, ethnicity, and material background all play a role. For instance, foreign maids live in Saudi families' houses, which would be inconceivable if they were Saudi women.
18. In Hijaz, schools for boys have existed for a long time; in Riyadh, when the third Saudi state was established, there were almost no schools, even if many boys and girls attended informal groups called "circles" in order to learn the Qu'ran; the first 12 state schools for boys opened in 1926. See Alexei Vassiliev, *The History of Saudi Arabia* (New York: New York University Press, 2000), pp. 310, 576. State education spread at a broader scale almost at the same time for girls and boys.
19. Indeed, as Gilles Kepel underlines, "by the end of the 1960s, Saudi Arabia was the only country in the Muslim world in which the *ulama* had not lost control of the public debate over the central values of society." See Gilles Kepel, *Jihad: The Trail of Political Islam* (Cambridge: Harvard University Press, 2002), p. 52.
20. In the beginning, some *ulama* were hostile to girls' education: see the introduction in.. Saddeka Arebi, *Women and Words in Saudi Arabia: The Politics of Literary Discourse* (New York: Columbia University Press, 1994), p. 357. Moreover, the contents and programs differ between girls' and boys' schools; girls' education was under the Ministry of Religious Affairs' authority until 2002, when it was transferred to the Ministry of Education after a fire in a dilapidated girls' school in Mecca killed several pupils and created a scandal (whose details are exposed in Alain Gresh, *"Paroles libérées en Arabie Saoudite"* ["Freed Words in Saudi Arabia"], *Manière de voir,* No. 68 (April-May 2003), pp. 80-84.

21. This is mentioned in the 155th article of the "Policy of Teaching:" "Mixing between boys and girls is forbidden at every educational stage, except for day nurseries and kindergartens." See Fawziyya Bakr Al Bakr, *Al-mar'a al-sa'udiyya wa al-ta'lim* [Saudi Women and Education] (Riyadh: Maktabat al-Malik Al Fahd al-wataniyya, 1998), pp. 20, 224.
22. It also bans women's working in dangerous fields and perilous activities. See Vassiliev, *The History of Saudi Arabia*, p. 432.
23. In Arabic: *al-Dukhul mamnu' lil-nisa' bidun mahram*.
24. Before, women would have had problems with the Committee for the Promotion of Virtue and the Repression of Vice. Cafes in Riyadh are generally along the lines of an American, Starbucks-like model, rather than "traditional" cafes.
25. In Arabic: *li-l-nisa' faqat.*
26. Women are allowed to enter the family section (qism al-'a'ilat) of restaurants and cafés but the existence of a familial or contractual link between the members of a group is rarely controlled, except when the religious police intervenes in the place.
27. The religious police are only present in the big cities; they are largely absent from the villages.
28. Such as the death of a man in the custody of the religious police in May 2007 in Riyadh. See Ebtihal Mubarak, "Al-Lahem Files Second Appeal in Huraisi Murder Case," *Arab News,* June 12, 2008,http://www.arabnews.com/?page=1&section=0&article=11 0814&d=12&m=6&y=2008.
29. See Mahmoud Ahmad, "Prince Naif Curbs Power of Virtue Commission," *Arab News,* May 25, 2006.
30. In this sense, globalization has participated in reinforcing sex segregation, according to Eleanor A. Doumato, "Education in Saudi Arabia: Gender, Jobs, and the Price of Religion," in Eleanor A. Doumato and Marsha Pripstein Posusney, eds., *Women and Globalization in the Arab Middle East: Gender, Economy and Society* (London: Lynne Rienner Publishers, Inc., 2003), pp. 239-257.
31. Cf. Vassiliev, *The History of Saudi Arabia,* p. 434.
32. She was then a PhD candidate. Interview by author, Riyadh, April 2005.
33. In the Hijaz, women used to wear a colored veil, according to Yamani, *Cradle of Islam.*

34. Eric Hobsbawm and Terence Ranger, *The Invention of Tradition* (Cambridge: Cambridge University Press, 1996).
35. Center of Research in Human Sciences, *Masirat al mar'a al-su'udiyya wal-tanmiyya fi ma'at 'am.*
36. Yamani, *Cradle of Islam.*
37. The family's consent is also needed for boys' education, which is not compulsory.
38. Before 2001, women were mentioned on their male relatives' identity card. Now they can have their own personal card, including a photo with their face uncovered.
39. This is what people who commit bombings are called in the official discourse.
40. National dialogues were launched in 2003 by the Crown Prince. There have been several sessions, about national unity (Summer 2003), extremism (December 2003), women (June 2004), the young (December 2004), "we and the other" (December 2005), education (November 2006), and employment (April 2008). About these dialogues, see Steffen Hertog, "Building the Body Politic: Emerging Corporatism in Saudi Arabia," *Chroniques Yéménites*, No. 12 (2004), pp. 103-118 and the website of the King Abdulaziz Center for National Dialogue, http://www.kacnd.org. For a list of the participants and the titles of the papers prepared for the national dialogue, see http://www.kacnd.org/third_national_meeting.asp.
41. Cf. Hertog, "Building the Body Politic: Emerging Corporatism in Saudi Arabia."
42. *"Al-hiwar al-watani al-su'udi al-thalith: 18 bahthan 'ala arbi 'a mahawir fi mawdu' al-mar'a"* ["Saudi Third National Dialogue: 18 Researches Following Four Axes about Women"], *'Ukaz*, June 12, 2004. In Saudi Arabia, there is a great deal of research underway in the social sciences on subjects linked to women and gender, a phenomenon reinforced by segregation rules which condition the female students' choices.
43. *"Musharikun yuhaddidun bi-l-insihab wa-l-'uqala' yatadakhkhalun li-isti'naf al-hiwar al-watani ba'd marhala 'asifa min yawmihi al-thani"* ["Participants Threaten Withdrawing and Reasonable People Interfere in Order to Return to National Dialogue after the Storm Which Began the Second Day"], *Al-Watan,* June 14, 2004.

44. In 1990, 47 women drove in Riyadh, challenging a social norm prohibiting female drivers. Since then, a fatwa and a law have forbidden women from driving. The protagonists were arrested and lost their jobs for a few years, during which time they still received their salaries. Among them, several are now well-known intellectuals, often writing in the newspapers.
45. *"Musharikun yuhaddidun bi-l-insihab wa-l-'uqala' yatadakhkhalun li-isti'naf al-hiwar al-watani ba'd marhala 'asifa min yawmihi al-thani".*
46. *"Hiwar al-su'udiyya: manh al-mar'a huquqha al-shar'iyya"* ["Saudi Dialogue: Give Women Their Legitimate Rights"] Islam Online, June 14, 2004, http://www.islamonline. net/ Arabic/ news/ 200406/14/ article10.shtml.
47. Interview by author with female participant of the dialogue, Riyadh, April 2005.
48. Six new female consultants in the *majlis al-Shura* were appointed in June 2006. Before, there were three. Cf. Maha Akeel, "More women consultants join shoura," *Arab News*, June 29, 2006, http://www. arabnews.com/?page=1& section=0 &article= 84524&d=29&m=6&y=2006. The Consultative Council was created in 1991. Its members, supposed to represent the different constituencies of the Saudi population, are appointed by the government. See Camille Ammoun, *Le Majlis Al Shûra en Arabie Saoudite, de l'illusion participative à l'invention d'un watan* [The Majlis Al-Shura in Saudi Arabia: From the Participative Illusion to the Invention of a Watan], Master's thesis, Paris, Institut d'Etudes Politiques, 2004.
49. Akeel, "More women consultants join shoura."
50. Faye Bowers, "Saudi women, long silent, gain a quiet voice," *The Christian Science Monitor*, January12, 2004, http://www.csmonitor.com/2004/0113/p07s01-wome.html.
51. Bowers, "Saudi women, long silent, gain a quiet voice."
52. Interview by author with Saudi businesswoman, Jeddah, April 2005.
53. The Committee was created in 2004.
54. Interview by author with Saudi journalist, Riyadh, April 2005.
55. Michel Camau, *"Remarques sur la consolidation autoritaire et ses limites"* ["Remarks on Authoritarian Consolidation and Its Limits"], CEDEJ, http://www.cedej.org.eg/article.php3?id_ article=294.

56. For instance, women's joblessness: the difficulty the young have in finding a job is exacerbated for young women, given sex segregation and the limited number of jobs within female institutions.
57. In 2005, Prince Saud al-Faysal, the Minister of Foreign Affairs, declared that he would appoint women to his ministry; this declaration took place at the inauguration of a Saudi-British forum. In fact, the initiative was not such a change, as female employees at the Ministry of Foreign Affairs told me in 2007 that Saudi women had been working in the Ministry for more than ten years, but the female section, which was in another building, has been transferred in the Ministry building and more women have been hired. *"Su'ud al-faysal: intabahu ya rijal ... al-nisa' sayadkhulna al-kharijiyya hadhihi al-sana"* ["Saud al-Faysal: Be Careful Men ... Women Will Enter the Ministry of Foreign Affairs This Year"], *Al-Hayat*, February 24, 2005.
58. The list exclusively composed of female candidates (significantly called "the national list") in the Eastern Region Chamber of Commerce was faced with substantial abstention by businesswomen in this region. Among 470 registered, only 45 voted. To explain this high rate of abstention, the newspapers mentioned the low number of active and committed businesswomen, since many of them lent their name to a male relative, or worked together with their family and considered the other members' vote to be enough. *"Sayyidat a 'mal al-sharqiyya yakhayyibna zann al-murashshihat"* ["The Eastern Province Businesswomen Deceive the Candidates' Hopes"], *Al-Sharq Al-Awsat,* February 22, 2006.
59. Umm al-Qurra University opened a female section in 1971 and Imam Muhammad bin Saud University did so in 1984.
60. Doumato, *Getting God's Ear*.
61. In this period the most well-known were Nura al-Sa'ad, Fatma Nasif, and Suhayla Zayn al-'Abidin.
62. The World Association for Muslim Youth (WAMY, *al-Nadwat al-'alamiyya lil-shabab al-Islami*) opened women's sections in the beginning of the 1990s, first in Jeddah, then in Riyadh. Subsequently there were other organizations such as the Mecca Foundation (*Mu'assasat Makka al-mukarrama)* or the Foundation for Construction and Development (*Mu'assasa lil-i'mar wa al-tanmiyya*). For Saudi female preachers' travel to

Afghanistan in order to preach, see Amal Zahid, *"al-da'iyyat al-sa'udiyyat"* ["Saudi Female Preachers"], *Al-Majalla*, No. 1339, October 9-15, 2005, pp. 24-32. Interview by author with a female witness who went to Afghanistan in this period, April 2006.

63. Interview by author with female student at the Imam Muhammad bin Saud (Islamic) University, April 2006.
64. The Ministry of Islamic Affairs made this decision: see *Al-Arabiya,* April 19, 2006, http:// www. alarabiya.net/ Articlep. aspx? P=23003.
65. Interview by author with a young Saudi woman, April 2006.
66. What Saudis call the "Western" way of life generally refers to the United States due to the historical and contemporary links between both countries.
67. Plans are partly accessible on the Ministry of Economy and Planning's website, http://www.mep.gov.sa.
68. Monica Malik and Tim Niblock, "Saudi Arabia's Economy: the Challenge of Reform," in Paul Aarts and Gerd Nonneman, eds., *Saudi Arabia in the Balance* (London: Hurst & Co., 2005), pp. 85-110.
69. Those are their own words.
70. Mona Almunajjed, *Women in Saudi Arabia Today* (Basingstoke: Macmillan, 1997).
71. On Saudi business women see "Top 20 Business Women," Arab News, http://www.arabnews.com/?mode=/supplements/Top20/Top20.htm.
72. Interview by author with woman who founded a computer training center in Riyadh, April 2005.
73. Interview by author with woman who founded a computer training center in Riyadh, April 2006.
74. See Decisions of the Council of Ministers: No. 63 (11/3/1424) and No. 120 (12/4/1425).
75. "Lingerie Shops to Employ Women," *Arab News,* June 30, 2005, http://www.arabnews.com/?page=1&section=0&article=66141&d= 30&m=6&y=2005.
76. "Kingdom Delays Plans to Replace Salesmen in Lingerie Shops," *Arab News,* May 15, 2006, http://www. arabnews.com/?page=1&section=0&article=82232&d=15&m=5&y=2006.

77. Nowadays, the majority of students registered in Saudi universities are female. But this figure must be considered along with the fact that many male students study abroad, which is much easier for them than for female students.
78. In Saudi Arabia, a wife can ask for divorce. However, in order to obtain the divorce, wives often have to pay financial compensation to their husbands — often part of the dowry that they received from their husbands when they got married — and they often lose custody of their children.
79. The oldest women's magazine was *Sayyidati*, a part of the daily newspaper *Al-Sharq Al-Awsat*, which is edited in London. In Saudi Arabia, the oldest one is *Majallat al-usra* (which has a Salafi tendency), which has been in existence for about 15 years; other magazines include *al-Mutamayyiza, Hayat* (a magazine with an Islamic tendency, targeting 15 to 25-year-old women), and *Majallat al-shaqa'iq*. All of these magazines follow an Islamic editorial line, unlike some other magazines, widespread in Saudi Arabia but edited outside (for instance *Laha*).
80. Interview by author with Saudi journalist from *Hayat*, Riyadh, April 2006.
81. Interview by author with a female professor at King Saud University, Riyadh, April 2005.
82. I attended the forum on March 17-18, 2007.
83. On this classical authoritarian proceeding, see Philippe Droz-Vincent, *"Quel avenir pour l'autoritarisme dans le monde arabe?"* ["What Future for Authoritarianism in the Arab World?"], *Revue française de science politique,* Vol. 54 (2004-6), pp. 945-979.
84. Except for hospitals and some banks where the absence of separation between men and women is increasingly accepted.
85. This is part of a wider research project, to be developed in my PhD dissertation.

8

A Gulf Merchant Synoecism: Dubai before Oil

Stephen J. Ramos

To understand Dubai's modern history since its founding in 1833, one must go further back in time to explore the regional history that frames its foundation. European powers, beginning with the Venetians, and, then subsequently, the Portuguese, the Dutch, and finally the British, were interested in the Gulf region as a means to secure trade routes to and from the Indian Subcontinent and points eastward. This meant that from the fifteenth century through the late nineteenth century, if trade routes could move uninterrupted through the Gulf region, European powers were not involved in the societal affairs of settlements as a traditionally colonial ruling class. European merchants didn't bother to extensively explore trade within the region, believing that it required more effort than either the climate or the local economies were worth.[2]

The region's local tribes were divided among the maritime coastal groups and those that were nomadic and land-bound, and conflict among these groups occurred in parallel with the larger European conflicts also playing out in the region. The intersection of the two came with the increase in piracy, which, in very basic terms, represented a kind of cultural disagreement on trade customs. The Europeans felt that they were unjustly looted and local groups simply sought to protect themselves from foreign incursion while taking what they believed was their share. Historians still debate this issue today, but in relation to Dubai, the piracy of the times serves as an example of how looser understandings of the licit and illicit, particularly in terms of trade, could be capitalized upon as a business venture. The smuggling of gold, weapons, and other goods throughout Dubai's history may have been seen as illicit from perspectives outside Dubai's ports, but the merchant-friendly environments of these ports and the adherence to local autonomy allowed them to trade freely.

British incursions into regional affairs increased as the pearl trade sector grew and, once oil was discovered in Persia and Saudi Arabia at the beginning of the twentieth century, British firms entered the region more actively. Inspired by oil profits and the gold trade after 1947, the British government and firms behaved more paternalistically, and established a more direct protectorate relationship with regional sheikhdoms, including Dubai. The interrelation of the British presence, resource exploration and wealth, and local aspirations for development define this period, which culminates in oil discovery in Dubai in 1966. The emphasis on infrastructural projects in Dubai marked its development pattern throughout this period, which would then serve as a blueprint for projects in its post-oil discovery phase.

In this paper, I will trace the regional history of the Gulf, along with the presence of a continuum of European powers, and then focus more closely on Dubai's relationship with the British and how this both influenced and determined the emerging sheikdom's urban development through oil discovery.

Geographical History of the Gulf Region

Dubai is an emirate within the greater United Arab Emirates (UAE), located in the eastern part of the Arabian Peninsula. The UAE is comprised of seven emirates (Abu Dhabi, Dubai, Sharjah, Ras al-Khaima, Fujairah, Umm al-Qaiwain, and Ajman), and of the total UAE land area of 83,600 square kilometers (32,270 square miles), Dubai occupies 4,114 square kilometers (1,588 square miles), and is second in size after the significantly larger Abu Dhabi.[2] This land, in section, falls into four geographic categories; coast and coastal plain, interior desert, an upland plain, and interior rugged mountains.[3] Traditionally, this geographic diversity has marked two distinct cultures: coastal settlements dedicated to trade, fishing and pearling and other socio-economic activities oriented toward the sea, and interior settlements and nomadic Bedouin communities based on agriculture and animal husbandry. In her work on the geographic and economic conditions of the lower Gulf region before oil was discovered, Dr. Frauke Heard-Bey points out that tribes of the region included many subsections that were individually sea-oriented or nomadic, but intermingled with one another in tribal confederation as the basis for "the creation of a nation-state within a large and geographically very varied territory." [4] This intermingling included marriage within the different sections and intensive trade based on seasonal pearl and date harvests. I will look further at the subsections of the regions below, but it is important to recognize that these two forms of economic cultures within the territory, within larger tribes, were often collaborative and, taking into account the region's resource scarcity, both in terms of limited arable land and seasonal fishing possibilities, this mutual interaction and dependence was a pragmatic survival mechanism.

Though the UAE was only formed officially in 1971, the history of the region is rich, wherein recent discoveries are only now beginning to fill in wide gaps in the knowledge of this past. For Dubai in particular, in 1981 Iraqi scholars discovered evidence of a trading center there from 3,000 years ago, which is unsurprising, both in light of its geographic location and its subsequent maritime trade history.[5] As pointed out by Geoffrey R. King, the voids in the historical knowledge of the region appear mainly between the arrival of Islam, the Prophet Muhammad and the first caliphs in the seventh century, and the encounter with the Portuguese in the late fifteenth and early sixteenth centuries. Despite historical accounts that seem limited to speculation on changing landscapes of local tribe settlement and power struggles, the coastal trading settlements of Julfar (present Ras al-Khaimah) and Dibba (present Fujairah and Sharjah) are mentioned in Arab accounts of this period and archaeologists believe that the Al-Jumayra settlement, just west of Dubai (and now the name of a Dubai neighbourhood), was settled in the ninth century.[6]

Venetian trade within the larger Middle Eastern region, particularly in Damascus, Aleppo, and Alexandria is recorded in the fifteenth century with some evidence of contact with the Gulf for pearl trading.[7] But it was the Portuguese who were the European power able to take control of the Gulf through the maritime dominance of their powerful men-of-war fleet in the sixteenth century. Rather than colonial imposition or re-settlement of the area, their principal objective was to control spice trade routes from the Indian Subcontinent to Europe. The sea route around the Cape of Good Hope, which they had discovered, helped the Portuguese to access the Indian Ocean and, by taking over the Island of Hormuz in the Straits of Hormuz, the Portuguese could strategically control trade routes throughout the region. As a precursor to the later British experience, the Portuguese signed a treaty with the Sheikh of Hormuz to pacify local opposition to their occupancy in exchange for

Portuguese support for the Sheikh in controlling local matters.[8] The maritime focus of the Portuguese period in the Gulf meant that local institutions remained essentially unchanged throughout the sixteenth century.[9]

The decline of Portuguese power in the Gulf came with the aid of both the Dutch and the British, though each would eventually enjoy power in the region at different moments. Each country established East Indies companies in the early seventeenth century, and in line with these trade pursuits, the British and Dutch helped the Persians recapture the Island of Hormuz from the Portuguese in 1622.[10] As was often the case in European political intrigue and shifting allegiances, the British and Dutch allied to defeat the Portuguese fleet in the Indian Ocean, only to then fight each other for power over regional trade supremacy. A British-Dutch war in the mid-seventeenth century extended to the Gulf region, causing damage and losses for the British fleet.[11] Though the Dutch achieved power over trade routes during the seventeenth century, their power slowly waned both in Europe and then internationally, ending symbolically when they abandoned Bandar Abbas and Kharg Island in 1765.[12]

The British commercial interests in the region increased, particularly in India and along their East Indies Company trade routes. But with the fall of Dutch power, the rise of what was called "piracy"—Omani, and later Qawasim attacks on trade ships—created instability for the Gulf. Omani "piracy," or local Gulf maritime power, held sway through the first half of the eighteenth century, but a civil war between the Hinawi and the Ghafiri factions weakened Omani power, and the Qawasim were the principal group attacking British trade ships, particularly in the lower Gulf area. The Qawasim origins are debated, but it is believed that they were the Hawala who came from central Arabia in the seventh century and migrated to lower Persia.[13]

Eventually crossing the Gulf to Oman through maritime battle and by taking advantage of Omani internal power struggles, the Qawasim took control of the area between present-day Ras al-Khaimah down to Sharjah. Inspired by both strategic and religious interests, the Qawasim allied with the Wahhabis and intensified their sea attacks. The British and the British-Indian fleets allied with the Omanis in retaliation against the Qawasim, but their joint expeditions between 1808 and 1819 were unsuccessful. It was not until

November 1819, when a group of 3,000 British and Indian forces attacked the Qawasim naval base at Ras al-Khaimah, were the British able to assume control of the region, and a mixture of treaties, truces, indirect rule, and canon diplomacy would maintain this rule until their departure from the region 150 years later. In his book on the form of British rule within what he terms "the Arabian frontier of the British Raj" in the nineteenth and twentieth centuries, James Onley describes this policy of informal or indirect rule decided according to their strategic economic interests in the region, based on the principle of 'informal control if possible, formal control when necessary.' As he states:

> The method of control the British adopted was largely determined by the success they had in attracting local collaborators and mediators. The greater their success, the more indirect their control. Therefore it is the Empire and its periphery, rather than the imperial capital of London, that holds the key to understanding both the timing and the nature of (British) imperialism.[14]

The particular "local collaborators" were tribal families that signed Trucial protectorate agreements that, at least through oil exploration, enabled a more distant and preferred British participation, within the regional southern Gulf periphery around the central British interests in India.

In January 1820, the British marked the defeat of the Qawasim with the signing of the General Treaty of Peace with the regional sheikhs of Bahrain and what was then northern Oman (which included present-day UAE), where all agreed to end "piracy" attacks both among each other and on British trade ships. This treaty would commit Britain to maintain and enforce this peace, mostly in the interest of their trade pursuits. The "Trucial System" was coined officially in 1835 when the British declared a truce between the Bani Yas tribe from the lower Shakhbut area (present-day Abu Dhabi) and the Qawasim, as a means to secure a peaceful pearling season for merchants of the lower Gulf. This truce was signed again by all factions in the Ten Year Maritime Truce of 1843, and then finally ratified into perpetuity (over the next century) through the Perpetual Treaty of Truce in 1853, which stipulated for the British government to "watch over and protect" the southern Gulf region "for evermore."[15] The Treaty also renamed the region as Trucial Oman, or the Trucial States, which was of course, better than the region's previous British title, the "Pirate Coast."

Malcolm Peck points out that the British agreed to back regional sheikhs in power militarily at that particular moment in exchange for a guarantee of peace, most importantly for their trade routes through to India, but also for the pearling sector of the lower Gulf.

> By freezing the power relationships that existed between tribes or tribal confederations, thereby preserving a number of small states that otherwise would probably have been swallowed by larger neighbors. Eventually the British role in the affairs of the Trucial States would carry their evolution toward western-style statehood a step further by defining territorial boundaries.[16]

With a few strokes, a mix of British magnanimousness and clear economic self-interest established a static territorial, political, and social structure for the Trucial States, which were previously characterized by far more fluid inter-tribal power relationships. The British officially installed a Political Resident in Bushire (Persia), which had already served as a diplomatic base since 1778,[17] and in Sharjah in 1823 to "meet the treaty commitments."[18] The treaties established a precedent for an increasingly paternalistic British intervention into the inter-tribal affairs of the lower Gulf as both mediator and military enforcer, wherein British colonial obligations were not as specifically defined as in other areas of the Empire. These treaties brought the region into the sphere of British colonial administration at a point when many in London believed that the region was not worth what it would cost to oversee. The resulting "'cut-price' imperial system of indirect control required local rulers to sign anti-piracy peace treaties and to accept the authority of small British residencies" in exchange for British Trucial protection.[19] The military backing of local sheikhs in exchange for peace for British maritime routes was a low price for Britain to pay for hegemonic and exclusive control of the lower Gulf, particularly with regard to other competing European powers, along with Russia and the United States.

The Bani Yas and the Qawasim were rival tribes in the late eighteenth and early nineteenth century. Because the British treaties focused specifically on maritime truce, the Bani Yas (not coincidentally given the British predisposition against the "pirating"

Qawasim) were benefited due to their land-based power, in contrast to the Qawasim sea prowess. Though the treaties sought to end the warring factions of the region, the Qawasim and Bani Yas would continue their inter-tribal battling until the end of the nineteenth century. The Bani Yas were originally from the Najd region, and were comprised of many sections, both seafaring and Bedouin.[20] During this time, the Bani Yas controlled Shakhbut and areas south, and in addition to fighting the Qawasim, they were also battling against the Wahhabi, which resulted in a strained tribal power structure at its base in Shakhbut. In 1833, 800 members of the Al Bu Falasa subsection of the Bani Yas left to settle in a point between Sharjah and Shakhbut led by Maktoum bin Buti and Ubaid bin Said Al-Falasi.

By the late 1820s, the British Political Resident had already reported that the creek of Dubai had approximately 1,200 residents, so the new arrivals nearly doubled the population, and this is generally recognized as the official foundation of Dubai.[21] Al-Falasi died soon after in 1836, thus consolidating dynastic rule of the Maktoum family with the official recognition and security of the 1835 British treaty. The Maktoum dynasty has been the ruling family in Dubai ever since.

Dubai of the Nineteenth Century

The Al-Maktoum dynasty was established in Dubai in 1836, with the associate monarchical intrigues of loyalty, lineage and succession. In spite of the overarching Trucial treaties, which focused principally on the sea peace, Dubai's tenuous status between the Qawasim and the Bani Yas required a mix of political cunning and natural luck to keep each group at bay from overtaking the fledging Dubai. Similar to the larger political intrigues of the previous centuries among the Portuguese, Dutch and British, the three factions frequently shifted allegiances for their own benefit. By 1840, the Qawasim and Bani Yas resolved some of their larger conflicts and sought to overthrow the Maktoum in Dubai, agreeing to split it along its creek line, with Bur Dubai on the western side to go to the Bani Yas and Deira for the Qawasim.[22] An outbreak of smallpox in Dubai made this acquisition less appealing and Sheikh Maktoum bin Buti was also able to counter-strategize against the two to divert their attacks. This kind of plotting would occur continuously, albeit mostly under the somewhat myopic radar of the

Trucial agreements, but as the century wore on, Dubai's condition as a buffer zone between the two tribes was generally accepted as beneficial to all in its existence. The division certainly helped the British solidify control of the region, and the 1853 Perpetual Treaty and its ratification sought again to freeze a regional power structure toward British benefit.

The second half of the nineteenth century proved to be more prosperous for the lower Gulf region, particularly for the pearling sector run by the merchants. The maritime truce offered a calmer environment for pearling, and the increased business demonstrated how the sector benefited from this. Between the 1870s and the late 1890s, pearl exports from Dubai grew ten-fold,[23] and the harvests drew regional attention that boosted immigration to Dubai, particularly among Persians and *Banians*, British Indian Hindu merchants.[24] Dubai merchants were well-integrated into the distribution patterns of the lower Gulf, and operated principally out of the Persian Lingah port, which was a key hub for British trade between India, Persia, and Europe. Because banking was considered to be against the Muslim law, it was the Banians, with the support of Bombay banks, who took up the banking sector in Dubai and funded the yearly pearling expeditions. The Persian community was involved mainly in retail and food trade, and the Arab bourgeoisie focused mainly on pearling and trading.[25] The 40 shops and 100 traders in the *souq* recognized by Sheikh Maktoum in the 1840s grew steadily,[26] and by the end of the century, Dubai claimed the highest number of men employed in the pearling sector in the region (6,936), 335 pearling ships, and was clearly becoming the economic and commercial center of the Trucial States.[27]

While successful pearling expeditions intensified trade for Dubai, during the latter part of the nineteenth century it was still the Persian port of Lingah on the other side of the Gulf that served as the principal distribution center for Indian goods for the region. Lingah's hub status was established since the eighteenth century and continued throughout the nineteenth century, which attracted many Indian traders to settle in Lingah and mix in with the Persian trade community. Over time, Dubai traders also mixed with this trading group, and from 1873 through 1902 they controlled distribution trade from Lingah to the Trucial Coast.[28] At the turn of the century, however, Lingah's fate would suffer drastically due to the imposition of Tehran's restrictive Imperial Customs tariffs and controls for re-exported goods, which reached up to 400 percent on some goods, particularly for Arab traders.[29]

In 1904, in what would prove to be a regional coup, the ruler of Dubai, Maktoum bin Hashar, at the *majlis*, declared the Dubai port to be tax-free and control-free by removing the already low 5 percent customs fees, and this quickly attracted re-export activities from Lingah across the Gulf to the Dubai Port.[30] All commerce between Great Britain and India would then pass through Dubai, such that by 1905, some 34 steamers were calling regularly, raising the annual volume of cargo to 70,000 tons.[31] The prominent British India Steam Navigation Company essentially shifted its distribution center, firmly establishing Dubai's vocation as a strategic *entrepôt* for British imperial trade routes. As a result, the merchant class greatly benefited from the rapid increase in trade throughput, and large sectors of the Lingah Persian and Indian trading communities migrated to Dubai along with the trade route business.

Maktoum bin Hashar's free port policy announcement at the *majlis* was not coincidental, as it was this council that was chaired by the leaders of the merchant community. Fatmah Al-Sayegh's research explores the relationship between the Dubai merchant class and the ruler throughout the twentieth century, and underscores the importance of this sometimes delicate relationship in understanding the development projects of the emirate. The free port policy attracted a larger merchant community from Lingah, which meant that this tacit balance of power needed to be cared for all the more prudently. Al-Sayegh describes this understanding between ruler and merchant class at the beginning of the twentieth century as such:

> Since the ruler's income was not as high as that of the pearl merchants, and sometimes fluctuated with the market, the ruler often turned to the merchant for financial assistance, a fact which increased his dependency on them. This caused a unique situation where in fact the merchants were often in a position to dictate their wishes. The ruler was fully aware of this fact, and in return for merchants' financial contributions he appointed them to his Majlis, or advisory board.[32]

The *majlis* then served as a kind of pre-municipal group, led by the ruler, wherein merchants' financial power gave them significant sway over governing issues. The merchant leaders promoted certain civic initiatives through philanthropic projects for several schools and a hospital, which established a precedent both for specific concern for these kinds of foundational infrastructures, and to a more general degree, a blurring of public and private spheres within the ruling system.

Urban Morphology at the Beginning of Twentieth Century

While the port was taking on increased international trade functions, at the turn of the century Dubai was still a town of 10,000 people, of which almost 7,000 were involved in the pearling sector. The urban layout included three areas located around the mouth of the Creek: Deira, consisting of 1,600 houses and 350 *souq* shops for the Arab merchant community, Al Shindagah, a residence of the ruling family that included 250 houses, and Bur Dubai, the smallest of the settlement areas with 200 houses and 50 *souq* shops, mostly populated by Persian and Indian merchants.[33] Spatially, the town was perhaps more divided than the blurred public and private functions mentioned above, with the ruler's fortress located in Al Shindagah, across the creek from the merchant area of Deira. Oddly, the Bur Dubai area was perhaps the lesser important of three areas in terms of Dubai's political economy, but it housed the cemetery, which holds symbolic importance for many urban cultures.[34]

It is important also to underscore the morphological precedent of this outlay in order to better understand subsequent urban development. First, the simultaneous separation and agglomeration of the three settlements around the water element of the creek required a transportation mechanism (*dhow* river transport, later enhanced through bridge and tunnel construction) in order to communicate each area. While the silt accumulation allowed residents to cross the creek during seasonal low tides, the creek generally required a form of transportation to cross. Furthermore, the creek served as *center,* because it was the essential entry and exit point for the pearling economy, and because it was the element that joined the three separate settlements.

Second, the spatial separation of function, maintaining the Al Shindagah area dedicated to the ruler and his family, and the Deira area for the merchant class, along with Bur Dubai, though to a lesser extent. While this would eventually change, with a mixing of spatial functions among the three settlements and beyond, the initial urban layout served as a blueprint for later modern and modernization projects that spatially isolated districts for specific functions, and equally importantly, while always subordinate to the final power of the ruler, different areas of the burgeoning town could be understood as overseen and associated with certain communities in addition to the ruler. Finally, and related to each of the previous points, Dubai was a megalopolitan urban structure. By this I mean that while the creek must be understood as a central urban element and a structuring mechanism for urban articulation and development, these three settlements were also separated by the creek, and each settlement required a transportation armature for functional coherence.[35]

Thus, the fluid nature of the creek as center was essentially centrifugal, such that as development moved beyond the walled areas of the city with infrastructural developments during the latter part of the twentieth century, Dubai's polycentric character, and its ability to have a moving or shifting center hierarchy, was established within Dubai's initial settlement pattern.

The Dubai Reform Movement

While World War I had little impact on Dubai, it was the period between the wars that would greatly alter Dubai's economic structure. The worldwide crisis precipitated by financial events in October 1929 would devastate international markets, and Dubai was hit heavily, essentially ending the pearling sector and the associate ancillary activities. As early as July 1929 there were already signs of pearling fleets that could not go out because of lack of financing, and by 1933, the international price for pearls had dropped by 20 percent.[36] Once the crisis hit, sectors of the merchant class felt part of the blame should be directed toward Britain. The British treaties had prevented other countries from investing in the local pearling industry, and merchant leaders felt that this had denied them access to improved technology for more competitive and efficient pearling.[37] Indeed, Britain sought to prevent international interlopers into their Gulf "lake," but also consciously wanted to block excessive economic success for the Gulf, particularly in a sector that they did not benefit from directly. The Banians, who were hit particularly hard by the crisis as the principal financiers, requested that Britain intervene to pursue their debtors, but these pleas went unanswered.[38] The introduction of the cultured pearl by the Japanese would also bring international prices down for pearls, and mark the end of this long pearling history in the lower Gulf which had lasted thousands of years.

The end of the pearling industry also interrupted the tacit governing agreement between the ruler and the merchant class in Dubai. This occurred for two reasons. First, while sectors of the merchant class and the *majlis* were involved in port and regional distribution activities, most of the merchant class wealth was based on profits from pearling. Once this ended, they no longer controlled Dubai's purse strings, and thus, there was a shift in the balance of power established during the pearling era to the benefit of the ruler. Second, this shift also occurred because of concessions for oil exploration and air use. In 1939, the British Political Resident for the lower Gulf remarked, "…a key reason for the goodwill between the British and the rulers was that negotiations over air and oil gave the rulers a square deal which carried a money bag rather than a big stick."[39] British oil exploration throughout the Gulf region dated back to the turn of the century, as I will explore in greater detail later, but similar preventative strategies that inspired the 1892 Gulf treaties to keep Russia and other European countries away from Gulf resources also drove the British to establish oil exploration concession agreements with countries in the region.

In 1935, the London-based Anglo-Iraqi Petroleum Company (later renamed Petroleum Development (Trucial States)) formed a subsidiary company called Petroleum Concessions Ltd., which was responsible for signing exclusive oil exploration concession agreements in the lower Gulf.[40] In 1937, Dubai's ruler Sheikh Said Al-Maktoum signed a twenty-five-year oil concession agreement with Petroleum Concessions Ltd., wherein the ruler received 60,000 rupees at signing, an annual income of 300,000 rupees, with an additional 200,000 rupees if oil were discovered, and an export price of 3 rupees per barrel.[41]

In addition, the British sought exclusive air rights in the region for their Imperial Airways line to be able to land and refuel for flights from Basra to Bombay and Cairo to Karachi. Again, these concessions were signed directly with the rulers, beginning in the early 1930s with Ras-al Khaimah and Sharjah, and then again in 1937, with Sheikh Said in Dubai. While it was initially believed that there was no appropriate land site for an airstrip, the agreement took advantage of the linear form of the Dubai creek as a landing site for water planes. Sheikh Said received 5,000 rupees in the first year of this agreement, and it is believed that in order to secure this agreement, he would buy up all empty seats on planes that were not full when leaving Dubai to retain Imperial Airways patronage.[42]

With direct passive revenue streams coming from air and oil concessions, Sheikh Said assumed a much stronger position vis-à-vis the *majlis* and the merchant class, placing him in a position of greater financial power after having to depend on pearling merchants for an income. Other Gulf countries that also depended on pearling faced similar shifts in the ruler/*majlis* power shares, which precipitated a wave of reform movements in the region, particularly in Kuwait and Bahrain. Clearly these movements were the result of disgruntled merchants that had previously controlled local affairs, who, with the end of the pearling industry, lost much of their wealth, but perhaps even more importantly, much of their power and status. Merchant leaders in Dubai emboldened by the success of the reform movement in Kuwait and Bahrain sought similar reforms.

In October 1938, four hundred merchants from various families, including the ruler's, tried to impose a set of political and economic reforms on Sheikh Said. The reforms included a new fifteen-member consultative *majlis*, of which the ruler would be president, whose main functions would be to administer the public coffer consisting of 85 percent of the concession revenues. Importantly, the reforms also included a list of infrastructure investments, such as the dredging and widening of the creek to help boost trade throughput and increase economic activity for the merchants, still reeling from the end of pearl trade, particularly to create advantage over the competing port of Sharjah, which also silted heavily. While comprised of disgruntled, status-stripped merchant leaders, the democratic aims of the reforms strove to extend the political and economic decisions of Dubai beyond simply those of the ruler. The reform movement enjoyed some initial success, but Sheikh Said, with the continued support of the British, along with Bedouin tribes on the outskirts of Dubai, was able to regain power. While the power had shifted locally in Dubai because of the end of pearling, the power agreement between the British and the regional rulers, and Sheikh Said in particular, had not changed. And the British, at least at this point, preferred to continue to conduct their business with one person and not a potentially quarrelsome, elected *majlis*. A combination of gun-boat diplomacy (several ships from the Royal Navy were stationed within sight of Deira), several low-flying Royal Air Force planes, and the kind of Al-Maktoum cunning that had kept usurpers at bay for over a century, helped Sheikh Said to regain power.

On March 29, 1939, through what appeared to be a peace offering, Prince Rashid, son of Sheikh Said, was to marry the daughter of a prominent merchant class family involved in the reform movement. Since the October initiative, the Deira side of the creek, controlled by the merchants, had been guarded against any kind of retaliation from the ruler. After some months, this guard seemed un-necessary for the event of the March wedding. On the day of the wedding, however, Bedouin troops crossed the creek and declared that Dubai was once again unified.[43] Instead of the consultative *majlis* that the reform movement demanded, a *Majlis al-tujjar* was established, which would continue to include some selected merchant leaders, but only at the ruler's discretion. From this point forward, Prince Rashid took over the affairs of Dubai in the name of his father, though Sheikh Said would live on until 1958. Rashid was more sympathetic with the merchants' plight, and upon taking power officially, he would proceed to implement many of the infrastructural projects that the reform movement petitioned. Once Sheikh, Rashid would also establish a municipal council that would open some of the technocratic municipal decision-making processes.

The important difference, however, is that the merchant class could not force his hand into these projects, and he made sure that the projects were cleared and coordinated with the British political agents. The reform movement marks the beginning of the era of Prince, and subsequently Sheikh, Rashid, as a kind of trial by fire in political intrigue. His marriage into the reformist merchant family, and the intelligence to understand the logic in some of the requests of the reform movement, particular as a means to further Dubai's development, helped form a more cooperative collaboration with the merchant community.

Nevertheless, the outcome of the reform movement, the *counter-reform* if you will, signified that an unclear distinction between overall development objectives and those of individual merchant interests could continue to exist comfortably, with the very clear understanding that each was ultimately subordinate to the Al-Maktoum ruler and his British backing. The outcome also demonstrated that the infrastructural reforms to promote economic concerns for the merchant class were attended to (albeit not until the 1950s), but the political reforms calling for democratization were ignored, which again, would serve as a kind of *modus operandi* for what could and could not change within the regime, essentially until today.

Oil Exploration and Increased British Paternalism

The end of World War II marked the beginning of the Cold War, and soon after, Indian independence in 1947 ended the British colonial project in the Subcontinent. However, the British Raj remained in the Gulf region for twenty more years for various reasons: first, the oil interests pursued since the beginning of the twentieth century; second, cold war motives to keep Russian influence in the resource-rich region at bay; and finally, the remaining hubris of Empire, and an inertia that saw no reason to abandon a situation of good relations with the rulers of the region.[44] J.P. Bannerman suggests that before oil explorations, the political unit in the Trucial States was understood as "people-centered," based on personal agreements, and not territorially defined with specificity.[45]

Once oil exploration concessions were established with the British, however, territorial domain took on a much greater significance for Gulf rulers. We've already seen how this impacted local ruling dynamics, but at the same time, when oil concessions were signed with both Dubai and Abu Dhabi in the late 1930s, an initial disagreement on territorial boundaries was sparked. Though World War II temporarily halted explorations, they resumed in 1945, as did the border dispute, which flared in 1948 when a Dubai raiding group killed fifty-two Manasir allies of Abu Dhabi in a border battle.[46] British political intervention helped resolve the conflict by drawing up territorial boundaries from the coast to the interior that both Abu Dhabi and Dubai agreed to, but the border would remain a point of contention between Dubai and Abu Dhabi through the Emirates' formation in 1971. Clearly, the British understanding with Trucial rulers could be used to back those rulers against reformist merchants and to pit the rulers against one another, again with British paternalist intervention as the final word on matters.

As oil exploration resumed after World War II, British institutions moved to Dubai to establish a presence in the growing town. In 1947 a British political resident was set up in Dubai, and in the previous year the British Imperial Bank of Iran (which would change its name to British Bank of the Middle East—BBME—in 1952) signed an agreement with Dubai to set up an office there that would enjoy a banking monopoly until 1963. While profits for BBME were initially more modest in Dubai compared with other Gulf branches in Kuwait and Bahrain, the bank enjoyed good relations with Prince Rashid, and this would eventually pay off well for them. Beginning in the early 1950s, gold became the new resource to replace pearls in Dubai. While Kuwait had previously been the principal exporter of gold to India, their discovery and subsequent concentration on oil in 1950, along with Dubai's economic growth and geographic proximity to India, attracted gold trade flows southward.[47] After India's independence was declared, the sale of gold was officially outlawed for Indian merchants.

For the merchants of Dubai, who were forced to find other sectors for business opportunities (both legal and illicit) after the pearl decline, a market for the covert sale of gold to Indian merchants through *dhow* trade began. Thus, all international gold trade with India (including Britain's and Switzerland's) would pass first through Dubai, where its *dhow* traders would then transship the gold for the final trek to meet with Indian traders off their coasts. The BBME in Dubai would offer "free dollars" for gold trade, even though Dubai was still part of the sterling region, and in this way, a curious three-way exchange for currency and bullion traders emerged that generated profits of 300 percent or more. The BBME, of course, also profited handsomely. With the same vision and flexibility demonstrated in competition with Persia, Dubai, again, utilized a lax regulatory system and a willingness to encourage business to solidify its economic geographic position.[48]

Dubai Urban Infrastructure

The historical relationship between Dubai and the British government, and their associate interests in promoting British banking through institutions like the BBME as well as British consulting groups, as we shall see cannot be overemphasized as part and parcel of the modernization project of the emirate. Geoffrey Jones's history of the BBME underscores the kind of unorthodox relationship established between the Bank and Sheikh Rashid:

> As in Kuwait, BBME had a monopoly of banking in Dubai after opening in 1946. In Dubai, as elsewhere, the responsibilities of monopoly encouraged BBME to undertake functions beyond the scope of a normal commercial bank...Moreover, from the late 1950s

BBME played an important part in the Ruler's plans to modernize Dubai.[49]

Since proposed in the *majlis* reform movement of the late 1930s, the dredging and widening of the creek was understood as Dubai's most imperative infrastructural project to help increase throughput of traffic, as well as accommodate the landing of heavier equipment necessary for oil exploration. In 1954, using contacts both through the political agencies of the British Raj along with those of BBME, Prince Rashid called upon Neville Allen, an engineer for the British Sir William Halcrow firm who was working on hydrographic surveys for the development of the Shuwaikh Port in Kuwait, to carry out similar surveys for the creek for its eventual dredging scheme. Allen's survey determined that the cost for dredging would be £388,000, and in 1955 Prince Rashid and the British political agent approached BBME to try to secure a loan for the project. The Bank would not agree to the loan without the British government's guarantee that it would pay in case of default, which was not immediately forthcoming.

An alternative route through this same network helped to secure a £400,000 loan from the Ruler of Kuwait, under the auspices of the Kuwait Development Fund that offered regional help to developing neighbors since Kuwait's discovery in 1938. The BBME helped to negotiate favorable lending conditions and also agreed to guarantee payments in case Dubai defaulted.[50] The initial dredging and widening of the creek was completed by the end of the decade, and increased throughput capacity to allow local vessels and coastal steamers of up to 800 tons to enter. Grey Mackenzie & Sons, also a British firm working in the Gulf since the late nineteenth century, operated barges that unloaded cargo in the creek for offshore ships over the 800-ton limit.[51] The Sharjah creek had silted to a point beyond use, long enough for Dubai to secure the infrastructural advantage.

In addition to creek dredging, through the same regional networks, Dubai also contracted the British architect/planner John R. Harris to draft the first 1960 master plan to direct booming expansion and infrastructure projects. Harris had also been involved in architecture and planning work in Kuwait, but as creek activity and development increased, Sheikh Rashid either foresaw, or was persuaded, that this kind of urban development and expansion needed proper planning to guide it. The sources on this matter diverge according to who is writing the history, but whether Sheikh Rashid saw what was happening in Kuwait and Bahrain and wanted to follow their example with the advice of British institutions and consultants who would benefit, or whether these infrastructure projects were part of his larger vision for Dubai is conjectural. Clearly Sheikh Rashid's political cunning, along with a family history of business-friendly policy to facilitate trade, demonstrated the intelligence to both identify and create opportunities for Dubai. But it was with the financing and technical expertise of both British and Gulf networks that these projects were ultimately realized.

Harris's 1960 document was principally a road map outlining the transportation armature to help structure the city's growth, which also included general land use indications for industrial, residential, commercial, and public (future schools, hospitals) use, but these were broad-brushed, and could later be changed circumstantially according to new project and investment requirements. A 1968 promotional booklet on Dubai announces as much in its "Town Planning" section: "The whole plan has an inbuilt flexibility enabling it to be adapted to new conditions and major development projects."[52] Again, while initially a part of the reform movement's petitions, the Dubai Municipality was officially established in 1957 as the institution in charge of carrying out the indications of the Harris plan. By the end of the decade, the small fishing town began to grow southward along the creek's natural urban axis with the help of muscular, ambitious engineering projects to guide expansion.

Dredging and land reclamation, and Harris's first master plan, occurred at the same time as Sheikh Rashid promulgated the Land Law of 1960, which essentially was a homestead declaration giving land ownership to those Dubai nationals who could prove that they had lived on their property for a certain period of time. All other land belonged to the ruler, land could not be owned by non-nationals and if the municipality needed private land for infrastructural purposes, it was committed to paying the appropriate price. Prince Maktoum bin Rashid Al Maktoum headed the land regulation committee, with the Land Law structured specifically on the Sudanese land law, which had recently been completed after Sudanese independence in 1956,[53] and Sudanese consultants were contracted to help formulate the law based on their recent experience.[54] The Land Law is another example, though in a different sector, of consulting expertise contracted through regional networks based on British spheres of influence (the Sudan was also a part of the British Raj at this time). The law was also an essential step to define land capitalization for wealth accumulation and should be understood as directly linked to the first master plan as part of the larger strategy to both invest in Dubai as a territory through large infrastructure projects and take advantage of the resulting land value increase from these projects. The law also helped to guarantee the loans needed for these projects by capitalizing land for wealth accumulation.

Other infrastructural projects were also initiated during this period with financial help from the above-mentioned networks, including the Qatari ruling family, which like Kuwait, had also recently discovered oil within its territory. Projects included drilling for additional fresh water resources for the growing population (the site of Al-Awir would become an important water resource, along with the enhanced Bedouin well systems),[55] the Dubai State Telephone Co., along with the founding of the Dubai Electric Company, which the BBME also helped form based on the foundational structure and articles of the Baghdad Electric Company.[56] The British Halcrow firm, which by this point was firmly established as the chief engineering group for Sheikh Rashid's plans, was also contracted to build the first bridge across the creek. The Al-Maktoum Bridge finally connected Bur Dubai with Deira, facilitating alternative passage for vehicles beyond the creek water passage through *dhows* and *abras*.

Sheikh Rashid initiated many infrastructural projects during this boom period between 1958, when he assumed the title of ruler, and 1966, when oil was struck. It is important to underscore that, along with the more traditional infrastructural and municipal services projects mentioned, there was also a conscious effort to establish a banking and hotel infrastructure to further attract trade and diversify financial possibilities. The financial arrangements with local and British contacts to finance the engineering projects often resulted in Dubai's use of borrowed money to pay international (mostly British) consultants to carry out ambitious projects, such as creek dredging and road construction. But Sheikh Rashid also understood that at some point, these institutions would need to be created locally.

The BBME had enjoyed a monopoly in the banking sector in Dubai since the late 1940s and, though officially their profits where less than in other parts of the region, gold trade throughout the 1950s earned the bank an important income. During a trip to London in

1959, Sheikh Rashid is said to have made an agreement with the BBME to extend their monopoly banking privileges, which were previously scheduled to end in 1967, for an additional seven years, or through 1974. Nevertheless, beginning in 1962, Dubai representatives went to Kuwait to study the National Bank of Kuwait and to offer them a 30 percent share in the establishment of a National Bank of Dubai in 1963.[57] The National Bank of Dubai, to the BBME's surprise, opened in May 1963. In Geoffrey Jones's history of the BBME, with an obvious bias, he states, "BBME's decision not to oppose the formation of the National Bank was the only practical choice...There was great disappointment, however, when further breaches of BBME's monopoly followed."[58]

These "further breaches" included the opening of the First National City Bank of New York (Citibank) in January 1964 as a part of the 1963 oil concession agreement with the United States firm the Continental Oil Company. By 1968, along with these three banks, six other banks from neighboring Gulf countries, the U.K. and the U.S. had opened offices, and this number, of course, would continue to grow apace with Dubai's economic prosperity.[59] Sheikh Rashid's decision to first establish a National Bank and then to diversify the international bank presence in Dubai may have origins in the fact that the BBME had initially refused his petition for a loan to widen and deepen the creek, and that his desire to use their presence as a quasi-public coffer had clear limits. The merchant community, which had a history of anti-British sentiment, may also have influenced Sheikh Rashid's decision but it seems just as likely that he observed the moves of neighboring Gulf countries and believed that Dubai's financial autonomy would require the founding of a national bank as well.

Dubai also saw the beginnings of its hotel sector in the early 1960s, with an increasing number of visits from international businessmen attracted by the prospect of oil exploration, along with gold trade activities. The three first-class hotels, the Carlton (112 rooms) on the Deira side of the creek, the Bustan (32 rooms) by the airport, and the Airlines Hotel (26 rooms) in Bur Dubai, were advertised with swimming pools and tennis courts.[60] Additional hotels included the Ambassador (46 rooms) and the Oasis (36 rooms).[61] In the following decade, international hotels would become towers lining the creek, but at this point, they were still ground+nine buildings. Foreshadowing future supply-side infrastructural decisions, hotel construction preceded the demand capacity, and many rooms were initially vacant. As the decade would progress and investments increase, these kinds of vacancies would not last.

Air and Seaports

The municipal services, financial institutions, and nascent tourist infrastructure projects sought to complement those core elements of Dubai's trade and *entrepôt* functions, but Sheikh Rashid's projects still centered on large-scale trade infrastructure. Though the creek had been widened and dredged in the late 1950s, the 1930s air concessions agreement with the British R.A.F. to use the creek as a landing strip for water planes was signed mainly with the interest of warding off other international courters. The creek's actual use as an airstrip is recorded only from 1942-1947.[62] The principal airport for the lower Gulf was the Sharjah International Airport established in 1939, but just as Dubai wanted to compete for maritime trade with Sharjah by dredging the creek, Sheikh Rashid realized quickly that an airport would be necessary to attract international business directly to the city.

When presenting the idea to the merchant community, however, he made sure to underscore his firm belief in an "open skies" policy,[63] and not repeat the exclusive agreement signed in the late 1930s by Sheikh Said. Sheikh Rashid also emphasized these different circumstances to downplay any bad memories of the power change that the air concessions deal of the 1930s had caused the *majlis*. Easa Saleh Al-Gurg, who served as an advisor to Sheikh Rashid and an early employee of the BBME, recounts in his autobiography how he and Sheikh Rashid, during their 1959 trip to London, met with International Airadio Limited, the British air-traffic control firm, where they committed to running a new Dubai International Airport. They identified a plot of land between the Al-Ghusais and Al-Rashidya areas in early 1960 and, by the end of the year, the terminal and air tower were complete. The airport was managed by International Airadio Limited, and flights from Gulf Aviation and Kuwait Airways immediately began routing through Dubai. British Overseas Aviation Company, though initially reluctant, also eventually began flying through Dubai, as the result of Sheikh Rashid incorporating his father's policy of buying up any vacant seats on flights so that the BOAC could meet its minimum of 60 percent occupancy.[64]

By 1965, increased trade along the creek continued to serve the construction and oil exploration boom of the 1960 and it was clear that a deep-water port was needed to alleviate month-long queues of ships waiting to unload cargo for the city. While forty Grey and Mackenzie barges worked to unload offshore ships, it simply could not keep apace, and, in several cases, helicopters were contracted to help throughput. In 1965, Halcrow was summoned once again to begin surveys for a deep-water port just south of the creek's entrance in Al Shindagah. The initial plans for the new Port Rashid were complete in 1967, but based on conservative British growth projects for trade, included only four berths. As we will see, even Sheikh Rashid's insistence on sixteen berths proved below the mark, and all berths were oversubscribed when Port Rashid opened in 1971, which would then have to be expanded to thirty-seven berths by the end of the 1970s.

Oil Discovery

By the early 1960s, the twenty-five year oil concessions contract that Sheikh Said had signed in the late 1930s with Petroleum Concessions Limited (PCL) was ending. The first round of concessions contracts throughout the Gulf, roughly from 1910 through World War II, were generally forced on rulers through the British political agencies, wherein the oil exploration was not required to train nor include local labor, offer participation of the host country, foster any commitments toward industrialization development, and were generally established on unjust financial arrangements.[65] In the case of Dubai, the end of the pearl trade, and the financial advantage of direct payments to Sheikh Said, offered a politically attractive way to strike a new power contract with the local *majlis*, but this is not to say that the concessions contracts were just. After PCL acquired the concession rights, World War II interrupted oil exploration in Dubai but when it resumed, PCL explored three separate sites for onshore drilling (notably, Jebel Ali) during the 1950s. By the time the contract was up, oil had been discovered in commercial quantities in other regions of the Gulf and the frustration of unsuccessful drilling meant that the British were not as eager to renew the existing contract.

In 1963, Dubai signed an oil exploration contract with the U.S. Continental Oil Company (CONOCO), and set up the Dubai Petroleum Company (DPC) to run the onshore concession. The

Dubai Marine Areas Limited was also set up as a joint venture with British Petroleum and Compagnie Française de Pétroles for offshore exploration.[66] This arrangement would change several times through quick sales of percentages within these joint ventures from one international oil company to another, but on June 6th, 1966, the DPC discovered crude oil in the offshore "Fateh" field (meaning "good fortune" in Arabic) at 7,600 feet below sea level. Subsequent fields known as "Fateh South" and "Rashid" were also successful, and oil production began three years later in 1969. On September 22, 1969, the first shipment of 180,000 barrels arrived at the U.K. CONOCO refineries, and on October 15, 1970, Dubai became an official member of the club of oil exporting countries.[67] By the end of the first year, the Dubai oil fields yielded 3,561,094 barrels of crude oil, with revenues of US$ 376,114. By the end of 1970, revenue jumped to US$ 11,556,000 and by the end of 1975 estimated revenue reached US$ 600,000,000.[68]

Conclusion

While oil discovery brought revenue to Dubai and would change the city's physiognomy, moving it beyond the initial three settlements along the creek, it is clear that Dubai's status as a dynamic *entrepôt* for international trade and transshipment, its foundational infrastructure projects, and its "free port" policies to attract merchant communities from throughout the Gulf and the Indian Ocean, along with licit and illicit trade for re-export to Persia/Iran and India, were solidly established before "black gold" was struck in Fateh field. Dubai's trade vocation existed before the arrival of the British, but their indirect protection (with clear costs and benefits to Dubai), along with the fact that British merchants were not at-tracted to local Gulf trade because profits were considered too low for their efforts, allowed for a community of Banian, Persian and Arab merchants to settle in Dubai and assume their own positions of power and influence.[69] Though before the arrival of oil, because of the ruler's dependence on the merchant community for their pearl trade wealth and subsequently because of Sheikh Rashid's sympathies with the importance of trade for the emirate, Dubai was, as Enseng Ho states, "a 'trading state' in which the ruling family, the Maktoums, combined the role of both ruler and chief merchant."[70] Indeed, through both marriage and family, Sheikh Rashid is perhaps the best example of this, so much so that his example would become imbued in both the responsibilities and political understandings expected of the sheikhdom title itself.

Sheikh Rashid was able to carry out the infrastructure projects solicited by the *majlis* in their reform movement, and though the merchant community was hit strongly by the end of pearling, gold trade profits for the Dubai merchant community helped to quell reform rumblings. Once the creek was dredged and widened, with Harris's master plan and the 1960s Land Law in place, the Dubai municipality saw the strategic opportunity to reclaim land on the Deira side of the creek by using what was removed from the dredging project. Creek dredging and land reclamation in the late 1950s and early 1960s provided a new surface on which to guide southern creek development. This reclaimed land then became the corridor for office, hotel, and municipal development, which the municipality was in turn able to either lease or sell without having to buy out any existing landowner plots within Deira—one of the densest parts of the city. Thus Baniyas Road would become the city's central business district, mixing heavier industry with commercial and office uses. This strategic use of ambitious infrastructural projects, and those institutions that would help establish future economic sectors for Dubai (i.e., numerous banks as a financial infrastructure, hotels as a tourism infrastructure) with multiple developmental objectives, would also mark future infrastructural projects and overarching developmental strategies. Thus Dubai's development blueprint was being forged while the city was still a Gulf outpost and British protectorate up through oil discovery: large-scale engineering projects to facilitate trade movement (which, in turn, attracted more trade); urban expansion along the new trade route (initially, the creek); and spatial planning reduced essentially to providing transportation infrastructure to facilitate and loosely structure growth.

Notes

1. Owen, 2008.
2. Kassar, 2007. Land reclamation projects in Dubai and throughout the UAE will expand this total land area significantly, but this is the latest published data.
3. Peck, 1986, p. 6.
4. Heard-Bey, 1982, p. 34.
5. Peck, 1986, p. 24.

6. King, 1997, p. 76, Wilson, 2006, p. 22.
7. Nyrop, 1977, p. 21.
8. Nyrop, 1977, p.22.
9. Peck, 1986, p. 27.
10. Ibid.
11. Nyrop, 1977, p. 23.
12. Ibid.
13. Peck, 1986, p. 29.
14. Onley, 2007, p. 30.
15. Heard-Bey, 1982, p. 164.
16. Peck, 1986, p. 32.
17. See Onley, 2007 for more detailed explanation of British political structure within the region.
18. Nyrop, 1977, p.24. Hamza, 1968.
19. Davidson, 2008, p. 17.
20. Heard-Bey enumerates the many Bani Yas subsections, which along with the Al Bu Falasa, Al Bu Mahair, the Rumaithat, the Qubaisat, the Mazari, the Hawamil, the Maharibah, the Al Mishaghin, and the Sudan. In addition to the Bani Yas tribe, she also enumerates the subsections of the Manasir and Dhawahir tribes, who were less numerous than the dominant Bani Yas in the region. For a more elaborate discussion, see Heard-Bey, 1982 Chapter Two.
21. Davidson, 2008, p. 12-13. Wilson, 2006, p. 29.
22. Davidson, 2008, p. 15.
23. Davidson, 2008, pp. 22-23. Gabriel, 1987, p.139. Lorimer, 1970.
24. Onley, 2007, p. xviii.
25. Al-Sayegh, 1998, p. 88.
26. Davidson, 2008, p. 68.
27. Al-Sayegh, 1998, p. 89.
28. Al-Saleh, 1998, p. 89.
29. Ibid.
30. Gabriel, 1987, p. 71.
31. Fairservice, 2002, p. 23.
32. Al-Sayegh, 1998, p. 90.
33. Heard-Bey, 1982, p. 242.
34. Mumford, 1961. See discussion of the "necropolis" on p. 7.
35. Gottmann, 1961, introduces the concept of the "megalopolis," and Pope, 2008, describes Dubai's contemporary form as "megalopolitan."

36. Al-Sayegh, 1998, p. 94.
37. Davidson, 2008, Chapter 2.
38. Ibid.
39. Davidson, 2008, p. 24.
40. Peck, 1986, p.3 7.
41. Davidson, 2008, p. 27.
42. Davidson, 2008, pp. 25-26.
43. Davidson, 2008, p. 34.
44. Peck, 1986, p. 40.
45. Bannerman, 1986, pp. 76-77.
46. Peck, 1986, p. 41.
47. Green, 1973.
48. Gabriel, 1987, p. 142. Green, 1973.
49. Jones, 1987, p. 150.
50. Jones, 1987, p. 154.
51. Gabriel, 1987, p. 141. Jones, 1986.
52. Hamza, 1968. The Engineering Department of the Dubai Municipality was responsible for the Plan's implementation.
53. Balfour-Paul, 1991, Chapter 2.
54. Hamza, 1968.
55. Davidson, 2008, p. 92. Wilson, 2006 p. 177.
56. Jones, 1987, p. 155.
57. Jones, 1987, p. 156.
58. Ibid.
59. Hamza, 1968.
60. Wilson, 2006, p. 186. Gabriel, 1987, p. 143. Hamza, 1968.
61. Harris, 1994, Section 4.2.8.
62. Al-Gurg, 1998.
63. Davidson, 2008, p. 94.
64. Davidson, 2008, p. 95.
65. Al-Otaiba, 1977, pp. 39-40.
66. Ibid.
67. Ibid.
68. Al-Otaiba, 1977, p. 67.
69. Owen, 2008.
70. Owen, 2008, p. 7. Ho, 2008.

References

Al-Gurg, Easah Saleh, *The Wells of Memory*, London: John Murray, 1998.

Al-Otaiba, Mana Saeed, *Petroleum and the Economy of the United Arab Emirates,* London: Croom Helm, 1977.

Al-Sayegh, Fatma, "Merchants' Role in a Changing Society: The Case of Dubai, 1900-90," *Middle Eastern Studies* Vol. 34, No.1, January, 1998.

Balfour-Paul, Glen. *The End of Empire in the Middle East: Britain's Relinquishment of Power in Her Last three Arab Dependencies.* Cambridge: Cambridge University Press, 1991.

Bannerman, J.P., "The Impact of the Early Oil Concessions in the Gulf States," in Lawless, R.I. (ed.), *The Gulf in the Early Twentieth Century: Foreign Institutions and Local Responses*, Durham: Centre for Middle Eastern & Islamic Studies, 1986.

Davidson, Christopher M., *Dubai: The Vulnerability of Success,* New York: Columbia University Press, 2008.

Fairservice, Ian, (ed.), *Dubai: Gateway to the Gulf.* London: Motivate Publishing, 2002.

Gabriel, E. F., (ed.), *The Dubai Handbook.* Ahrensburg: Institute for Applied Economic Geography, 1987.

Gottmann, Jean, *Megalopolis: The Urbanized Northeastern Seaboard of the United States.* New York: Twentieth Century Foundation, 1961.

Green, Timothy, *The World of Gold Today*, New York: Walker and Company, 1973.

Hamza, Kamal, *Dubai: The Pearl of the Coast*, Beirut: Al Massaref Magazine, 1968.

Harris, John R., "Dubai Development Plan May 1971," in *Development Plans of the GCC States 1962-1995*, London: Archive Editions, 1994.

Heard-Bey, Frauke, *From Trucial States to United Arab Emirates,* New York: Longman, 1982.

Ho, Enseng, "Dubai and Singapore: Inter-Asian Connections Through Indian Ocean Port Cities," Paper presented to SSRC-Dubai School of Government Conference on Inter-Asian Connections, Dubai, February, 2008.

Jones, Geoffrey, *Banking and Oil: The History of the British Bank of the Middle East Volume 2*, London: Cambridge University Press, 1987.

Jones, Stephanie. *Two Centuries of Overseas Trading: The Origins and Growth of the Inchcape Group*, London: MacMillan Press, 1986.

Kassar, Khaled, (ed.), *1000 Numbers and Reasons Why Dubai,* 2nd ed., Beirut: BISC Group, 2007.

King, Geoffrey R, "The History of the UAE: The Eve of Islam and Islam Period," in Ghareeb, Edmund and Ibrahim Al Abed, (eds.), *Perspectives on the United Arab Emirates,* Abu Dhabi: Trident Press, 1997.

Lorimer, John G., *Gazetteer of the Persian Gulf, Oman, and Central Arabia*, London: Gregg International Publishers, 1970.

Mumford, Lewis, *The City in History: Its Origins, Its Transformations, and Its Prospects*, New York: Harcourt Brace Jovanovich, 1961.

Nyrop, Richard F., et al., *Area Handbook for the Persian Gulf States*, Washington: American University, 1977.

Onley, James. *The Arabian Frontier of the British Raj: Merchants, Rulers, and the British in the Nineteenth Century Gulf*, New York: Oxford University Press, 2007.

Owen, Roger, "Cities of the Persian Gulf: Past, Present and Future," Lectured delivered at the University of Nicosia, Nicosia, Cyprus, 14 October, 2008.

Peck, Malcom C., *The United Arab Emirates: A Venture in Unity*, Boulder: Westview Press, 1986.

Pope, Albert. "we are all bridge–and –tunnel people...*Log",* Vol. 12, Spring/Summer 2008.

Rammin, Thomas, "The Ensemble of Port Development Factors in the Mediterranean Region: 1815-1999" Doctoral Dissertation, Harvard University Graduate School of Design, 1999.

Wilson, Graeme, *Father of Dubai: Sheikh Rashid bin Saeed Al Maktoum*, Dubai: Media Prima, 1999.

Wilson, Graeme, *Rashid's Legacy: the Genesis of the Maktoum Family and the History of Dubai*, Dubai: Media Prima, 2006.

9

Dubai: The City and Sacredness

M.H. Ilias

Dubai is a city with rare sense and character. Its transformation from a humble fishing and pearling community to a busy modern city of the 'new millennium' and a prosperous port of the Gulf has been, of course, dramatic. The city's uniqueness, however, lies in its 'superlative' structures[1] that become the means through which Dubai mediates meaning. Through world-class infrastructure, 'business-friendly' climate and 'politically neutral' setting Dubai city is negotiating its identity. The architectural splendors in Dubai have collectively set in motion an interesting politico-spatial practice. Much is written about the new mode of urbanity emerging in Dubai. The developments in Dubai, speak eloquently of a radical re-imaging of conventional notions associated with space and politics. So, scholars now view the city not just a spatial entity but as a medium of socio-political discourse.

The mega projects have become a source of media debates and arguments and most importantly, a model to be emulated throughout the region and even in some parts of South Asia which contributes majority of labourers in the Gulf[2]. Interestingly, Dubai has become a point of reference for all the Middle Eastern states--a model that everyone wants to replicate. Countries of the region, no matter whether they are politically on the opposite side, are not indifferent to the success of Dubai.[3] No other city captures such an amount of exaggeration, fantasy and imagination. The so-called 'Dubai model' has become a wide-spread term, connoting the exportability of its particular mode of development.[4]

The transformation of Dubai as the major commercial centre in the Middle East also marks a shift of focus from Bagdad and Cairo to Dubai as the gatekeepers of 'Arab culture' and sites for debates and experiments. One particularly potent argument in this context is of Elshetawy. The structural makeover of Dubai, according to him, opens scope for a postcolonial reading.[5] He presents Dubai as a "shining example of society in transformation." Dubai can be placed as a gateway between the newly emerging centres of the east and the west, a "crucial staging post" in the shift in economic might and cultural epicenter from the west to emerging Asia.[6] Dubai's mode of urbanism is a response to this postcolonial positioning. It is evident from Dubai's changing cultural landscape, wherein there is an increasing blurring of the distinctions of east and west, orient and occident and colonial and postcolonial.

While talking about architecture, one can see that the buildings, on the one hand, respect the vernacular Arab city fabric, on the other they attempt to insert a different, a distinct, and an elevated style to the cities of similar sort in the region. On the identity front also Dubai has emerged as a strategic site to endorse a transnational diversity. Dubai is unique because of its ability to accept people from around the world with different, and often contradictory values, provided they adhere to the lifestyle range that Dubai is willing to accept in the public sphere.

There are two major questions to be addressed here; where does Dubai stand in terms of global urban imagination and has Dubai been elevated to a higher space or still in an uncertain space, caught between old and new? The scope of enquiry, however, should not be limited to the traditional binaries, traditional or modern, old or new, orient or occident, etc., as such a line of approach may fail to assess the dynamic synthesis representing a set of new experiments in spatiality and urbanity.

The city is a living metaphor for the neo-liberal globalized world. At a popular level the word 'Dubai' is synonymous with unabashed consumerism. With proliferation of themed shopping malls and 'spectacular' events, the city's name evokes a sort of artificiality. The city obsessively uses the 'spectacle' as a way of making an edge over other cities in the region, who are trying to emulate its success. Dubai itself, therefore, maintains a wish to be defined primarily by its commercial character.[7] Interestingly, the city's recent fame comes from its projection as a 'uniquely apolitical' city in the Gulf region.[8] This adjective may be to make a new strategic asset out of it and thereby to attract business minded people and multinational corporations. Besides, it also helps rewriting the spatial history of the land and disengaging old 'socio-political' narratives that the land possessed in the past.

The economic downturn might be having a substantial impact on Dubai's ambitious plans, but the city continuously captures a high amount of exaggeration and fantasy. So, than just being a global city, Dubai connects to a larger theme-- a hyperspace[9] in which we find ourselves caught as individual spectators. This spectacular nature of the city produces a specific geography of 'sacredness'. What makes an object sacred in the capitalist discourse, normally, is its unavailability for ordinary use[10]. Such spaces are meant for display; seldom for common use or the consumption of the ordinary people. Being removed from the common use, these spaces have acquired immunity from the rules of the land. With less use value, high exhibitory value and greater political immunity, they become the sacred spaces of capitalism.

Dubai is a space where the parallel between capitalism and religion becomes very pertinent. It is interesting in this context to have a detailed discussion about the nature of 'religiosity' attached to the city as it occupies exactly the space, function and exclusiveness once reserved for 'sacred spaces' of religion. Such a space is integral to the understanding of social reality and political process. This work posits the removal of living spaces from the use of common people in Dubai as the formation of new geographies of 'profanation'. It also discusses some of the elements that precipitate into the formation of new socio-spatial order in Dubai. Finally, it seeks to make an understanding of Dubai as a nexus where the various spatial trends come together to produce new political alignments and geographical meanings.

City as Spectacle

With globalization of the monarchies, the urban social formation in the Gulf States is moving on a different trajectory and rendering specific patterns and directions. As Khalaf observes, this urban social formation differs markedly in its sociological characteristics and evolution from other societal types dominant in most industrialized capitalist or the least industrialized developing countries.[11] The city design is the major theatre wherein economic globalization enacts its drama and generates specific spatial patterns that organize life ways of local cultures throughout the Arab Gulf in a diverse way. The speed, pattern and policies of urban development have been fairly similar across the Gulf, but making a comparison between other developing countries where urbanization was slow and associated with industrialization and sound economic development and the Gulf countries in this regard seems to be a bit difficult.[12] Riad's coinage "petro-urbanism" appears to be more appropriate to describe particular socio-spatial development took place alongside the process of globalization and consequent urbanization in this region.[13] These cities evolved not only as the capitals of their countries but also as urban centres where multiple functions are performed, such as managing all aspects of the "political economy" of oil wealth[14], which itself is encapsulated within the global capitalist economy and culture. Their social formation manifested in rapid development of multi-ethnic character and peculiar housing pattern.[15]

One of the significant impacts on physical infrastructure in recent years has been the construction of spectacular buildings like colossal malls and commercial clusters, high, prestige-inspiring towers, grand exhibition and conference centres, internet cities, media cities, knowledge cities, recreational theme parks, of which the most diagnostic feature of Gulf capital cities is the immensity and centrality of showrooms, large malls, and exhibition centres.[16] Burj al-Arab (constructed in the shape of a boat), palm islands (largest artificial islands), Burj al-Khalifa (world's tallest building)[17]- all add up to this spectacle in Dubai and increasingly spectacular nature of their designs are dubbed as 'iconic'. Perhaps the most obvious example of Dubai's ongoing growth was the amount of construction of such amenities which came to a standstill due to the economic slump.[18]

With greater amount of prominence and centrality, these new socio-economic spaces of market, of course, have successfully replaced the old social spaces like mosques, souks, majlis and streets in the region. The earlier social spaces had represented first of all, a public space and as a space of ordinary people, that was, neither as a divine territory nor as a no-man's land, but a circulation, an exchange and a sharing, that is at once multiple and mobile.

Another prominent trend is to recreate the pre-oil spaces in the form of heritage villages, but these efforts always end up with re-creating such old spaces in the midst of modern skyscrapers. The ordinary people never identify with them as many of these spaces are tailored to cater the needs of transnational elites and many of these developments have caused considerable downgrading and displacement of neighborhood settlements of ordinary people.[19] What we, generally, see happening today is movement of Gulf cities away from the anecdotal image and they now generally lack public spaces for socializing or public realm allowing for gathering as there is increased transformation of such spaces architecturally into towers, high-rise buildings and malls as there was surplus money to be invested in.[20] Dubai, in particular, prides itself on its appellation of the "Shopping Capital of the Middle East."

As we discussed earlier, the malls are no longer the places only to purchase goods[21], but the major meeting points and socializing spaces for an increasing army of expatriate labourers. As a major hang-out for Asian expatriates, large number of people coming in for browsing not necessarily for shopping. Mall users engage in activities that do not necessarily have to be described as consumerist.[22] Ordinary people, especially South Asian expatriate labourers, gather in these 'cathedrals of consumerism' for socialization or to meet their acquaintances and share news coming from home countries. With their peculiar kind of design, the malls also become a liberating space for many.

Malls as places, where people can display their ethnicity, engage in various work related activities, or simply socialize with others, also celebrate a form of multiculturalism.[23] One clue is given by the ad slogan of Lulu Centre, the largest retailing network in the UAE which reads "the world comes to shop here." Crawford's usage "the world is in a shopping mall"[24] could apply to any mall, particularly in Dubai, where shopping malls have turned out to be a sort of public space for expatriate labourers.

The malls in Dubai, among others, are designed in a way that entice and entertain consumers by offering them a pleasure-giving 'experience'.[25] As a major source of entertainment, the malls as such attract shoppers and onlookers by the thousands every day. A consumer turns to be a passive spectator as the malls embody the goods and seduction of global capitalism. With their adventurous design and aesthetics of display and spectacle, the malls create and "focus the dream images of the global capital economy and help produce global subjectivities by shaping everyday people's imagination and discourse about globalization[26]."

The showcase image of Dubai also leads to a specific form of operation--the spectaularization of urban space-- in which the ordinary practitioners of the city become on-lookers in the new spatial process. As Michel de Certeau sketches out in New York City's case, they live "down below" the thresholds at which visibility begins.[27] In a completely 'visible terrain', these practitioners make use of the spaces that cannot be seen. This spectacularization has permeated all sorts of social relations and perceptions. Dubai is using the 'spectacle'[28] as a way of asserting its identity and a way to fix its position on the map of globally significant cities. The spectacle puts ordinary people at a distance and the mass accepts it in passivity. Elsheshtawy argues that the spectacle in Dubai is "not just the product of urbanization but a system of alienation produced by the new forms of urbanity[29]." "With this `peculiar formation," he continues, "the spectacle does not become a device goading spectators into consuming, but instead spectators actively adapt the spectacle to shape their own perceptions and expectations."

Sacred Spaces of Capitalism

The special stature of new market spaces in the Gulf, especially in Dubai involves two major considerations. Firstly, they are meant mainly for display; not for common use or the consumption of the ordinary people.[30] Secondly, being removed from the use of ordinary people, such spaces have acquired immunity from the rules of the land. With less use value, high exhibitory value and greater political immunity, they become the sacred spaces of capitalism.[31]

However, to fully comprehend these developments, it would be appropriate to define what a sacred space is. The sacred spaces are conventionally the spaces that in some way belonged to religion and ultimately to God. They are removed from the free use of human being and having only exhibitory value and no real use value.[32] A sacred space, thus, is not merely discovered, or founded; it is claimed, owned, and operated by people advancing specific interests.[33] 'Sacredness' as a property intrinsic to space is, therefore, constructed, not 'given' and necessarily inscribed by people. Foucault focuses on this aspect of sacred geographies. For him, sacred site is an instrument of power, that is, the area controlled by certain kind of juridico-political or cultural powers.[34] As contested spaces, they are tied up with, and draws meaning from hegemonic and hierarchical social and political practices. Bordieu also has used the term 'sacred space' in a similar connotation in order to mean the peculiar 'spatial order', which legitimates the systemic social inequality, by means of special spatial practices, signs and codes.[35]

The most significant aspects of sacred spaces are their "hierarchical power relations of domination and subordination, inclusion and exclusion, appropriation and dispossession."[36] Van der Leeuw has identified four kinds of politics in the construction of sacred space. He outlined a politics of procession whereby every establishment of "a sacred place is a conquest of space; a politics of property whereby a sacred place is appropriated, possessed and owned."[37] The sacredness is maintained through claims and counterclaims on a place's ownership. There is "a politics of exclusion also, whereby the sanctity of sacred place is preserved by maintaining boundaries."[38] The other significant issue to be discussed along with sacredness is desire. The desire for space inevitably leads to the monopolizing of geography where the space can best be manipulated and the spaces of others are rendered invisible.

Sacred spaces may be, therefore, read, not only as divine or religious, but also as the reflections and reproductions of social, political or economic desires. Agamben points out to this aspect of sacredness and opens up the possibilities of extending the site of analysis beyond conventional sacred spaces.[39] For him, every object, which is placed in a separate sphere and kept far from popular use, is 'sacred'. Removing commodities largely from the popular use, capitalism also shows the salience of sacredness. It is therefore important to analyze the 'entrepreneurial, social, political and other 'profane forces' that constitute the construction of sacred space.

Dubai itself is such a big space where the parallel between capitalism and religion becomes very pertinent. With high amount of autonomy and independence, the City occupies exactly the space, function and exclusiveness once reserved for 'sacred spaces' of religion. The politico-juridical autonomy being enjoyed by the special economic areas and free zones, expansion of which is the key factor in Dubai's successful economic performance, illustrate the sacredness given to the commercial spaces in Dubai better. It also illustrates how a specific geography of sacredness is being produced around the market places.

Jabal Ali Free Zone, the most prominent commercial space, for instance, has been given special powers and legal incentives regarding some of the otherwise sensitive matters like immigration. Aiming to attract global commerce, Jabal Ali boasts of minimal restrictions only. To achieve this objective, the local authority has command over a wide range of affairs including financial regulations in the region, labour issues, environmental protection, and project licensing as well as municipal affairs. Jabal Ali allows business to operate without having a local partner, *kafil,* which is otherwise unimaginable all around the GCC and possesses more liberal immigration regime and visa laws.

Building on the success of the Jebel Ali Free Trade Zone, Dubai currently has a wide range of such specialized free zones with greater legal immunity.[40] As Dubai recognizes the minor importance of oil and gas production to its economic performance, development of free zones receives a major focus of the UAE's strategic policy for economic diversification.[41] Some of the zones cater to service sectors (e.g. Dubai Internet City, Dubai Media City, Dubai Health Care City, Knowledge Village and Dubai International Finance Centre) and enjoy special laws that are more liberal than the country's typical laws. These free zones are exempt from the licensing, agency, Emiratization, and national majority-ownership obligations that are applicable to other sectors in the domestic economy. "Minimum state control and bureaucracy and maximum efficiency" are two shibboleths that Dubai wants to spread.

Swift issuance of government permits and licenses, allocation of prime lands for industrial plants, a fully developed infrastructure and a wide range of state support services are further aspects of free zones. They are home to thousands of companies who take advantage of strategic location and incentives. Companies in free zones generally enjoy 100 percent foreign ownership, corporate tax holidays, personal tax exemption, no restrictions on the repatriation of capital and profits, and freedom from import duties and currency restrictions. The land department in Dubai is now endeavouring to frame new liberalized regime as the liberalized real estate and property laws in the new economic zones have generated unprecedented inflow of foreign companies.

The economic zones in the region, in general, have a different structure of governance and political accountability and participation. In other words, they can be defined as something which is maintained separately with greater amount of immunity from the country's juridical domain. As a sphere transferred to the exclusive use of 'economic elites', economic zones attain high 'display value' rather than the real 'use value'. Given over to spectacular exhibition, 'use of all' and popular participation become impossible. 'Religiosity' emanates, by and large, from these immunities. Global finance sanctions 'the sacredness' of such spaces further and facilitates a passage from the 'use of all' to the use of 'miniscule few', from 'the profane to the sacred', or from 'human sphere to the divine'.

Issues of specific rights and exclusive claims over the SEZs illuminate the affinities between religious and capitalist discourses over the 'divine spaces'. One way to examine this affinity is to compare the legal autonomy being enjoyed by the sacred spaces of both; religion and capitalism. This autonomous stature involves a consideration of two manifestations of internal sovereignty, namely political and legal sovereignty. Internal political sovereignty refers to the ability of state to conduct political business independent of pressures or compulsions from within. Internal legal sovereignty denotes to the ability of state to make its own laws without limitations imposed by an outside agency.

The state sovereignty in the Middle East, in general, encounters massive threat from various sources. The processes and phenomenon like economic liberalization, integration of states politically and economically into regional forums (like the GCC) and rise of political Islam have contributed much to the erosion of state sovereignty. When post-colonial states surrender much of their political and monetary sovereignty to the 'neo-liberal' forces, Islam has seized the popular imagination by capturing the mantle of 'anti-imperialist', populist ideology in most Muslim majority states. But the developments in the oil-rich Arab Gulf speak particularly of a shift of focus from tribal/religious structure to the economic zones as the major force to challenge the state sovereignty. With a wide range of manifestations, they promise a new equation to the relationship between the 'sacred' and 'sovereign'. With similar sort of independence and autonomy being possessed by holy spaces of religion, these spaces are more or less free from constrains of the local political units and their spatial determinations.

At a moment, when the GCC states have lost innumerable sovereign powers to neo-liberal global restructuring, market serves an indispensable role in consolidating and demarcating 'sacred' geographies. When landscapes are created to replicate 'sacred worlds' as understood by particular groups, physical factors contribute to the 'sacredness' of spaces. The sacred spaces of capitalism push religion in principle away to the infra--or supra civic spheres, at the risk of proposing a substitute, a "civic religion".[42] This civic religion keeps sanctity of commerce over religion.

Consumption, symbolic exchange, simulations and signs are important for this civic religion to survive.[43]

The issue of politico-juridical immunity of sacred spaces of capitalism is evident in the special property laws enforced in such spaces. As in other Emirates in UAE, the strict property laws in Dubai regulate the sale and lease of land to expatriates. The foreign ownership is generally restricted or set at a ceiling. But this stringent property regime is conveniently waived and Dubai permits foreign residents to purchase freehold properties in designated areas. With the new motto of 'open doors, open minds', Dubai allows foreign ownership of properties and real estate investments in strategic locations like Palm Islands.

'Uniquely Apolitical' City

As discussed earlier, Dubai's popularity in the region derives from its projection as a 'politically neutral' city in the Gulf region.[44] Sheikh Mohammed Bin Rashid, the ruler of Dubai, himself admits that Dubai has no 'political ambitions'. Dubai's 'ethos', according to him is commerce.[45] The political neutralization of place may generally constitute the master image in the currently dominant account about economic globalization, but in Dubai's case, this adjective makes a new strategic asset out of it and thereby it was possible to attract business minded people and multinational corporations. Dubai is a success story because it is a business friendly and politically neutral place.

Political neutrality of the city is the major attraction in the post-liberalization era. Dubai can hardly be seen as a major player in regional or international politics. Should this apparent lack of political aura be seen as a weakness? No, one might instead be tempted to view this weakness as more of an asset than a liability.[46] The lack of political prominence allows a form of strategic opportunity by which politics and economics could be handled within a loose ideological constituency.[47]

This political neutrality assumes many forms and operates in many arenas. It is undoubtedly a strategic asset of profound value besides being a market asset.[48] Dubai gets benefit out of being such an apolitical city. No other city in the region can claim such 'positive' political neutrality. The relatively weak political status of Dubai is, thus, an advantage that a politically powerful Dubai would lack. Another politically worth-fetching position of Dubai is its neutral stand in many of the sensitive issues.

Dubai actually benefits out of political instability in the region and attracts even warring groups to sit and negotiate on many contentious issues over a table. As Abdulkhaleq Abdullah puts it; "it is only in Dubai where Americans and Iranians can meet amicably, talk to each other decently and spy on each other's intentions with relative ease"[49]. The same political neutrality brought a team of Iraqi politicians to Dubai to negotiate the highly contentious oil law. The Iraqi participants could not meet in highly volatile Iraq and would not agree on any other city in the region as a venue for their close door meeting.[50] India-Pakistan secret negotiations have taken place in Dubai in the year 2009 add long up to its increasing international popularity as a politically neutral place. Briefly put, it hardly matters for Dubai, whoever comes in and negotiates, as long as they stay away from politics and do not contribute to the politicalization of the Emirate[51].

New Map and Blurred Spaces of Others

The projection of Dubai as 'uniquely apolitical' city helps rewriting the spatial history of the land and disengaging old 'politico-religious' narratives that the land possessed in the past. This catchphrase also facilitates deconstructing Dubai's old map and the City becomes the site of an active replacement of old landmarks with the new ones. The basic idea of political locatability has disappeared as a reference point in an effort to remap the old geography. The cartographic representation of Palm Islands[52] offers a 'textbook sort' example to this new practice.

Palm Islands primarily offer a counter-image to the clichéd image of Arabian Desert. Tourists' imagination of Arabian Peninsula normally hinges around the anecdotal images of the desert, camels roaming its endless horizons, oases miraculously appearing within desolate landscapes and the like. The move here is to attract tourists by providing an alternative to this imagination. Relying on sketches, the map of Palm Island enmeshes us in diverse levels of reality. Apart from serving the purpose of 'exhibition of its property', the diagrammatic representation of Palm Island helps achieving and maintaining the cartographic balance in favour of the new identity of Dubai.

The images as seemingly benign and apolitical, thus, become highly contested symbols used to assert this new identity. So the new map, in addition to their theoretical usefulness, has a high degree of practical applicability to depoliticize the landscape. It is through the production of new map, the new political embellishment of the city is achieved. Map serves here as a tool to re-write the spatial history of the land and as a significant function of deployment of power and the legitimization of it. The new map in Dubai's case is not merely a cartographic practice that marks the land, but a political sign system constructing distinct modes of spatial arrangements.

The question of new spatial formation in Dubai is also raised and illustrated by various examples of absence or presence. A number of social scientists have commented on the "social formations" of the Gulf cities with their social and economic segregation patterns.[53] The new city map, in Dubai, has engendered its own set of hierarchies that produce distinctive codes of inclusion and exclusion.

It seems to be appropriate to give a gist of current cleavages in the GCC societies, since this must perhaps be the major source of spatial exclusion. Historically, the line of division was demarcated between citizen *watani* and foreigner *wafid*. Class and ethnic/national stratification systems were overlapping in a more confused state here. The division between citizens and foreigners still runs deep in the Gulf but is taking new turns.[54] In addition, the societies are now stratified in terms of class and what matters more now, is the different forms of separation and control in tune with the new mode of social stratification.[55]

Gavrielides sketches out the situation in a lucid manner: "Christians from Goa work exclusively as maids and governesses for urban Kuwaiti families…Baluchis are employed as door keepers by Kuwaiti families."[56] Nepalese and Tamils form Sri Lanka generally fill up the slots of security personnel and office boys respectively, while America and Western European countries contribute many well paid managers.[57] The middle stratum is comprised mainly of South and East Asian clerks and middle level government employees. It, sometimes, turns to be racist as Sri Lankan or Filipino women do the same job and get quarter of the wages in relation to European or Lebanese women.

What strike as more significant are the different forms of separation and control which assume many forms and operate in many arenas. Being an outcome of a dynamic specific to current forms of economic growth, this new geography has reproduced new forms of social and spatial inequalities. The adoption of neo-liberal economic policies, all along the region, has led to the creation of a series of urban inequalities and spaces which cater to diverse range of social groups. Looking at various forms of urbanity emerging in the city, one can see Dubai making progressive detachment from the old concentric Arab model and is constituted as a series of decentralized neighborhood or fragments.[58]

These developments, in Dubai, have collectively fragmented the city further and skewed development in favour of new areas. The organization and use of space by different groups for their favour make the things more clear. Dubai is, thus, not a merely neutral space in spatial terms but an eclectic mix of contested spaces and representations. There is a multiplicity of geographical expression, despite the city's continues effort to homogenize it. Tantamount almost to a sort of *ghettoization*, there has been the issue of distinctive spatial segregation. There are specially designated areas or exclusive enclaves for locals and each category of expatriates and there are a variety of areas demarcated ethnically for different groups or sub cultural enclaves without much of cultural autonomy.[59]

The housing patterns of the Gulf city, according to Khalaf, reflect the recent stratification based on ethnicity and social class.[60] Khalaf has identified three main types of national housing each associated with particular social class: houses of the (1) political and economic elite, (2) new middle class and (3) low-income social starta.[61] While national elites dwell in special properties like villas, independent quarters or farm houses, the construction and industrial workers live in residential camps, porto-cabins, and make-shift shanty housing compounds that are isolated on the margins of city. However, it is not just expatriate workers occupational category, but their ethnicity and nationality also become a deciding factor.[62] The multistoried high-rise residential buildings and suburban villas rented by foreign professionals represent another pattern of housing.[63]

Under the conditions of sharp social segmentation, the labour camps and other poverty pockets[64] which represent stark contrast to the spectacular malls are kept away from the swankiest quarters. Viewed as a cheap, easily deportable workforce, they are generally kept out of sight by housing them in work camps located on the outskirts of the city.[65] In Dubai, there are "areas labelled frankly on bus route maps as labour camps."[66]

The process of spatial exclusion, however, may not be unique to Dubai, but it is a characteristic of Arab world, where formal cities are, generally, composed of certain parts such as the historical core, the colonial enclave and areas of post-independence growth.[67] The process of globalization sharpened this new geography of centres and margins. The ascendance of new technologies and new social networks, both inextricably linked, also have contributed to this spatial segregation. As happened elsewhere, for last two decades, urban spaces in the GCC states have lost their geopolitical reality to the exclusive benefit of transnational elites.

Paying much attention to spectacle, maps tend to paint the city with a single brush, favouring the new formal areas and ignoring the informal. With a lifestyle promoted through the sheer power of imagery, social spaces of majority expatriate workers is often rendered invisible and their lifeworlds with less spectacular aspects are hidden away. While immigration and ethnicity constitute as otherness, alternative spaces of South Asian labourers do exist as not being part of city's official image. The only expatriate community, which is immune to this selective spatial control, is of highly-paid Americans or Western Europeans.

Rapid urban growth from migration since 1980s has provided a multi-ethnic character for Dubai.[68] An immense 'array of cultures from around the world', each rooted in a particular country, now are claimed to be 're-territorialized in Dubai' in the form of little ethnic enclaves.[69] Many of these 'localizations' are embedded in the transition evident, when a majority of resident workers are today immigrants. However, it is still enigmatic, how far this multi-ethnic global social and cultural make-up has been fully appropriated nationally. As Khalaf notes, though the presence of exorbitant number of foreign labourers created an ethnic/cultural mosaic, it is seldom being caught up by national political or cultural imagination.[70] This slippage is evident from the lack of role for expatriates in social or cultural process and the tendency of dominant culture is not to encompass others. An amalgam of corporate and national elite cultures inscribes a multiplicity of other cultures and identities with social and spatial 'otherness'. The reconfiguration of social spaces associated with globalization in Dubai also has made differential impacts on immigrants.

This division is becoming more profound with the government's effort to institutionalize this socio-spatial segregation with complex sponsorship legislation, unequal compensation structure and nationalization and controlled access to opportunity for non-nationals. Relations among nationals and migrants are also affected by specific laws and conditions that relegate most migrant groups to subordination. Nationals, in addition to their national and ethnic consciousness, now, have a clear perception of their status in the class hierarchy. This differential treatment help maintain sharp economic disparities that favour nationals and other privileged groups and render large numbers of immigrants susceptible to exploitation. While exploitation is manifested at multiple class/ ethnicity levels, the semi-skilled and unskilled Asian and African workers experience various levels of exploitation.[71] The recent cases of labour unrest by South Asian labourers have exposed the critical situation and brought into focus the hostile relationships inherent in new post-oil/post-globalization social structure. Scholars see this as a political opening through which the marginalized people find their voice and are making claims.

Conclusion

A close look at Dubai's development would reveal that there are some factors instrumental in the making of contemporary city. Most notable among these is spectacularization, which integrates amusement, recreation and leisure as important components. The physical appearance of the city itself makes striking resemblance with colossal showroom or museum, with significant absence of real users and presence of merely passive spectators. Likewise, the economic re-configuration, which we always associate with globalization, in the city can be identified in terms of the emergence of a long array of sacred sites of capitalism, where display becomes the norm. These sites enjoy greater immunity from the rules of the land and cater mostly to a transnational elite clientele. Among such sites there are shopping malls, mega building projects and on a far more complex level, special economic zones, which represent not just buildings or architecture style but spectacular, unique and iconic.

In order to attract such a clientele and to attract foreign investment, Dubai engages in significant image-makeover. The strategy of spectacular architecture which has been adopted for this purpose has become Dubai's trademark. Dubai engages in developing an identity makeover relevant to tourism which takes the place of pilgrimage legitimizing the sacredness.

The general inaccessibility to the 'museumized spaces of market' eventually leads to dissatisfaction of a large chunk of population. These are unwelcome developments for a significant population of Emirati natives, who think these projects, these buildings and these businesses – who are they for? For most of the residents these ultra-luxurious settings are quite remote from their daily lives. Many feel a sense of alienation as these developments are not meant for them and the entire city is being created for foreigners. The massive trend towards the radical spatial reorganization has contributed to the emergence of new forms of territorial centralization. The geographies of sacredness and centrality leads to new forms marginality that cuts across the old divide of poor/rich and sets in motion a whole series of new dynamics of inequality. The massive economic transformation has culminated in forging a new societal type in which there is a clear national/ethnic hierarchy with Emiratis, the British and other Westerners at the top. While the Filipinos and Indians constitute the middle level, South Asian labourers are at the bottom.

Similarly, Dubai is not a unified spatial entity merely composed of megaprojects; its everyday life shows a place full of sufferings, struggles and encounters taking place in all sorts of settings. The city can never be a single whole; it is rather a contested space with contesting spaces and identities. There are different 'Dubais-for Emiratis, for Westerners and for South Asian underclass labourers who constitute the lowest echelons of the Gulf society.

Notes

The superlatives include the tallest building (Burj Khalifa) and the largest man-made island (Palm Island).
Osella, 2007.
This is very evident from Iran's attempt to replicate the Dubai model in many places including Kish Island which shares border with UAE.
Elshetawy, 2010, p. 3.
Ibid.
Ibid.

7. Ibid., p. 8.
8. Abdulla, 2008.
9. Hyperspace refers to the space in which individuals are unable to deal with the global economic elites and multinational corporations. Frederic Jameson, 1991.
10. Agamben, 2007, p.73.
11. Khalaf.
12. Qutub, 1985, p. 175.
13. Riad, 1981, p. 1.
14. The definitive aspects of the Gulf city type, according to Khalaf are to be viewed within the context of the dynamics of the oil economy and globalization processes. Khalaf, pp. 244-246.
15. Khalaf,2006, pp. 244-266.
16. Khalaf, p. 256.
17. Burj al-Arab (tower of the Arabs) world's tallest hotel has become the major landmark of the city. The brochure itself reads "it really is fit for kings, queens and Sheikhs!"
18. A new multi-billion dollar seems to be announced on daily basis. Each one was more ambitious than the last. These projects were creating hundreds of new residential, leisure and entertainment developments aimed at increasing number of tourists visiting Dubai. The economic slump has, of course, slowed down this trend.
19. As Khalaf points out "the reconstructed villages represent frozen slices of the region's history...the reconstruction of the cultural past appears as heritage shrines in similar ways in all of the modern Gulf metropolises... the reproduction of this eclipsed city life now preserves local roots that were bulldozed away under the frenzy of the oil boom."
20. Pappe, 2005, pp. 157-158.
21. Malls replaced the mosques as the major place of socialization. Ahmed, 1994.
22. Elsheshtway, 2010, p.183.
23. Ibid.
24. Margret Crawford popularized this usage in her 1992 article "The world is in a shopping mall". See Crawford, 1992, pp.124-140.
25. When you are in Dubai, the place where people take you first will be malls than any historically important places or cultural monuments.
26. Kanna, 2003, pp. 9-10.
27. Certeau, 1988, pp. 91-93.

28. Guy Debord defines the spectacle as a world vision that has become objectified, splitting up the world into 'reality and image'. He also suggests that the spectacle can contribute to a general sense of alienation by emphasizing the disconnectedness between observers and the material object. Debord, 1967.
29. Elsheshtawy, 2010, pp. 140-41.
30. Gulf cities are primarily "centres of display than centres of production". Kanna, 2003, pp. 9-10.
31. Agamben, 2007.
32. Ibid., p. 73.
33. Chidester and Linenthal, 1995, p.15.
34. Due to the unequal access to the space and representative nature of some groups, the spaces become the site for certain groups to exert their power. Foucault (1980).
35. Bordieu, 1994.
36. Chidester and Linenthal, 1995, p. 17.
37. Van der Leeuw, 1986.
38. Ibid.
39. Agamben, 2007.
40. Existence of numerous free zones, where conditions for operating business enterprises are considered highly attractive remains an important factor attracting companies to invest in Dubai.
41. Since the contribution of oil to GDP is merely 3 per cent, Dubai focuses on economic sectors where it holds a strong competitive advantage and ones that are expected to grow globally. The emirates key strengths are tourism, trade, transport, construction and financial services.
42. Nancy,1993, p. 105.
43. Baudillard, 1972.
44. Abdulla, 2008.
45. *Wall Street Journal,* 12 January 2008, "Our Ambitions for the Middle East."
46. Marchal, 2005.
47. The apparent weakness of Dubai reflects in backing up its sovereignty claims over its own territory. Dubai does not want to allow spoiling the party with Iran by raising the issue of disputed islands, though there are concerns from GCC.
48. Abdulla, n. 32.
49. Ibid.
50. Ibid.

51. Ibid.
52. The largest reclamation project in the world that will result in the world's largest artificial islands with a cosmopolitan city.
53. Abu-Lughod, 1983, pp. 223-231.
54. These cities exhibit an unprecedented pace of change, greater population heterogeneity, and greater magnitude in development, leading to demographic imbalances (e.g. nationals versus non-nationals and gender ratios) and disparities in privilege and life conditions among the various ethnicities and classes. Khalaf, 2006, p. 250.
55. For details see Dresch, 2006 and Longva, 1997.
56. Gavrielides, 1987, p. 162.
57. There is a clear national/ethnic hierarchy in which Emiratis with the British and other Westerners at the top. While the Filipinos and Indians constitute the middle level at the bottom you have got the South Asian labourers.
58. Elsheshtawy, 2010, pp. 4-5.
59. Multi-ethnic diversity and segregated housing patterns are urban features not particular or unique to the oil-rich Gulf cities. Khalaf, 2006, p. 250.
60. The multi-ethnic population of the Gulf city is segregated by housing areas and neighbourhoods. For each community there is specific area, the South Asian community, which makes up 75 per cent of population is associated with the places such as Meena Bazar, Souk Naif and Sabkh area. See Elsheshtway,2010, p.189. One may analyze the housing patterns within the context of inclusion and exclusion. See Khalaf, 2006, pp. 251, 256.
61. Khalaf, 2006, pp. 253-256.
62. Ibid., p. 251, Dresch, 2006.
63. Al- Najjar, 1996, pp. 28-37.
64. Arab cities are complex composites. Alongside each formal city, there exists a large and an equally important informal city inhabited by the poor. See Abu-Lughod, 1967, p. 161.
65. Dresch, 2006 and Elsheshtawy, 2010, p. 165.
66. Spatial segregation is very pertinent and accommodations are arranged in relation to status, which we can be analyzed in class terms or ethnic-national terms. See Dresch, 2006.
67. Abu-Lughod, 1967.
68. Dubai is a unique, unprecedented experiment. No other city houses more than 200 nationalities, nor is there one whose population

represents less than 10 per cent of its residents. See Elsheshtawy, 2010, pp. 1-2.

69. Cities are the terrain where people's diversity is celebrated. Dubai city of today concentrates on diversity. But the linkage of people to territory as constituted in Dubai as a global city is far less likely to be intermediated by the state or national culture.
70. Khalaf, 2006, p. 248.
71. Ibid., p. 256.

References

Abdulla, Abdulkhaleq, "A Politically Neutral City", *Gulf News*, 13 February, 2008.

Abu-Lughod, Janet, "Varieties of Urban Experience: Contrast, Co-existence and Coalescence in Cairo", in Ira M. Lapidus (ed.), *Middle Eastern Cities: A Symposium on Ancient, Islamic and Contemporary Middle Eastern Urbanism,* Berkeley, University of California Press, 1967.

Abu-Lughod, Janet, "Urbanization and Social Change in the Arab World", *Ekistics* 50, No. 300, 1983.

Abu-Lughod, J., "Book Review (*What Drives Third World City Growth? A Dynamic General Equilibrium Approach* by Allen C. Kelley; Jeffrey G. Williamson)", *Contemporary Sociology*, Vol. 14, No. 4 (Jul., 1985), 1985, pp. 528-530.

Agamben, Georgio, *Profanations,* New York: Zone Books, 2007.

Ahmad, Akber S. and Hastings Donnan, "Islam in the Age of Postmodernity" in Akbar S. Ahmad and Hastings Donnan (eds.), *Islam, Globalization and Postmodernity,* London: Routledge, 1994.

Al- Najjar, Baqer, "The Gulf: Multinational, Multicultural, Multi-ethnicity City: Research into the Social Formation of the Gulf city", in *The City and the Country*, Al-Rafed Book no. 5, 28-37. Sharjah, UAE: Ministry of Culture and Information Publications, 1996.

Baudillard, *For a Critique of the Political Economy of the Sign* (Trans. Charles Levin, St. Louis, M.O: Telo Press, 1972.

Bordieu, Piere, *Outline of a Theory of Practice*, Cambridge: Cambridge University Press, 1977.

Chidester, D. and Linenthal, E.T. 1995."Introduction", in Chidester, D. and Linenthal, E.T., (ed.), *American sacred space*, Bloomington, IN: Indiana University Press, 1995, pp.1-42.

Crawford, Margret, "The world is in a shopping mall", in Borden, Iain, Hall, Tim and Miles, Malcom (eds.), *The City Cultures Reader,* 2nd ed. London: Routledge, 1996, pp. 124-140.

Debord, Guy, *The Society of Spectacle*, Brooklyn, New York: Zone Books, 1967.

de Certeau, Michel, *The Practice of Everyday Life*, trans. Steven Rendall, Berkeley: University of California Press,1988.

Dresch, Paul, 'Foreign Matter: The Place of strangers in Gulf Society', in John W. Fox et al (ed.), *Globalization and the Gulf*, London: Routledge, 2006, pp. 200-219.

Elshetawy, Yasser, *Dubai: Behind the Urban Spectacle,* London: Routledge, 2010.

Foucault, Michel.1980. "Geography and Power", in Colin Gordon (ed.), *Power/Knowledge: Selected Interviews and Other Writings 1972-1977*, New York: Pantheon, pp. 69-70.

Gavrielides, G. 'The Anatomy of Parliamentary Elections in Kuwait' in L. Layne (ed.), *Elections in the Middle East: Implications of Recent Trends,* London: Boulder and Co, 1987.

Jameson, Frederic, *Postmodernism, or the Cultural Logic of Late Capitalism,* Durham: Duke University Press, 1991.

Kanna, Ahmed, "Dream Images of the Global: Dubai as and Ethnographic Site in the Global Economy", Paper presented at *Dubai Conglomerated: A Conference on Dubai* at Harvard School of Design", April 18-19, 2003.

Khalaf, Suleiman, "The Evolution of the Gulf city type, oil and globalization", John W. Fox et al. *Globalization and the Gulf*, Oxon: Routledge, 2006, pp. 244-266.

Longva, Ann Nag, *Wells Built on Sand: Migration, Exclusion and Society in Kuwait*, London: Boulder, 1997.

Marchal, Roland, "Dubai: Global City and Transnational Hub", in Malawi Al-Rushed, *Transnational Connections and the Arab Gulf,* Oxford: Routledge, 2005.

Nancy, Jean-Luc, *The Sense of the World*, Jeffrey S. Libert (trans.), University of Minnesota Press, Minneapolis, 1993.

Osella, Filippo and Osella, Caroline, "Muslim Entrepreneurs between d the Gulf", ISIM Review, 19 Spring, 2007, pp. 8-9.

Pappe, Ilan, *The Modern Middle East*, London: Routledge, 2005.

Qutub, Ishaq, *Characteristics of Urban Growth in Arab Gulf States*, Kuwait: Kazima Publications, 1985.

Riad, Mohammed, "Some aspects Petro-urbanism in the Arab Gulf States", *Bulletin of the Faculty of Humanities and Social Sciences* 4, 1981.

Van der Leeuw, G., *Religion in essence and manifestation.* Princeton, NJ: Princeton University Press, 1986.

10

Reaching a Threshold: The Stagnation of the Reform Process in Bahrain[1]

Edward Burke

Introduction: The Accession of King Hamad and the Promise of Reform

Bahrain, an island state situated in the strategically vital Persian Gulf, has a population of approximately 1 million, including 350,000 foreign residents. Sixty percent of Bahrain's citizens are Shia, although the country is ruled by a Sunni dynasty, the al-Khalifa family.[2] At the tip of the "Shia crescent", a concept crudely outlined by King Abdullah of Jordan in 2004, Bahrain has been viewed as a key reform test to ease sectarian tensions in the region, an opportunity for shared values and a common Bahraini identity to overcome discrimination on religious lines.[3] The reforms begun by King[4] Hamad bin Isa al-Khalifa upon his accession to the throne in 1999 were greeted with relief by a Bahraini population weary of the systematic repression practiced during the latter years of the region of his father, Sheikh Isa, and the political and social space opened in Bahrain has been filled with debate as to the future direction of the country, not least upon the division of powers between the elected parliament, the Majlis al-Nuwwab and the royal family. Bahrain's experience is being observed with interest and a certain degree of wariness by other members of the Gulf Cooperation Council (GCC), who are concerned lest Bahrain act as a template for reform.[5]

Upon his accession in 1999, Sheikh Hamad bin Isa al-Khalifa, recognising a need to distance his rule from the abuses committed under his father since the dissolution of the Constituent Council, established a Supreme National Committee for Drafting a National Action Charter in order to begin a process of reconciliation and reform. On February 14th and 15th 2002, of a turnout of 90 percent of eligible voters, 98 percent voted to support a National Action Charter which outlined a reform path for Bahrain including an imprecise proposal for a bi-cameral parliament. The Charter also precipitated the dissolution of the State Security Courts and amendment of the State Security Law, thus removing the most repressive state legal architecture.[6] The high turnout and overwhelming support of Bahrainis for the National Charter was greatly helped by a recent meeting between King Hamad and Sheikh Abd al-Amir al-Jamri, a leading Shia cleric where the King agreed that legislative power would rest with a democratically elected chamber–the Majlis al Nuwwab–and that the Majlis al-Shura would have only an advisory role, powers which would be enshrined in Bahrain's constitution. The King signed a document agreeing to these recommendations, which was widely circulated as an assurance that he would keep his word in the future.[7]

The initial period of Bahrain's reform process appears to have been modelled on the Jordanian experience. Essentially it called for a National Charter to define a course for the country, facilitated the return of exiles, the release of political prisoners, reinstatement of employees who were dismissed from their jobs as a consequence of their political activities and the repealing of repressive state security laws. In February 2002, King Hamad used the overwhelming endorsement of the vaguely worded National Charter as a mandate to promulgate a constitution which fell short of most Bahrainis aspirations and consolidated power once again around the royal family, with the Constitution misleadingly citing Bahrain as a constitutional monarchy and changing the country from an Emirate to a Kingdom.[8] The King also reneged upon his public declaration that the democratically elected Majlis al-Nuwwab would be the principal legislative chamber, dividing legislative authority between the two houses of the Majlis al-Watani (National Assembly) and the Majlis al-Shura with 40 Members appointed by the King, and the Majlis al Nuwwab with an equivalent number of representatives elected directly by the populace.

Given that the Majlis al-Shura maintained a casting vote in the case of deadlock between the two houses and the subsequent gerrymandering that characterized the 2002 and 2006 elections, the trust placed in the King by many Bahrainis to empower a truly democratic legislature was felt to have been misplaced.[9] In addition the extensive influence still wielded by the King's uncle, Prime Minister Khalifa bin Salman al-Khalifa who was perceived as the key executive authority during the reign of his father Sheikh Isa, a period when thousands of opposition activists were imprisoned and many tortured, continues to cause much resentment and suspicion in what is almost his 40th year in office.

If the opposition viewed the new Constitution as a breach of faith on the part of the King, preparations for the elections of 2002 convinced them that the government was embarked on a strategy to provide a veneer of democracy while denying Bahrainis the opportunity to participate in fair and transparent elections.[10] The electoral districts of Bahrain for the 2002 elections, which remain substantially unaltered today, are a gross example of gerrymandering. In 2003 the Bahrain Human Rights Society (BHRS) pointed to the imbalance of constituents in the electoral districts, with one predominantly Sunni district containing barely 400 voters while a Shia district could have up to 14000. In protest at the promulgation of the new constitution and the fixing of boundaries to limit the impact of the Shia vote, the main Shia party, al-Wefaq, together with several secular opposition parties such as al-Waad, refused to participate in the 2002 elections to the Majlis al-Nuwwab. Shia clerics encouraged a boycott of the polls and national turnout for the second round of voting was low, registering barely 43 percent of eligible voters.

Democratic Hopes versus Political Reality

The boycott of elections by al-Wefaq did not last. The primary motivation for engaging in the political process appears to have been the lack of a viable alternative and a willingness to work with pragmatic reformist Ministers and members of the royal family to try and ease sectarian tensions. The reversal of the boycott in 2006 by al-Wefaq precipitated a split in their ranks, with a relatively small minority of members leaving to form the al-Haq movement, which continues to advocate non-participation in elections. Nevertheless, al-Wefaq, under the leadership of Sheikh Ali Salman, together with the support of the highest Shia religious authority in Bahrain, Sheikh Isa Qassim, and the blessing of significant Shia *Maraja* from outside Bahrain, including Ayatollahs al-Sistani and Fadlallah, retained the support of the majority of the Shia electorate and won 17 seats of the 40-seat Majlis al-Nuwwab in 2006.[11] During the elections al-Wefaq avoided overt sectarian references and in some cases offered support to liberal Sunni candidates. Blatant gerrymandering and vote-rigging however ensured that the opposition did not secure a majority of seats in the Majlis al-Nuwwab. The government can continue to generally rely on the support of the Sunni Islamist parties, al-Minbar and al-Asalah and independents, holding a parliamentary majority of 22 seats that is broadly supportive of the government.

Undoubtedly the most divisive issue of the 2006 campaign were the revelations published by a British-Sudanese adviser to the government, Salah al-Bandar, who alleged that the government had established a task force headed by the Minister for Cabinet Affairs, Sheikh Ahmed bin Attiyatallah al-Khalifa, to undermine the Shia community and implicated senior Sunni politicians including from the al-Minbar and al-Asalah parties as being in receipt of clandestine payments from the government. The allegations included a plan to increase naturalization of Sunnis from other countries, the infiltration of Shia civil society organisations (CSOs) and the setting up of fake non-governmental organisations (NGOs). These allegations and the banning of any discussion of the "Bandar report" in the media led to increased mistrust among the populace towards the government and indirectly damaged al-Wefaq for its engagement with the government.

The government has done little to allay mounting fears over its naturalization practices with regard to Sunni foreign citizens, which for many confirms that there is indeed a deliberate policy to engineer a Sunni majority.[12] The number of Shia representatives in top Government positions remains woefully under-representative, with opposition leaders alleging that Shia representation may be as low as 7 percent of the top 500 Government posts. Shia citizens are also almost completely excluded from any positions of command in security services, which is a profound demonstration of the lack of trust on the part of the State in the loyalty of the majority of its citizens. There are also serious allegations of Shia not being able to buy land in certain areas, exacerbated by a lack of transparency over land acquisitions or transactions made by senior royals. It is also widely believed that the royal family currently owns the majority of land in Bahrain and are distributing it both to reward supporters and for personal economic gain. The UN International Convention on the Elimination of All Forms of Racial Discrimination (CERD) has recently criticized Bahrain for the lack of economic social and cultural rights accorded to the Shia population and the UN Committee on the Rights of the Child (CRC) has also noted major disparities between social services provided in Sunni areas and Shia areas.[13] In addition to widespread anger over a lack of transparency over land transactions, there is also significant frustration that the reclamation of land from the sea is being treated as a personal project of the royal family.[14]

Under the Constitution, legislative authority is divided between the King and the National Assembly. The upper house - the Majlis al-Shura is appointed by the King, while the lower house - the Majlis al-Nuwwab, is elected by the popular vote.[15] Both houses consist of 40 Members and legislation must be passed by the King and the legislature. The King may veto laws passed by both the Majlis al-Shura and Majlis al-Nuwwab, but this may be overturned if both houses, meeting in a joint session of the Majlis al-Watani, vote by a two-thirds majority to reverse the King's veto, an event not easily envisaged due to the already described royal appointment of members of the Majlis al-Shura. While both the Majlis al-Shura and the Majlis al-Nuwwab can propose legislation, the official text of the legislation must be prepared by the Cabinet Office of Legal Affairs. There is a consistent trend however of the government rejecting bills originating from the Parliament outright, delaying legislation indefinitely and/or making substantial changes to the original bill before sending it back for ratification by parliament. As a consequence, the legislative process suffers from frequent and prolonged deadlock, frustrating both reformist Ministers and parliamentarians. Both houses of parliament also suffer from a lack of legal advice when trying to initiate legislation.[16] Bills originating from the elected Majlis al-Nuwwab are almost unfailingly rejected or deliberately stalled.

Under Article 66 of the Constitution a two-thirds majority of the Majlis al-Nuwwab can pass a vote of no-confidence in a Minster, except for the Prime Minister. This has not happened to date due to the lack of cooperation between al-Wefaq and the Sunni parties and independents and it remains to be seen whether this power can indeed be exercised. The Sunni parties seem to be especially reluctant to work with Al-Wefaq and those who have proposed doing so have suffered politically, most strikingly in 2005 when the leader of al-Asalah, Adel al-Mouwda, was replaced due to his perceived closeness to Shia Islamists.[17] Given the disharmony between the Sunni and Shia Islamist parties in the elected lower house of parliament, both the al-Khalifa family and the royally appointed upper-house of parliament have moved to present themselves as mediators between the Islamist parties and guardians of a more secular, tolerant form of government.

The Majlis al-Nuwwab does have the right to question Ministers, although this is frequently frustrated by the current Speaker of the Majlis al-Nuwwab, who refuses to assert the right of the Majlis al-Nuwwab to question certain Ministers including the unpopular Minister for Cabinet Affairs, Ahmed bin Attiyatallah, and is seen as overly obsequious to the Prime Minister.[18] Even when agreeing to be questioned, some Ministers have treated the elected house with contempt. The Finance Minister, Ahmed bin Mohammed al-Khalifa walking out of a session of parliament and the Minister for Muncipalities and Agriculture, Mansoor bin Rajab ignored calls for his resignation on corruption charges stating: "Why should I bow down to their demand when I have been appointed by the Kingdom's leadership and not by parliament?"[19] The Majlis al-Nuwwab does not receive a clear breakdown of state finances, although some Ministers have volunteered financial statistics when requested. According to royal decree, the Financial Control Bureau reports directly to the King and the parliament similarly has no oversight over the activities of the highly influential Economic Development Board (EDB). Other Ministries are exempt from financial oversight including the Ministry for the Interior, Defence and the Prime Minister's office.

The conservative Sunni political society, al-Asalah, advocates the strict observance of a narrow interpretation of Sharia law and often finds itself in broad agreement with leading figures from al-Wefaq in their opposition to the more secular instincts of the royally-appointed Majlis al-Shura. The other Sunni political society in the Majlis al-Nuwwab, al-Minbar, led opposition to the government's signing of the International Convention on Civil and Political Rights (ICCPR), citing as part of their opposition their rejection of the freedom to convert to another religion, an offence against Islam which in the opinion of their President should carry the death penalty.[20] The Sunni Islamist parties have also stated their support for restrictive media laws that would allow a broader interpretation of offences against Islam. The Islamist success in the 2002 and 2006 elections has allowed the Government to sow seeds of doubt among Bahrainis and external observers who favour a more secular state and the codifying by the state of women's rights and family law as to whether many of Bahrain's civil liberties could paradoxically be lost through the empowerment of its elected institutions. This discussion has intensified in the aftermath of the Bahraini government drafting a code of family law in December 2008, a decision opposed by leading Islamists who believe that such matters be decided by local Sharia law.[21]

The Judiciary

Bahrain's legal system derives from laws inherited from British Common Law, Sharia law and tribal precedents.[22] The higher civil and criminal courts are presided over by three judges, whose decisions can be referred to a court of cassation which is the final appellate court. Bahraini law does not allow for trial by jury. The application of Sharia law is divided into parallel courts for Shia and Sunni citizens, which rule on personal status cases. Rulings by Sharia courts can be appealed to the High Sharia court of appeal. The decisions of the Sharia courts are frequently criticized by women's groups, including the Supreme Council of Women, the Women's Union and the Women's Petition Committee, which have aimed at securing a codified personal status law to protect women's rights. Bahrain's Constitutional Court has jurisdiction over interpreting the constitutionality of laws and statutes and it's President and six members are directly appointed by the King.

While the constitution establishes the nominal independence of the Bahraini courts, in practice there is extensive interference from the Executive where key interests to the government are at stake. The King continues to chair the Higher Judicial Council, appoints judges by decree and many members of the judiciary are members of the al-Khalifa family. There is a significant lack of judges to hear the amount of cases before the courts, resulting extended delays in the hearing of cases. The Government also employs judges from abroad, who do not have a deep knowledge of Bahraini law and may bring malpractice from other courts systems to Bahrain. The Constitutional Court has been subjected by particularly sharp criticism from civil society activists for its lack of expertise and is widely perceived as a tool to protect the King and the Cabinet rather than as a safeguard of citizens' rights.[23] The Office of the Public Prosecutor (OPP) is similarly viewed as a tool of Government rather than an independent state agency. The judiciary has proved to be unwilling or unable to rigorously uphold citizens' rights in challenging sectarian practices, whereas, paradoxically when allegations of sectarianism have been the subject of discussion in the media, the judiciary has not hesitated to invoke anti-sectarian legislation to censor newspapers and close websites in the name of protecting the unity of Bahrain.

Political Societies Law/Electoral Law

The Political Societies Law promulgated by King Hamad in 2005 has been criticized for banning the establishment of parties, its restrictions on societies with regard to fund-raising and the vague proviso that parties could not be established on the basis of class, sectarian, ethnic or professional grounds. Political societies are also opposed to the articles in the law that require societies to request permission from the Ministry for Justice and Islamic Affairs (MOJIA) prior to contacting overseas political parties or institutions or travelling abroad to attend an international conference. The law also places a ban on foreign funding or training, raises the required membership age from 18-21 and gives the MOJIA discretion over whether to reject an application, without clear legal recourse to the courts.[24] Despite being ratified by both houses of parliament, both al-Wefaq and al-Waad asked the King not to sign the law, a request the King ultimately refused.

The Election Law of 2002 grants the right to vote to all Bahraini citizens over the age of 21. Citizens of GCC countries who are Bahraini residents as well as GCC non-residents who own property in Bahrain are also allowed to vote. Citizens of non-GCC countries are not allowed to vote, although extensive naturalization of Sunni citizens from non-GCC countries has been a feature of government policy in recent years. Al-Wefaq, al-Waad and other opposition groups are now urging significant reform of the electoral laws including the establishment of an independent electoral commission to curtail gerrymandering and other electoral infringements, the right for international organisations to observe the election and the expansion of the powers of the Majlis al-Nuwwab.

The Associations' Law

There are just over 460 CSOs operating in Bahrain, most of which have become operational only in the last few years. The inexperience of many of the leaders of these organisations and an unresolved internal debate in the Bahraini government on the extent to which CSOs should be monitored and regulated, has led to significant incoherence and mistrust between the government and civil society. CSOs in Bahrain currently operate under the 1989 Law of Associations (21/1989), which allows for significant Government interference in their activities. The law specifically prohibits associations from political involvement and grants the Ministry for Social Development intrusive powers over CSOs including the powers to nullify elections, appoint a board of directors, inspect headquarters, confiscate documentation and audit finances. Registration can also be refused if the Ministry for Social Development believes that the aims of the prospective association are already served by an existing body. If 60 days elapse without a response then the application is deemed to have been automatically denied. Funding from foreign sources is prohibited and affiliations or membership by an association of a foreign society, union or club is also forbidden, unless special permission from the government is secured. Employees of a society are not permitted to serve on the Board of Directors. CSO leaders complain that as well as granting overly intrusive powers to Government Ministries to inspect and regulate their activities the law does not provide for sufficient recourse to the courts. CSOs leaders have also frequently been threatened with prosecution by the government for comments made while abroad criticising the government under Article 134 of the penal code.[25]

In 2005, the UN Committee against Torture expressed its concern regarding serious restrictions placed on CSOs, including those dealing with human rights.[26] There have been successive attempts to draft a new associations' law, including in 2006 when the government introduced legislation which was heavily criticized for not addressing the concerns of CSOs and imposing further restrictions on their activities, and was withdrawn under public pressure.[27] The Ministry for Social Development is currently drafting a new associations' law in consultation with a broad range of civil society leaders and the International Center for Non-Profit Law (ICNL). The new draft law has been praised for allowing the de facto registration of a society, if the government does not reply to their application within 60 days. It also proposes to remove the ban on political activities for CSOs, and allow non-nationals to establish CSOs in Bahrain, which would constitute a significant breakthrough for migrant workers. The proposed law does not address however many of the serious restrictions placed on CSOs, including the obligation to seek Ministerial approval for fundraising activities.

Existing legislation governing fraud and ensuring transparency in financial transactions is sufficient to guard against possible abuses. Under the law the Minister for Social Development also retains the right to appoint Board members and annul elections, and does not sufficiently make reference to judicial oversight with regard to these powers. Furthermore, it imposes the requirement for informal voluntary groups to register with the government, defining such informal organisations as a group of people meeting to discuss issues of public concern or a "special interest".[28] The proposed law appears to have been based to some degree on legislation introduced in Jordan, where the government has continued to heavily restrict CSO activities, contrary to its obligations under the ICCPR. In drafting a new associations' law, CSO leaders contend that the government should not seek to impose specific criminal sanctions against CSOs, where pre-existing penal laws already suffice, including for offences such as fraud or sedition and punitive measures imposed by the Ministry for Social Development should be subject to expedient judicial oversight. Despite these reservations the new legislation drafted by the Ministry for Social Development is undoubtedly an improvement upon the existing law, which may explain why its passage has floundered of late.

The Public Gathering Law

The Public Gathering Law introduced as Law No. 32 of 2006 to amend the Public Gathering Law of 1973 (Law No. 18), is a continued source of controversy in Bahrain and was cited by Freedom House as a key reason for why Bahrain received a downward trend on its index of civil liberties in 2007.[29] Currently the law obliges organizers to seek permission for a public meeting at least 72 hours prior to it taking place and that a public demonstration cannot be held within 500 metres of certain state institutions, including airports, large commercial areas, schools and health facilities, as well as any locations deemed by the Minister of the Interior to be a sensitive to national security. Funeral processions cannot be used to organise political rallies. The law also imposes prison sentences of up to 6 months for breaking these regulations.

CSO and political opposition leaders argue that the public gatherings law is overly restrictive and can be used to deny permission to hold a meeting or a demonstration on political grounds. There are also occasional complaints of not receiving any communication from the government after they submit such a request. While the government points to its tolerance in not applying the law to those who organise meetings without official consent (in 2007 for example, of 324 marches and gatherings that took place in Bahrain, 104 applied for permission, 220 had not, with only a fraction of the latter being broken up), this is hardly conducive to confidence and clarity in the application of the law.[30] The Public Gatherings Law has therefore become another grey legal area in Bahrain, applied selectively rather than impartially. Furthermore, the definition of a public gathering is vague and potentially restrictive—a meeting of more than five persons to discuss an issue of public interest is deemed a public gathering. The organizers of a public gathering can also be held responsible for any "speech or discussion infringing on public order or morals."[31] In a submission to the UN Human Rights Council, the Bahraini Government defended the application process to hold a public meeting on the basis that the authorities needed ample time to prepare to protect the participants in such meetings.[32] Al-Wefaq introduced a number of amendments to the Public Gathering law on September 19 2007, seeking to reduce the notice period to 24 hours, remove geographical restrictions, and reduce the jail sentence to one month. So far these efforts have made little headway.

Media Freedom

The media is currently regulated by the 2002 Press and Publications Law (17/2002) and comes under the supervision of the Ministry for Information. This law has been widely criticized for its excessive restrictions on freedom of expression. As a direct consequence of the introduction of this law in 2002, Bahrain fell from 67th to 143rd between 2002 and 2008 in the "Reporters without Borders" international press freedom rankings.[33] The ratification of the law was suspended due to public protests but it continues to be used at the government's discretion. Under the terms of the law, journalists or civil society activists can be sentenced to prison sentences of up to 5 years for "inciting division, sectarianism and violence and attacking national unity."[34] The law also allows for fines of up to 2000 BD for other offences including publicizing statements by a foreign state or organization without government permission and making allegations against a foreign head of state that has diplomatic relations with Bahrain.[35] Occasionally the

Bahraini courts impose extended injunctions on publishing news stories on prosecutions before the courts, as has been the case with the Bandar Report, where a blanket ban on reporting remains in place. Due to lengthy delays in hearing cases in Bahrain, this ensures that cases alleging abuses by the government may be barred from discussion by the media for months, if not years. The Minister for Information has stated that increased measures taken against journalists in 2007 are a consequence of the irresponsibility of the press and has pointed to increased funding by his Ministry for media training as an attempt to improve standards and avoid further disputes.

The government exercises strict control over public broadcasting in Bahrain and all Bahraini television channels remain under the control of the state. Political websites are frequently censored when they discuss allegations of corruption by the government, including the hugely popular *Bahrain online* which was temporarily shut down in 2005 and the *Google Earth* was blocked as it allowed Bahrainis to get a rare view of the extensive palaces and secretive investments of the royal family. The government also actively monitors and censors media broadcasts and publications that offend public morality. The US State Department reported that 22 discussion forums and political website had been censored by the Ministry for Information in 2007, including the closing of websites of political societies such as al-Waad.[36] The government has recently stated that they are reviewing this practice and will refrain from exercising such intrusive censorship over the internet in the future.[37]

It is generally acknowledged that the editors-in-chief of Bahrain's six daily newspapers are appointed with the prior consent of the government and they are occasionally summoned to the Ministry for Cabinet Affairs for discussions on their editorial policy. Due to the vagueness of the media laws and a lack of trust in the independence of the judiciary, editors often exercise zealous self-censorship rather than risk prosecution or closure. The process of applying for a publication licence is complex and expensive, with a fee of 1 million BD being a major disincentive for prospective applicants. Books published in Bahrain also require pre-licensing from the Directorate of Printing and Publication at the Ministry for Information.[38]

In May 2008 the Ministry for Information published a new draft press law which, if ratified, would decriminalise press offences and ostensibly reduces the power of the Information Ministry to impose sanctions against publications without judicial oversight. There remains some concern over the rather vague offences of offending religion or threatening national unity, which may still carry prison terms to be imposed at the discretion of the judiciary. Furthermore, the Ministry for Information retains the power under Article 19 of the proposed new law to close a newspaper or a publication and then seek judicial permission retrospectively within 3 days, a practice that runs contrary to international practice. The Ministry for Information has also introduced plans to license private public broadcasting companies, under which registration of television and radio stations will be approved by the cabinet of Ministers, and overdue and important step towards improving freedom of expression in the broadcast media.[39] While improvements in Bahrain's media laws are obviously welcome, the competence of the Bahraini judiciary to protect freedom of expression is seriously in doubt.

Labour Rights

Labour rights in Bahrain are guaranteed by the Constitution and regulated by the Labour Law for the Private Sector of 1976 and the subsequent Workers Trade Union Law of 2002. The 2002 law was widely praised when it was introduced, including by the International Trade Union Confederation (ITUC) as a step forward in Bahrain labour relations. The right to strike is heavily restricted however and is denied to workers employed in "vital and important facilities such as security, civil defence, airports, ports, hospitals, transportation, telecommunications, electricity and water." Bahrain has also been slow to ratify international treaties regulating workers' rights, and to date has only ratified 4 of the 8 ILO core labour standards, including ILO Conventions 87 and 98, which protect freedom of association and collective bargaining.[40]

In October 2006, the King passed a decree prohibiting dismissal for trade union activities. This is not generally enforced however and there have been several well-documented instances where workers have been dismissed for union activities, including at Gulf Air and Batelco. The government retains wide-ranging powers to prohibit strikes under Article 21 of the Workers Trade Union law and the judiciary can also apply a broad interpretation to the existing ban on political activities by trade unions under labour legislation. The law also only provides for the establishment of only one trade union in the workplace, which the International Labour Organisation (ILO) Committee on Freedom of Association formally objected to in a letter to Bahrain.[41] Perhaps the most significant flaw in current legislation however, is the inability of public sector workers to form trade unions.[42] When public sector workers do engage in union activities, they can often face immediate dismissal or demotion.

Although they constitute up to 80 percent of the Bahraini private sector workforce, representation of migrants at the union level remains negligible. The Bahraini Government has moved towards addressing migrant worker rights in recent months, prompted to some degree by the recent review of Bahrain by the UN Human Rights Council and in January 2008, the King issued Decree No. 1 as an anti-trafficking measure to tighten the law on the exploitation of migrants. The Ministry for Foreign Affairs also leads a Government task force to combat human trafficking.[43] In contrast, the response by Bahrain's parliament to migrant abuse has been muted, reflective of a populist attitude that blames migrant workers for criminal activities and taking jobs from local Bahrainis.[44] Recourse to the judicial system by migrants is almost unheard of and labour cases often take over a year to process, during which time an employee is frequently suspended without pay. Approximately 50,000 foreign housemaids fall outside any labour law and their interests are not represented by any trade union. In 2007 the Embassy of the Philippines in Manama reported that 749 foreign housemaids ran away from their employers due to abusive working conditions.[45]

Anti-terrorism Legislation

In 2006, in an apparent contradiction of Constitutional protection against arbitrary arrest and detention, King Hamad signed a new Anti-Terrorism Bill that allows for up to 90 days of pre-trial detention without judicial oversight.[46] The UN Special Rapporteur on the promotion and protection of human rights and fundamental freedoms while countering terrorism and the UN Committee against Torture expressed their concern regarding certain provisions of the bill, most particularly the transfer from the judiciary to the public prosecutor of the authority to arrest and detain, including the authority to the extend of pre-trial detention. The Committee against Torture expressed its concern that the law could allow for a repeat of abuses committed under the notorious State Security Law.[47] The government responded that the legislation was consistent with international legislation and met the definition of terrorism defined under the Arab Convention for the Suppression of Terrorism.[48] However, the lengthy incarceration without trial of activists amid allegations of torture in 2007 and 2008 suspected of inciting revolt in Bahrain resurrected memories of the State Security laws during the repression of the 1990s.[49]

Targeted/Excluded Groups

During the turbulent 1990s, the Bahraini state practised systematic repression of opposition activity and groups, resulting in the imprisonment, torture and exile of thousands of political and civil society activists. King Hamad finally put an end to this traumatic and brutal era and there is now a limited political and social sphere within which the activities of the opposition, both legal and illegal, are tolerated. Social groups such as those advocating women's rights often meet more stringent opposition from the Islamist political societies than from the government, who nevertheless continue to restrict the activities of certain women's rights activists.

The vast majority of Bahraini exiles have now returned home, and some have even accepted positions in government, including the Minister for Labour, Majid al-Allawi. However, the external opposition remains in the form of the Bahrain Freedom Movement (BFM) which is based in London has little support from both the Bahraini diaspora and inside the country. The most significant and organised illegal CSO is the Bahrain Centre for Human Rights (BCHR), led by its President Abdulhadi al-Khawaja and Vice-President Nabeel Rajab. According to leading members of the BCHR, a large part of their activities is directed towards winning external support to pressurize for change within Bahrain. The BCHR issues more frequent allegations of torture and mistreatment of prisoners than alleged by other human rights groups and it has undoubtedly played a leading role in highlighting abuses taking place within Bahrain. Its ability to operate is in itself indicative of the support it enjoys domestically but also and, perhaps even more importantly, is a reflection of its international profile, including its strong links with international human rights organisations, such the International Federation for Human Rights (FIDH), Human Rights Watch (HRW) and Front Line Defenders, as well as support from parliamentarians such as Lord Avebury in the United Kingdom. In contrast, the Bahrain Human Rights Society (BHRS), although retaining close ties to the BCHR, has employed an approach that engages government leaders while retaining its objective independence.

The Bahraini government alleges that the BCHR has ties with the Iranian regime, pointing to statements by its President affirming his admiration for Ayatollah al-Khomeini, which clearly underlines the regime's discomfort regarding the Shia population's high spiritual regard for *maraja* both in Iran and more broadly in the Shia world. Alleging an Iranian link to Shia leaders is also a strategic means of obfuscating the government's obvious reluctance to cede more executive or legislative power to the Shia majority. However, this tactic is becoming less feasible as Bahrain become more dependent on trade with Iran and the government has of late adopted an increasingly conciliatory tone towards Tehran not least in order to secure an agreement to build a gas pipeline from Iran to Bahrain that will double the country's gas supplies.[50]

Strongly linked to the activities of the BCHR is the Women's Petition Committee led by Ghada Jamsheer, which is highly critical of the application of Sharia law, and in contrast to other women's groups, does not see a possibility for constructive engagement with the government. Confrontational demonstrations and appeals to western audiences have become a hallmark of the group's activities and, while its advocacy of a personal status law for women is not in accordance with some Islamists in the BCHR, they are a useful addition to the broader coalition of radical opposition groups, which seeks to maximize international condemnation of the government. It should be noted that the women's group with the most financial largesse in Bahrain is the government-funded Supreme Council for Women, patronized by Shaika Sabika, although Islamist women's groups generally have more influence at a community level.

The Bahrain Youth Society for Human Rights (BYSHR) is a relatively new and increasingly popular organisation which ostensibly serves as a human rights organisation but essentially aims to mobilize political opposition against the government on a wide range of political, social and economic issues. The BYSHR is led by the charismatic Mohamed al-Maskati, who has of late convened a number of youth workshops to advocate peaceful methods of opposing the regime. While the BYSHR certainly adopts a highly critical and confrontational approach, excluding the use of violence however, this in itself hardly warrants the tactics of the government, who have refused to register the BYSHR on questionable grounds, citing the age of its members. The government also seems to have had a hand in al-Maskati's recent deportation from Egypt where he travelled to attend a conference, and in late 2007 charged him with operating an illegal organisation, actions which have seen his profile soar both domestically and internationally.

Of the banned political groups in Bahrain, the most significant is the al-Haq Movement led by Hasan Mushaima, that refuses to recognise the legitimacy of the 2002 Constitution and by extension the Political Societies Law. Al-Haq represents the non-participatory wing that fractured from al-Wefaq in 2006 after the latter decided to reverse their position of not contesting national elections. Al-Haq operate a sophisticated domestic and foreign public relations campaign but so far have relied upon the support of disaffected Shia youth rather than securing the support of the Shia mainstream, including the Shia ulama who remain broadly supportive of al-Wefaq. They have also been condemned by other opposition groups for statements advocating the use of violence if peaceful efforts to advocate reform fail.[51] The government has so far avoided a heavy crackdown upon al-Haq, most likely out of concern for a destabilizing violent backlash, but continue to restrict their activities through other means including infiltration, censorship and breaking up public meetings.

Conclusion

The growth in Bahrain's economy is linked to the perception of Bahrain as a relatively liberal and stable haven in a troubled but economically and strategically vital region. This favourable view of Bahrain has encouraged investment from the Gulf region from Europe and the United States and increasingly from South and East Asia. There is currently an almost total absence of international pressure to reform - recently in 2008, the then President of the US George Bush praised Bahrain as a reforming role model for the region and the US has come to view Bahrain as a key ally in a vital area of US military commitment, not least due to its hosting of the US Fifth Fleet.[52] Bahrain has excelled at portraying itself as a country of moderation and reform, easily securing election to the UN Human Rights Council for the second time in May 2008 with the support of 142 out of 191 votes cast by UN Member States.[53] This lack of international pressure has hampered efforts to persuade the government to progress beyond a tendency to over-legislate and interfere in the activities of civil society.

While King Hamad is known for his relatively benign attitude towards freedom of expression and association, these rights are not yet protected by concrete legislation and an independent judiciary rather than by royal favour. Bahrain can be justifiably proud of its transformation since the turbulent years of the mid-1990s, but it is becoming increasingly obvious that Bahrain's reform process has reached a precarious impasse. The wave of optimism which swept Bahrain in 2001 after the publication of the National Charter is now remembered bitterly by many Bahrainis as a period of unfulfilled promises. In late April 2008, the Prime Minister ridiculed any suggestion that sectarianism exists within Bahrain and refused to acknowledge that discrimination needed to be addressed.[54] This failure of the government to address institutionalised discrimination against Shia citizens in Bahrain is leading to the increasing perception that the royal family and the government of Bahrain are not representative of the interests of the majority of Bahraini citizens. The complex relationship and division of power between the King, the Prime Minister and the Crown Prince has also served to preserve a system of clientelist factionalism. The moderate leadership of al-Wefaq senses that time is running out, that they must begin to deliver for their constituents who trusted their decision to engage within Bahrain's flawed parliamentary institutions. Bi-partisan cooperation in the Majlis al-Nuwwab remains gravely deficient and Bahrain's representatives must lead from within the parliamentary chamber to ease sectarian tensions and work on issues of common interest. A key dilemma for the more secular supporters of reform in Bahrain is whether they are willing to support the empowerment of a democratically elected legislature in a state with "an arguably illiberal majority and a liberal minority?"[55]

Impatient with what they see as a state conspiracy to deny them rights and jobs, some sections of the Shia youth are beginning to look outside Bahrain to Iraq and Lebanon for inspiration from Shia movements there.[56] It remains to be seen whether escalating violence in Bahrain is indeed manageable while simultaneously preserving Bahrain's image abroad. Some in government are optimistic that future economic growth combined with initiatives to address housing and other social problems will be sufficient to ease current unrest but this may not be enough to mollify Shia demands for equal treatment.

But by allowing for the construction of a strong civil society that advocates for the transfer of power away from the monarch, the King must eventually face a choice: cede some of the powers of government to the country's elected representatives or try to cling to the status quo through co-option and repression. The government's response to the mounting calls for democratic reform has been erratic, ranging from threats and penalties against activists to conciliation. More pragmatic senior officials realise that the status quo cannot continue indefinitely, that rising social tensions present a threat to the stability to the country and that faith in the country's reform process must be restored, including allowing elected representatives a share in the government of the country. Ultimately stability in Bahrain rests on a compromise being reached whereby elected representatives can co-govern with the ruling family. To strike such a balance of power will require difficult concessions and much wisdom from Bahrain's leaders.

Notes

1. "Reaching a Threshold" refers to a FRIDE interview with Sadig al-Mahdi, former Prime Minster of Sudan: *"The process of political reform is coming towards a threshold. What needs to be done now is to go beyond the general slogans of reform to the specific such as the separation of powers and the need to guarantee human rights..."* Interview with Sadig al-Mahdi, Madrid, 11 April 2008.
2. The overwhelming majority of Bahrain's Shia population follows the Twelver branch and the Jafari School of Islamic jurisprudence or *fiqh*. The Bahraini Shia populace can be subdivided into *Baharna* and *Ajam,* with the *Ajam* in the minority and identified as being of Persian origin. Sunni citizens follow both the Malik and Shafi'i schools of *fiqh*, the latter traditionally associated with the *Huwala* or those who had historic associations with Persia while the former is the *fiqh* practiced by the ruling al-Khalifa family and their allies. The al-Khalifa trace to their origins to the al-Najd central region of Saudi Arabia, from where they migrated to Kuwait in the 18th century before laying claim to Bahrain in 1783 after a turbulent preceding two centuries of Portuguese, Persian and Omani rule. While the al-Khalifa later ceded much of their sovereignty to the United Kingdom, beginning in the early 19th century and continuing up

until independence in 1971, their astute pragmatism ensured their survival as the most powerful dynasty in Bahrain for over two centuries.

3. *The Guardian*, "Fears of a Shia Full Moon", 26 January 2007.
4. Under the 2002 Constitution, Bahrain was formally declared a Kingdom rather than an Emirate. Therefore, King Hamad's father's title was that of Emir and King Hamad initially ruled Bahrain as Emir from 1999 to 2002.
5. Saudi Arabia's influence over Bahraini affairs is extensive, not only through its effective granting to Bahrain much of its current oil fields and pumping oil to Bahraini refineries, but also through Saudi investment in the Bahraini financial sector. While revenues from oil and gas currently account for only 11 percent of GDP, this constitutes 76 percent of Government income. Economist Intelligence Unit. *"Country Report 2007: Bahrain"* London: December 2007 p. 4.
6. The International Crisis Group (ICG), *"Bahrain's Sectarian Challenge"* Middle East Report No. 40, Brussels: 2005 p. 5.
7. Peterson, J.E. *"The Promise and Reality of Bahraini Reforms"*, *www.jepeterson.net/sitebuildercontent/sitebuilderfiles/Promise_of_Bahrain_Reforms.pdf.*
8. ICG, p. 5.
9. A. Ehteshami, and S. Wright, *"Political Change in the Arab Oil Monarchies: From Liberalization to Enfranchisement." International Affairs* (83:5), 2007. London: Chatham House, p. 919.
10. "Opposition" is a relative term in Bahrain which generally applies to those groups who oppose the current system of government and seek to expand the powers of the elected lower house. These groups are careful not to overtly criticize the King personally. Any criticism of the Prime Minister is usually also offered indirectly, reflecting the pronounced degree of caution exercised by the Opposition in relation to the royal family – the more senior a royal the less room for direct criticism.
11. The external influence of foreign *Maraja* is frequently used as a means to question the national loyalty of Bahraini Shia. However alleging external control of al-Wefaq ignores the more significant influence of Sheikh Isa Qassim and other spiritual leaders in issuing guidance on political questions, and

diminishes the internal debate that takes place within the Shia *ulama* of Bahrain.

12. Population statistics have been woefully inadequate in Bahrain for many years with a glaring lack of transparency over the naturalization of foreign citizens. On 14 May 2008, Bahrain's Opposition walked out of parliament in protest at a 42 percent jump in official population statistics from 740,000 to 1.05 million. *Reuters,* "Bahrain Shia MPs walk out over population row", 14 May 2008.
13. UN Human Rights Council, "*Compilation Prepared by the Office of the High Commissioner for Human Rights*", Doc. No. A/HRC/WG.6/1/BHR/2, Working Group on the Universal Periodic Review, First Session, 7-18 April 2008. Geneva: 25th February, 2008.
14. A. Khalaf, *"The King's Dilemma: Obstacles to Political Reforms in Bahrain"*, Fourth Mediterranean Social and Political Research Meeting, Lund University: March 2003, p. 6.
15. The Carnegie Endowment for International Peace, *Arab Political Systems: Baseline Information and Reforms – Bahrain,* Washington DC: 2008 p. 5 http://www. carnegieendowment. org/ files/ Bahrain_APS. Doc.
16. *The Bahrain Tribune*, "Grant right to Grill Ministers", 13 March 2008.
17. M. Zweiri, *"The victory of Al Wefaq: The Rise of Shiite Politics in Bahrain."* Research Paper No. 108. Athens: Research Institute for European and American Studies, April 2007.
18. In March 2008 the refusal of the Speaker to request certain Ministers to appear before parliament precipitated a walk-out of parliament by al-Wefaq in protest at their inability to question certain Ministers. The Bahrain Tribune, *"Grant us the right to grill Ministers"*, 13 March 2008.
19. The royal palace later replaced Mansoor bin Rajab in October 2008 in order to deflect mounting criticism. *The Bahrain Tribune* "I am only answerable to the leadership: Bahraini Minister" 15 May 2008 and *The Bahrain Tribune,* "Al Wefaq Chief Warns Deputies" 16 May 2008
20. *The Gulf Daily News*, "MPs refuse to ratify rights law", 22 February 2006 Al Minbar are generally percieved however as the less conservative of the two Sunni Islamist parties represented in the Majlis al-Nuwwab and were the only elected

political society to support the introduction of a personal status law which would have regulated women's rights.

21. The Gulf News, "Family law decision divides Bahrainis", December 15, 2008,
22. Carnegie Endowment, p. 6.
23. US State Department Country Report on Human Rights Practices – Bahrain 2007 www.state. gov/g/drl/rls/ hrrpt/2007/ 100593.htm.
24. US State Department Country Report on Human Rights Practices; Bahrain 2007.
25. Human Rights Watch, "End threats to rights activists", New York: 12 November 2008.
26. UN Human Rights Council, "*Compilation Prepared by the Office of the High Commissioner for Human Rights*", Geneva: February 2008 p. 9.
27. Carnegie Endowment, p. 9.
28. International Center for Not-for-Profit Law, "Comments on the Draft Law on Not-for-Profit Organisations and Foundations of Bahrain", Washington DC: December 2007.
29. Freedom House Country Reports 2007: Bahrain http://www. freedomhouse.org/modules/mod_call_dsp_country-fiw.cfm?year=2007&country=7131
30. Ministry of Foreign Affairs of Bahrain, The First Universal Periodic Review Report Presented by the Kingdom of Bahrain to the United Nations Human Rights Council, March 2008 http://www.mofa.gov.bh/mofa/en/upr.htm.
31. Human Rights Watch Country Report 2008: Bahrain 2007http://hrw.org/englishwr2k8/docs/2008/01/31/usint17940.ht m.
32. The First Universal Periodic Review Report Presented by the Kingdom of Bahrain to the United Nations Human Rights Council, March 2008.
33. Reporter without Borders, International Press Freedom Index http://www.rsf.org/article.php3?id_article=11715.
34. Reporters without Borders, "Bahrain: Tuning Promises into Reality"- March 2008 http:// www. rsf.org/article. php3? id_article =26040.
35. US State Department Country Report on Human Rights Practices 2007.
36. Ibid.

37. The First Universal Periodic Review Report Presented by the Kingdom of Bahrain to the United Nations Human Rights Council, March 2008 p. 9.
38. Bahrain: Turning Promises into Reality, Reporters without Borders Report, March 2008 http://www. rsf.org/ IMG/ pdf/ rapport_ en_bd-3.pdf.
39. *Reuters,* "New Bahrain press law ends jail for most offences", 6 May 2008 and *Khaleej Times*, "Bahrain plans to give television and radio stations full freedom", 13 April 2008.
40. International Trade Union Confederation (ITUC). *"Internationally-recognised core labour standards in Bahrain"*, Report for the WTO General Council Review of the Trade Policies of the Kingdom of Bahrain. Geneva: July 2007 p. 1.
41. International Trade Union Confederation (ITUC). "Internationally-recognised core labour standards in Bahrain", Report for the WTO General Council Review of the Trade Policies of the Kingdom of Bahrain. Geneva: July 2007 p. 3.
42. US Department of Labor. *Bahrain Labor Rights Report,* Bureau of International Labor Affairs, Washington DC: 2005.
43. *The First Universal Periodic Review Report Presented by the Kingdom of Bahrain to the United Nations Human Rights Council*, March 2008.
44. There are occasional demands in parliament for the widespread expulsion of migrants, particularly the 106,000 Bangladeshis working in Bahrain. *The Daily Star*, "Bahraini Islamist wants Bangladeshis expelled", 26 May 2008.
45. US State Department Country Report on Human Rights Practices: Bahrain 2007.
46. International Commission of Jurists (ICJ), E-Bulletin No. 12, 2006 http://www.icj.org/IMG/ICJBulletinjune06.pdf.
47. "*Compilation Prepared by the Office of the High Commissioner for Human Rights"*, Human Rights Council. Geneva: February 2008 p. 10.
48. *"Compilation Prepared by the Office of the High Commissioner for Human Rights"*, Human Rights Council. Geneva: February 2008 p. 7.
49. Human Rights Watch, "Bahrain: New Allegations of Detainee Abuse", 15 February 2008 http://www. hrw.org/ en/news/ 2008/02/15/ bahrain-new-allegations- detainee-abuse.

50. Middle East News, "Iranian parliamentary speaker begins two-day visit to Bahrain", 21 October 2008.
51. *Gulf News,* "Political Leader's call to take up arms against authorities draws flak", 16 July 2006.
52. White House Press Release – President Bush Visits Bahrain 13th January 2008 http://www. whitehouse.gov/ news/releases/ 2008/01/20080112-5.html.
53. *"Bahrain Wins Seat on UN Rights Panel", Khaleej Times,* 23rd May 2008.
54. The Bahrain Tribune, *"No discrimination says Bahraini Premier",* 23 April 2008.
55. G. Nonneman, "Political Reform in the Gulf Monarchies – From Liberalisation to Democratisation? A Comparative Perspective". Sir William Luce Paper No: 6, Durham University: 2006 p. 31.
56. The government has begun to demonstrate a sensitivity to Shia opinion in its reaction to events in Iraq and Lebanon, most recently with regards to the crisis in Lebanon in May 2008, when Bahrain went so far as to issue a joint statement with Syria that stated that both countries would not internationalize Hizbullah's recent seizure of strategic areas of Lebanon. Some leaders of the Sunni community remain concerned as to the potential ripple effect of these conflicts and an increasing Shia regional assertiveness. *Kuwait News Agency*, "Syria, Bahrain refuse to internationalize Lebanon crisis", May 11 2008 and *The New York Times*, "An island kingdom feels the ripple effects of Iraq and Iran", April 16 2006.

References

Carnegie Endowment for International Peace, *Arab Political Systems: Baseline Information and Reforms – Bahrain,* Washington DC: 2008.

Economist Intelligence Unit. *Country Report 2007: Bahrain,* London: December, 2007.

Ehteshami, Anoush and Wright, Stephen, "Political Change in the Arab Oil Monarchies: From Liberalization to Enfranchisement," *International Affairs,* Vol. 83, No. 5, London: Chatham House, 2007.

Freedom House, *Country Reports 2007: Bahrain,* New York: 2007.

Human Rights Watch, "Bahrain: New Allegations of Detainee Abuse," New York: 15 February, 2008.

Human Rights Watch, "End threats to rights activists," New York: 12 November, 2008.

Human Rights Watch, "Country Report 2008: Bahrain," New York: 2008.

International Center for Not-for-Profit Law, "Comments on the Draft Law on Not-for-Profit Organisations and Foundations of Bahrain", Washington DC: December, 2007.

International Commission of Jurists (ICJ), *E-Bulletin,* No. 12, 2006 http://www.icj.org/IMG/ICJBulletinjune06.pdf.

International Crisis Group (ICG), "Bahrain's Sectarian Challenge" *Middle East Report*, No. 40, Brussels, 2005.

International Trade Union Confederation (ITUC). "Internationally-recognised core labour standards in Bahrain", *Report for the WTO General Council Review of the Trade Policies of the Kingdom of Bahrain*, Geneva, July, 2007.

Khalaf, Abdulhadi, "The King's Dilemma: Obstacles to Political Reforms in Bahrain", Fourth Mediterranean Social and Political Research Meeting, Lund University, March, 2003.

Ministry of Foreign Affairs, "The First Universal Periodic Review Report Presented by the Kingdom of Bahrain to the United Nations Human Rights Council," March, Manama: MOFA, 2008.

Nonneman, Gerd., "Political Reform in the Gulf Monarchies – From Liberalisation to Democratisation? A Comparative Perspective," *Sir William Luce Paper,* No. 6, Durham University: 2006.

Office of the President of the United States, "Press Release: President Bush Visits Bahrain," 13 January, 2008, Washington DC: 2008.

Peterson, J.E, "The Promise and Reality of Bahrain's Reforms" in Joshua Teitelbaum, (ed.), *Political Liberalization in the Gulf,* New York: Columbia University Press, 2008.

Reporters without Borders, "Bahrain: Tuning Promises into Reality," Paris: March, 2008.

Reporters without Borders, International Press Freedom Index 2008, Paris: 2008.

UN Human Rights Council, "Compilation Prepared by the Office of the High Commissioner for Human Rights", Doc. No. A/HRC/WG.6/1/BHR/2, *Working Group on the Universal Periodic Review*, First Session, 7-18 April 2008. Geneva: 25 February, 2008.

US Department of Labor, "Bahrain Labor Rights Report", Bureau of International Labor Affairs, Washington DC: 2005.

US Department of State, "Country Report on Human Rights Practices – Bahrain 2007", Washington DC: Department of State, 2007.

Zweiri, Mohammed,"The victory of Al Wefaq: The Rise of Shiite Politics in Bahrain." *Research Paper* No. 108. Athens: Research Institute for European and American Studies, April 2007.

11

Changing Hues of Green in Bahrain

Gareth Doherty

As a color, green does not exist by itself: it is a mix of blue and yellow. Colors, though, have subjective boundaries and the point at which what we consider blue becomes green, or green becomes yellow, depends to a large extent on the culture and language of the perceiver, as well as the context. Anthropologists Brent Berlin and Paul Kay writing in 1969, speak of the relativity of color across cultures; they found that a word for green almost always exists, even when a word for blue does not.[1]

Green is more than color; it is vegetation, open space, a type of building or urbanism, an environmental cause, a political movement, "the new black." The color of photosynthesis and chlorophyll, green is mostly regarded as life–giving, bountiful, and healthy (except when referring to the tone of human skin). Talk–show hosts relax in green rooms and doctors' scrubs are often green (to contrast with red). As an adjective, green can mean naiveté, or something not yet ripe.

In attempting to find and describe green in its own right, independent of objects that happen to be green, let me ask you, the reader, to point to a green object, or part of a nearby object that happens to be green. That should be a relatively straightforward thing to do. However, when I ask you, the reader, to now point to the color green in that same object, things perhaps become a little bit more complicated?[2]

The Bahrain islands are the smallest, densest, and proportionately the greenest of the Arab states of the Persian Gulf. Ten miles wide by thirty miles long, the kingdom is smaller than London or New York and just about the same size as Singapore. As the city–state transitions to an intensely urban landscape driven by the demands of a growing population and limited land mass, the hues of Bahrain's greenery are changing and with them the ecologies of society, politics, and infrastructure with which green is inherently intertwined. The gray–greens of the native date–palm plantations are being replaced with bright grass greens of roadside shoulders, roundabouts, and the lawns of new residential and leisure developments. To have greenery in such an intensely urban environment is not very green from an environmental sense due to the resources often required to sustain the greenery. Bahrain represents an extreme example of the impulse for urban greenery, an impulse that is temperate and global as well as arid and particular to Bahrain.

Bahrain literally translates as "Two Seas" in Arabic. One sea, the Gulf, separates Bahrain from Iran on the east and Saudi Arabia on the west (to which it is linked by a 20 mile long causeway). The other freshwater "sea" springs up from the Dammam aquifer, which originates aboveground in Saudi Arabia and flows eastward, running under the sea and perforating the seabed around the Bahraini archipelago, as well as the land, with a plethora of springs.[3] As a result, Bahrain gained its regional importance disproportionate to its land area largely due to these sweet-water springs which sustained its greenery, and its urbanism.

Though often considered an antidote to the urban, in arid environments green, through cultivated areas, often indicates the presence of human settlements. The villages that punctuated Bahrain's greenery were sustained for millennia by the freshwater springs and agriculture, orchards and vegetable gardens, that existed between and within the grey–green date–palm groves, until the pressures of increasing population and development of the latter part of the twentieth century upset that relationship. Today Bahrain uses much of its water reserves on irrigating its remaining agricultural areas, which produce only 11 percent of the country's food and less than 0.05 percent of the national income. This agriculture is a remnant of a verdant past when the country was self–sufficient albeit with a much smaller population; Bahrain has grown from 70,000 in the 1920s to over one million residents today.

A complex system of irrigation channels, *qanats*, were fed by the freshwater springs and water distributed according to detailed customary irrigation laws that ensured fair access to water by farmers.[4] "The Adhari Pond starves the nearby and feeds the far beyond" goes a Bahraini proverb referring to the irrigation system that because of topography and the pull of gravity supplied faraway gardens rather than those close by.[5] The proximity between the springs and greenery was further disrupted by the artesian wells drilled during the 1920s and 1930s (leading indirectly to the discovery of oil) which led to a rapid increase in greenery in Bahrain—by some accounts almost doubling green areas between the 1930s and the early 1970s[6]—but eventually contributed to the over-extraction and subsequent depletion and salination of the underground water reserves. Some of the gardens that are still irrigated from the depleted and saline springs bear exceptionally pungent fruit.

Groves of date-palms are the most iconic and distinctive, yet rapidly diminishing, green spaces of Bahrain. Planning laws allow for the development of only 30 percent of agricultural areas (as opposed to all of non-agricultural areas), so many landowners seek to have land declassified as agricultural to be able to develop it. If the land is no longer green, it is no longer considered agricultural, so green must become as white as the desert sands through active neglect.

One property developer told me that it is easy to reconstruct the greenery of the palm groves, that even though date–palms are cut down for villas, green areas can be replanted with trees and greenery to regain the same effect. I wish it were that easy. There is something very green about these spaces, which is an indispensible part of their appeal: the richness of the hues of green, the range of textures, and the variety and intensity of the shadows. The allure of green is more than the pull of nostalgia; much more than the resonance of a bygone era that can never be recovered. Many of these spaces, whether maintained or neglected, feel timeless and dignified. They take much of their value from their history gathered over millennia of farming and gardening, as well as the microclimates that the plantations produce. The urbanity of that greenness cannot be recovered; it can be imitated, but not regained.

Writing about the social life of the Bahraini date–palms, Fuad Khuri states that the culture of palms in Bahrain used to be as elaborate as the culture of camels among the pastoral nomads in central Arabia.[7] There are more than 1,000 words for a camel in Arabic; I am not sure how many words there are for date–palms or for greenery but one Bahraini farmer told me that he gave the date–palms close to his house names, like his children, and in this way they are treated like family members. It is considered a great honor for a visitor to be served dates from these trees. It was common for farmers to plant trees to commemorate their child's birth and Shaikh Isa, the previous ruler, is credited with the saying, "The Palm tree is our mother, we can live under it". [8]

Date-palms provided building materials for traditional summer housing called *barasti*. Indeed every part of the palm had a use, the leaves, the trunk, the dates, all had particular roles and a diet of dates allegedly provides the basic nutrients the human body needs. The date season starts in May and extends through to October or November, depending on the variety. The date-palms offered just one layer in gardens with multiple levels of produce including pomegranates, bananas, mangoes, and alfalfa, all sheltered from the blazing sun by the trees. The date-palms have the capacity to be urban in that they penetrate so many aspects of Bahraini life, providing food, shelter, building materials, social spaces, and social status as well as facilitating ancillary industries and produce, and a focus for poetry and folklore.

While the date-palm groves offered sources of food and employment, they were also recreation grounds for the elite. With the shade they offer from the scorching sun, the palm groves create attractive spaces for social gatherings, especially during the summer months. Owning greenery in Bahrain had, and still has, complex social meanings. Large date-palm plantations were owned by city merchants, who invested in them not for income but for the status of ownership. Farmers were contracted to look after the gardens often at a low cost, such as a couple of baskets of dates a week for the owner. Wealthy merchants from Manama, the capital, would bring their families to the palm groves on Friday afternoons and issue invitations to relatives and friends to join them there until the *maghrib* prayers at sundown. Sometimes visiting cards would be issued, granting friends of the merchant permission to visit in their absence.[9]

It is important to note that the date–palm gardens of the past were not very profitable, as is the case today. One large property just outside Manama near Ain Adhari (a formerly important spring that has since dried up to be replaced in 2008 with an artificial pool) was sold in 1943 for 40,000 rupees (about US$ 1.2 million), while a shop in the souq in the center of Manama at that time cost 4,000 rupees. This land was then rented out at a rate of 27.5 rupees a month thereby netting an annual rent of 330 rupees, or approximately 1 percent of the value of the property. This was not a good financial investment, and thus it seems fair to deduce that the purchase must have been made for the social prestige that ownership of the greenery would confer.[10]

While the owners of the gardens historically belonged to an elite group of ruling family members and merchants, the farmers who worked in them invariably belonged to the Baḥarna, the local Arab Shi'i community, the largest social group, who by and large lived in the nearby villages. Green is also finely ingrained in Shi'i identity. During the commemoration of the martyrdom of Imam Hussein, on the first ten days of the month of Muharram, the center of Manama is clothed in green banners and flags and the streets strewn with sweet basil, *mashmoon*, since green is considered the color of Hussein, and Islam. Every Thursday evening it is still common to bring green shoots of *mashmoon* to graves in Shi'i cemeteries.

Those Bahrainis old enough to remember the mosaic of date-palm groves often lament their destruction. It is important however not to overly romanticize the past and to recognize that the destruction of the date–palm gardens is not just a recent phenomenon, although the scale and pace of destruction has certainly accelerated. Curtis Larsen, in *Life and Land Use on the Bahrain Islands: The Geoarchaeology of an Ancient Society*, cites E.L. Durand, the British Political Resident in Bushire who made the following observation when visiting Bahrain in 1879: "Foremost amongst the trees is of course the date, and some of the date gardens are extremely fine. Many, however, are going to ruin, the result of bad Government, and indeed in some places that were once flourishing gardens, not a bearing tree remains."[11]

Although the villages were intertwined with greenery, the center of Manama was not very green. Walking though the souq there today, one will not find much greenery apart from the odd tree or weed pushing its way through in the cracks in the pavement. There are many green shutters and occasional green doors, in partial compensation perhaps for the lack of soft greenery in the city. It was in the urbanization period of the early 1970s, right after full independence from the British, that greenery and city really started to mesh in Bahrain. Nelida Fuccaro links this to the oil crisis triggered by the Arab–Israeli war of 1973.[12] It was during this period when the green countryside with its villages and the gray and white city subsequently become one in the popular imagination that city people stopped going out to the gardens at weekends. The garden was no longer "the other" and instead became "corrupted" and considered part of the city. The special greenness of the gardens was disrupted by the extensive development that has taken place over the past thirty years. Bahrain's limited land mass makes the demand for land and the continuance of the past uses of greenery untenable. At the same time the extensive distribution infrastructures for water and Treated Sewage Effluent bring the possibility of greenery to much of Bahrain today.

Contemporary green residential compounds in Bahrain with names such as Green Oasis are partial compensation for the lost date-palm groves. Together with the date-palms of roundabouts, roadside shoulders and median strips of VIP roads (roads designed for extra-verdant greenery but also with security in mind), they represent the green of contemporary Bahrain. Such residential and transportation infrastructural spaces are important because they are the greenery that most people encounter in everyday life. These green roadsides represent not so much the past—although the palms do symbolize this past—but speak more about Bahrain's present, its place in the world, and its aspirations for the future. Typical ads for new developments, often on billboards positioned beside highways, will show an image as green rather than featuring the building they advertise.

At weekends and in the evenings, it is not unusual to see expatriates picnicking on the roadside shoulders despite the passing traffic. (I am told that Bahraini's would never do this.) The roadside palms, although of typically different species and hues of green than traditional plantings, still retain some of their social and agricultural value. The date–palms at the Bahrain Financial Harbour, built on reclaimed land on the site of the former port in the center of Manama, are pollinated in the spring and the dates harvested in the fall by low–income expatriate workers for their own personal use; public palms are appropriated and farmed by the low income workers.

The date-palm gardens and the roadside shoulders and roundabouts actually have similar types of social values. Roadside greenery can be seen as the date-palm groves of the present era. Both have a certain type of production, although those productive qualities are obviously different: the palm groves are agricultural, whereas the green roadsides indicate economic productivity, a production of development, a landscape of transformation. The plethora of green roundabouts and median strips lined with petunias of the national colors of red and white celebrate the power and benevolence of the state. As seen in the multitude of roadside billboards with pictures of the King, the Prime Minister and the Crown Prince, invariably situated beside greenery, the rulers are happy to be associated with green.

"Together let us make Bahrain Green" was the catch-phrase of the 2008 Riffa Views Bahrain International Garden Show. The organizers also sponsored a garden design competition among Bahraini schools called "The Riffa Views Eden Challenge." The International Garden Show, which runs for three days every year, is one of just three organizations in Bahrain under the direct patronage of the king, Hamad bin Isa Al-Khalifa. Green retains its position as a social catalyst, with the Gardening Club reflecting increased interest in things green and beautiful and, by association, royal.

The transformative power of turning desert to green is an extraordinarily potent one. To turn desert into luscious green is to prove that dreams do become reality, to achieve the impossible, to show that paradise can be constructed on earth. Writing in *The Social Life of Trees*, Maurice Bloch, invoking Lévi-Strauss, draws to our attention that to be effective a transformation needs to be of a certain magnitude.[13] For instance, turning arid desert into gravel or concrete is not as potent a transformation as desert into luscious green. The presence of the desert however is not easily forgotten.

Notes

This text is adapted from my doctoral research at Harvard Graduate School of Design.

1. See Brent Berlin and Paul Kay, *Basic Color Terms: Their Universality and Evolution* (Berkeley: University of California Press, 1969) 2–4.
2. See Alex Byrne and David Hilbert, *Readings on Color: The Philosophy of Color Vol. 1,* who outline four main positions of color in philosophy: eliminativists, they say, see color as a sort of illusion; for dispositionalists "the property green (for example) is a disposition to produce certain perceptual states: roughly the disposition to *look green*"; physicalists, such as Byrne and Hilbert themselves, regard green as a property of the selective reflection of incident light; meanwhile primitivists

agree that objects have colors but do not agree that the color is identical to the physical property of the object that is colored.

3. The sea–based springs induced a particular coloration of the green waters of the sea, as well as a particular luster on pearls which were a mainstay of Bahrain's economy until the 1930s.
4. See R. B. Serjeant, "Customary Irrigation Law among the Baharnah of Bahrain." *Bahrain Through the Ages: the History*, edited by Shaikh Abdullah bin Khalid Al-Khalifa and Michael Rice, (London and New York: Keegan Paul International, 1993), 471–496.
5. Ali Akbar Bushehri pers. comm., April 21, 2008. See also Nelida Fuccaro, *Histories of City and State in the Persian Gulf* (Cambridge: Cambridge University Press, 2009), 23. As Fuccaro suggests, the saying also cynically refers to the appropriation of Bahrain's resources by foreigners.
6. See Mustapha Ben Hamouche, "Land–Use Change and its Impact on Urban Planning in Bahrain: A GIS Approach," *Proceedings of the Middle East Spatial Technology Conference* (Bahrain: December 2007). Retrieved on June 26, 2009 from: http://www.gisdevelopment.net/proceedings/mest/2007/Remote SensingApplicationsLanduse.htm.
7. See Fuad Khuri, *Tribe and State in Bahrain: The Transformation of Social and Political Authority in an Arab State* (Chicago: University of Chicago Press, 1980), 39.
8. See Fareeda Mohammed Saleh Khunji, *The Story of the Palm Tree* (Bahrain: 2003), 45.
9. Ali Akbar Bushehri pers. comm., April 25, 2008.
10. From the archive of Ali Akbar Bushehri.
11. See Durand 1879 as cited in Curtis Larsen, *Life and Land Use on the Bahrain Islands: The Geoarchaeology of an Ancient Society* (Chicago: University of Chicago Press, 1983), 22.
12. See Fuccaro (2009), 229.
13. See Maurice Bloch, "Why Trees, Too, Are Good to Think With: Towards an Anthropology of the Meaning of Life". *The Social Life of Trees*, edited by Laura Rival, (New York: Berg Publishers, 1998) 39–40. Bloch suggests that to be effective, the transformation must be of a certain magnitude and cites the example of the transformation of wine to blood in the Catholic mass; the transformation would not be so intense if it were wine to whisky.

12

Globalization and Cosmopolitanism in Omani Society

Shelly Johny

Oman as a nation state is relatively younger than Saudi Arabia and even most of the Gulf sheikdoms in the region. Until 1970, Oman existed as a Sultanate union of different territories who were not yet, at least administratively, seen as one nation. This was reflected in the title of the country used until 1970, which was the Sultanate of Muscat and Oman. The southern province of Dhofar was seen as the private fiefdom of the Sultan and not even worthy of mention as a recognised political entity in any manner. But what makes Oman different from the other states in the region is that it has had a rather long history as a maritime empire with overseas territorial possessions and Muscat served as a major trading centre. This resulted in an ethnically and culturally diverse population especially in Muscat and the surrounding regions and along the Batina coast in Oman. While there exists a body of work which looks at the political and economic developments in Oman since 1970, especially the development in infrastructure and industry, lesser attention has been paid to the impact of the transformation of Omani society per say. The attempt here is to see how the endeavour to create an 'Omani national identity' as a part of the larger nation building project has had an influence on different segments of Omani society. Globalization has also had its impact on the different communities in Oman. Only a study on the impact that both state efforts and the phenomenon of globalization has had on Omani society will give a complete picture.

Ethnic and Cultural Diversity in Omani Society

John E. Peterson has given a detailed account of the diversity of Omani society in both southern and northern Oman. As mentioned above, the society in Muscat and the areas along the Batina coast reflect Oman's legacy as a maritime empire. The ethnic and linguistic communities include Hindu Kutchi Bhattia traders from Gujarat in India, Khoja Muslims from Sindh, Baluchis, and Zanzibaris from East Africa. While these communities constitute the major sections of society in these parts of Oman apart from Omani Arabs who form the much larger majority, there are other smaller groups like the Baharina Shias, Zadjalis and Persians. Most of these communities have had particular occupations in the general context of Oman's maritime empire during the previous centuries. The Gujarati traders conducted most of the trade at the ports and eventually came to wield economic and political influence during the nineteenth century because of their control over the treasury and customs and also the financing of the military campaigns of the Al Busaidi rulers of Oman in East Africa.

While the Gujarati Hindu merchants were in control of international trade, the Khoja Muslims, who were originally from Hyderabad in Sindh province, were in control of domestic trade[1] and they also traded in items like dried fish which the Hindu merchants would not because of their religious beliefs.[2] The Baluchis mostly served as mercenaries of the royal family and they form the largest non-Arab community in Oman.[3] Besides the Kutchi Bhattias, there are other groups of people of Indian origin who were formerly Hindus, but are Muslims presently. These include the Kumbhars and the Sonabaras.[4] While Oman has had strong links with East Africa even before the Yaariba and Al Busaidi dynasties, the present Zanzibari community in Oman mainly constitutes East Africans of Omani origin who fled from Zanzibar due to the political upheaval in the 1960s.

The society in the southern province of Dhofar is structured differently from northern Oman. There is no dominant ethnic group with smaller minorities as all the communities are organised as tribes and have close connections with other tribes. But the differences here are more based on language, territory and occupation rather than ethnicity.[5] There are a number of non-Arab speaking groups in this region. Because of its location, Dhofar has received waves of migration from nearby Yemen which was a centre of a magnificent pre-Islamic South Arabian civilization. The largest non-Arabic speaking group is the al-Qara who are *jabbalis* or mountain people. Other non-Arabic speaking groups include the al-Shahra, al-Mahra al-Baraima, al-Batahira, al-Harasis, and al-Hikman.[6] There are also descendents of former slaves and fishermen of mixed origin.[7]

State Formation and Culture in Oman: Contrast with the Gulf

Oman's cosmopolitan society does not conform to the general cultural template of the Gulf. The Gulf identity is mainly marked by a conservative tribal Arab element in concert with adherence to Sunni Islam. The Gulf Arab cultural identity is in marked contrast to the more westernised Arabs of Egypt, the Levant and Iraq who have a strong association with their national identities separate from the larger Arab identity. But Oman is a cultural aberration in the general social environment of the Gulf. This could be because of the manner in which the political segments which presently constitute the Sultanate of Oman evolved. This was different from the experiences of either Saudi Arabia or the Gulf sheikhdoms. Oman has existed as an entity for a much longer period then its Gulf neighbours. This does not mean that there are no minorities in the societies of the Gulf or that those societies are entirely homogenous.

As it is well known, there is a significant Shia minority population in Saudi Arabia and the Shias form the majority of the indigenous population in Bahrain albeit with little political influence. There are also other minorities in the societies of the Gulf sheikdoms who are associated with maritime trade and the pearl industry. But the predominant culture in all these cases is that of the Sunni Arab Bedouin tribes. The origin of the rulers of these states in Central Arabia allowed them unbroken access to their cultural homeland. This is true especially in the case of the states like Kuwait, Bahrain and Qatar where the ruling classes emerged from the tribes that migrated from the Najd to these new territories during the seventeenth and eighteenth centuries.[8]

When it comes to Oman, there are certain complications with regard to the creation of a singular Omani national identity. The present nation-state of the Sultanate of Oman consists of three territories which were not exactly united until the 1970s. These include Muscat and the coastal Batina region, interior Oman and the southern province of Dhofar. This is not to say that the divisions between these territories were very sharp as the Batina coast and interior Oman were often united under one political authority in various phases of Oman's history. But the political and socio-cultural characteristics of all the three territories were different. One of the ironies here is that the differences between the coast and interior became more pronounced during the nineteenth century in a period described as the heyday of Oman's maritime empire under Said bin

Sultan.

Ibadi Islam was the faith that was practised by the majority of Muslims in interior Oman and along the coast though there were a significant number of Sunnis as well. For a long period of Oman's history since the birth of Islam, Ibadi Islam was an essential component of Omani socio-cultural identity. The Ibadis are seen as a sect separate from the Sunnis and the Shias whose origins can be traced to the Khawarij who were the first dissenters from the main body of Muslims. Oman's interior contained the major centres of Ibadi Islam like Nizwa and Rustaq. One of the important characteristics of Ibadi Islam is its concept of government which Ibadi Muslims consider as the one most identical to the system of government that existed during the early Islamic period immediately after the death of the Prophet Muhammad. This system of government was also seen as the one most suited to the requirements of humankind.

According to this system, the Imam who was the ruler of the Muslims was elected from among worthy candidates by a group of learned religious scholars with support from the chiefs of the major tribes.[9] In this manner, the Imamate system of government of Ibadi Islam did not sanction hereditary succession to the position of Imam.[10] The Ibadi concept of government clashed with the interests of the Al Busaidi dynasty which ruled Oman during the nineteenth century and continue to rule Oman in the present time. Though the Al Busaidis are also Ibadi, they are more secular in their outlook and Al Busaidi rulers during the nineteenth century were more interested in fostering trade and their oversees territorial possessions. The differences between the Al Busaidis and conservative Ibadi elements in the interior were accentuated by the close interaction that the former had with the non-Ibadi cosmopolitan population at Muscat and the ports of the Batina coast as part of the culture of maritime trade and commerce.

The opposition against the Al Busaidis grew into an Ibadi Imamate movement consisting of the ulema and tribal forces. They captured Muscat in 1868[11] and established an Ibadi theocratic regime under Azzan bin Qays, a descendent of the first Al Busaidi ruler.[12] Azzan's rule lasted only till 1871 when he was toppled and the ruling Al Busaidi branch was reinstated. The twentieth century saw a revival of the Ibadiyya movement and two Imams in succession were elected and they governed in interior Oman separately from the

Sultanate who governed Muscat and the Batina coast. When the Imamate began to be a threat to the Sultanate, the Sultan's forces with considerable help from the British defeated the interior tribes during the 1950s.[13] The Sultanate finally managed to bring under firm control all the territory in the northern parts of present day Oman. The troubles of the Omani ruler, Said bin Taimur was by no means over. In 1965, a Marxist insurgency broke out in the southern province of Dhofar. Dhofar had not been recognised as a political entity and was regarded by Said as his personal possession.[14] The desperate political and economic conditions in that province provided the fuel for the outbreak of the insurgency. In 1970, Said bin Taimur was deposed and his son, Qabus bin Said became the Sultan. The early years of Qabus's rule were spent trying to fight the insurgency in Dhofar. Finally with significant help from Britain and Iran, the Omani armed forces quelled the insurgency in 1975. It was only from then on that Oman could truly begin its nation-building exercise.

Constructing Omani National Identity

While the authorities were clear about the kind of political and economic system that the new nation would have, there was a problem with the construction of an Omani national identity. This was because of the relationship that the Al Busaidi dynasty had with all the three major territories constituting the Sultanate of Oman. Prudence would naturally favour an Arab-Ibadi identity being the core theme of an Omani national identity. This was because the cultural and political heartland of Oman throughout its history has been in interior Oman despite the vibrant maritime commercial culture on the coast. The political support bases of Omani ruling authorities controlling the coast were in the tribal heartland of interior Oman. This is with the exception of times when the coast was under the control of foreign occupiers. The Ibadi element also gives Oman a uniqueness within a larger Sunni dominated Gulf region.

Interior Oman ceased to be the political centre only under the Al Busaidis who shifted the capital to Muscat. The Al Busaidis themselves being Ibadi, it would have been the natural choice to stress on Ibadi Islam as being an integral part of the Omani identity. But the troubled history between Ibadi forces in the interior and the Al Busaidi rulers prevented such a possibility. While publicly claiming that Ibadi Islam forms an integral part of the Omani identity, the Omani government under Qabus during the 1970s and 1980s preferred projecting the Arab characteristic of Oman's identity and adopting a more generalised version of Islam. The Qabus mosques with their domes and minarets resemble those in other parts of the Muslim world rather than the Ibadi tradition of mosques consisting of plain square buildings without domes and minarets.[15]

By stressing the Arabness of Oman's identity and sidestepping the Ibadi element, the government under Qabus effectively avoided a problem that bedevilled the Al Busaidis ever since it began to lay stress on maritime trade and expanding its oversees territories. One of the criticisms that were levelled against the Al Busaidis was their dependence on non-Ibadi communities like Baluchis and Hindu Gujarati merchants for maintaining their rule and conducting commercial activities. In fact, the domination of the Indian merchants on Oman's economy was resented by the Ibadi forces in the interior and the Indian merchants were targeted by tribal raids against Muscat and other settlements along the coast during the nineteenth century.[16] Oman's nation-building exercise had begun after major threats to its unity, like the Imam's rebellion in the 1950s and the Marxist insurgency of the 1960s and 1970s, had been put down. There was a general movement towards giving more representation to Arab Omanis during this period. Through the method of projecting an Arab identity, the Omani government managed to appease the sentiments of Arab Omanis while at the same time preventing space to a pro-Ibadi sentiment which had been dormant since the 1950s.

The government's policy of promoting Omani Arabs in its development activities led to the rise of a new class of Omani Arab entrepreneurs who could take advantage of the new environment. These groups include the likes of the Zawawi[17] and the Shanfari business groups. In stark contrast to the time when the Indian merchants financed the Al Busaidi military campaigns in places like East Africa, the political influence of the Indians have declined while members of the Zawawi and Shanfari business families hold ministerial positions in Oman.[18] These changes did not mean that the social standing of the non-Arab communities in Muscat have totally declined and important families and individuals from among the Gujarati Muslims, Zanzibaris, Khoja Muslims and Baluchis continue to have good relations with the royal family. The projection of the

Arab element of Oman's identity over that of the Ibadi has actually worked in favour of the cultural minorities in Oman.

The external adoption of the symbols of Arab identity has proved to be much easier. This would not have been the scenario if the government was actively bent upon advocating a particular sectarian belief as the official faith of the country. The non-Arab communities in Oman have adopted the Omani national dress[19] while outside their homes, and there is an increased tendency to use Arabic. This phenomenon is not just limited to the Muslim minorities in Oman but is also practiced by the Indian merchant community in Oman. The presence of a large number of expatriate workers from around the world has also helped the ethnic and sectarian minorities in Oman. As the expatriates markedly do not wear the national dress it has helped the minorities to stress their identities as Omani nationals. The identification that the minorities could make with the Omani national identity during the 1970s and 1980s was very crucial because of the increased importance that Ibadi Islam was to have later on as a result of the government reaction to particular events.

But there have also been complications in Omani society arising from an attempt to promote Arab identity. A major portion of the Baluchi community is economically and socially marginalised in Omani society. Their inability to speak Arabic proficiently has additionally contributed to their marginalisation. At the same time, immigrants from Zanzibar who fled the island because of political disturbances during the 1960s also faced problems when they initially arrived in Oman because of their lack of proficiency in Arabic. But they managed to attain good positions and jobs because of their English-speaking skills which came in handy when Oman began to build its economy and infrastructural capabilities. Having gone through an education system that favours Arabic, the younger generations belonging to ethnic and sectarian minorities do not speak their community languages in public as much as their elders. For example, the descendents of the generation that fled from Zanzibar tend to speak more in Arabic outside their homes while Swahili is mostly spoken at home. Because the Gujarati community have their own schools, they have been able to better preserve their language in comparison to other communities.

The region that was most affected by the government's effort to promote Arabic was the southern province of Dhofar. There is criticism that the government has concentrated its development activities in Dhofar and that a disproportionate amount of funds have been spent for a province like Dhofar which has lesser population in comparison to the other parts of Oman. This could have occurred because of the insecurity that the government has with regard to Dhofar because of the insurgency of the past and a necessity to prevent such an event from happening again. Also, Dhofar was economically backward and had few facilities like roads, schools and hospitals when the insurgency ended in 1975. John E. Peterson has accounted how the government's efforts have affected the non-Arabic speaking communities in the province. There are a number of communities in Dhofar who migrated from the Yemen in the past and speak old languages of the civilizations of southern Arabia. Because of the lack of facilities, Dhofaris are heavily dependent on government schools for the education of their children. The result has been a homogenisation of society in that province as only the elders continue to speak the old languages while the younger generation tend to speak more in Arabic. The non-Arabic languages are under threat of extinction in Dhofar.[20]

Globalization and Cosmopolitanism in Omani Society

As in the case of many littoral states, it is difficult to mark the exact time when globalization began to have its impact on Omani society in the twentieth century. This is after keeping in mind the distinction that many scholars make between the globalization of the eighteenth century and the one that began in the early nineteen nineties. Because of its maritime history, the cosmopolitan society in Muscat and the surrounding areas have always remained open to influences from other parts of the Indian Ocean. One of the biggest influences on Oman has been that of India. If we leave out the maritime trade and cultural links that existed between Oman and India since ancient times, we see that India began to become a cultural icon in Oman in the modern age since the nineteenth century during British colonial rule in India. Turki bin Said, the Sultan of Oman in the 1970s and 1880s and whose descendents continued to rule Oman since then was under British protection in Bombay before he became the ruler.[21] The Al Busaidi rulers began to send their sons to India for their education. During the course of their education and due to their conditioning they were heavily influenced by Indian administrative and cultural practices.

India continued to be an influence on Omani society long after

Oman ceased to be a maritime empire. When they first began migrating to Oman in the 1960s and 1970s, Malayalee expatriates from the south Indian state of Kerala encountered non-Arab Omanis like Baluchis and Khoja Muslims who spoke Hindi more fluently than themselves. In fact, the Omanis were also surprised by such encounters as it was expected that all Indians would be proficient in Hindi. Very soon, the Malayalees began to be addressed as 'Malabaris' to differentiate them from other Indians. For the Omanis, Malabar was familiar since long as the port of Beypore, a major ship-building centre where most of the Omani ships and sailing crafts were built, is located in that region of Kerala. Hindi films (or what is popularly referred to as Bollywood films) were popular among the Omanis in Muscat during the 1970s and 1980s with the actor Amitabh Bachchan having a huge amount of fan following.

If globalization means better connectivity to the rest of the world through the leap in communications technology, then satellite television and the internet has helped Omanis to keep abreast of the latest trends and happenings in Indian popular culture in comparison to the previous generation. A recent example of this is the case of Aaasma Mohammad, an eighteen-year old singer from Oman who enjoys singing Hindi film songs. She got the opportunity to take part in a singing contest on an Indian television channel and later did playback singing for a Hindi film. Her father, Muhammad Rafi became the fan of a popular Indian singer by the same name after he realised that his father had named him after the singer.[22] It is not just Oman's links with India that has been reinforced due to globalization. In what is described as a 'translocal' phenomenon, Erik Gilbert has described how the Zanzibaris in Oman who fled Zanzibar after the revolution that happened there in 1964 started re-developing their links with relatives and friends back in Zanzibar from the early nineteen nineties through the use of communication and transportation facilities. Gilbert states that though there is no relocation of the Zanzibaris from Oman back to the island, the spatial differences between the Zanzibaris in both the locations have become less of a problem due to globalization.[23] In the same manner, the Gujarati merchants in Oman who originated from the Kutch region of Gujarat continue to maintain their links with relatives back home in India and continue to make frequent trips to Mumbai for business purposes. Among the Baluchis, who do not retain such links with their place of origin in the Pakistani province of Baluchistan, globalization has helped them in identifying themselves with cultures that face a similar predicament. The younger generation of Baluchis during the 1990s began to be influenced by Rap and Hip-Hop music and notions of 'Black Power'.

A focus on the wider links that Muscat and the surrounding regions have with the outside world gives the impression that interior Oman and Dhofar have been isolated from the rest of the world since time immemorial. This is not entirely true. Ibadi beliefs were carried over to Oman from the cosmopolitan port of Basra where it was supported and financed by Ibadi merchants. During the Ibadi *nahda* or renaissance during the nineteenth century, the religious scholars of the Ibadi movement in centres in interior Oman nurtured links with fellow brethren in the Mazab region in Algeria and Zanzibar. There was much exchange of knowledge regarding Ibadi theology and jurisprudence between these areas. Likewise, Dhofaris who went to different parts of the Gulf for employment during the 1950s were influenced by Arab nationalism and socialism. They got the inspiration from these experiences to begin a pro-Marxist insurgency against the Sultan during the 1960s. The formation of an effective state system in Oman actually curtailed their access to the outside world.

This is not to say that the Omani government follows a deliberate policy of isolating interior Oman and Dhofar from the outside world. The government has become involved in a number of projects with other countries with the aim of developing the education and skills of un-employed Omanis from all over the country. For example, the Omani government has tied-up with the Galfar Construction Company in a programme which trains Omanis from different parts of the country including the interior and Dhofar in technical courses in the South Indian state of Kerala. They are provided with training in construction technology and computer applications.[24] At the same time, no amount of government effort can replicate in Dhofar and interior Oman the wide-spanning links that the cosmopolitan society in Muscat has with the outside world. While retaining their links with the outside world, the ethnic and sectarian minorities have also successfully adapted themselves to a predominantly Arab-based Omani national identity before the 1990s. But there are also new challenges for Oman's cosmopolitan society.

In 1987, the Wahhabis of Saudi Arabia attacked the authenticity of Ibadi Islam and commented that it could not be regarded as a true version of Islam. This accusation resulted in a counter-reaction by the Omani government where it resolved to defend Ibadi Islam as a vital part of Omani heritage in the context of a predominantly Sunni Muslim Gulf region. The government began to establish Ibadi-oriented 'Islamic cultural institutions'. These efforts have had its impact especially in terms of defining the role of women in Omani society.[25] Women in Oman who were earlier westernized in their style of dressing have now adopted a conservative mode of dressing due to the greater importance given to religion in the cultural environment of Oman.[26] The new situation has also begun to have its impact on political and security situation in Oman. Most of the members of a clandestine group who were arrested by Omani security forces in 2005 and accused of plotting against the government were Ibadi Muslims and were from the interior areas.[27] A higher profile for Ibadi Islam in Oman's cultural environment can create complications for Oman's minorities.

Notes

1. Mark Speece, "Aspects of Economic Dualism in Oman", *International Journal of Middle East Studies*, Vol. 21, No. 4 (1989), pp. 497, 504.
2. Calvin H. Allen, "The Indian Merchant Community in Masqat", *Bulletin of the School of Oriental and African Studies*, Vol. 44, No. 1 (1981), p. 50.
3. J.E. Peterson, "Oman's Diverse Society: Northern Oman", *Middle East Journal*, Vol. 58, No. 1 (Winter, 2004), p. 35.
4. Ibid, p. 40.
5. J.E. Peterson, "Oman's Diverse Society: Southern Oman", *Middle East Journal*, Vol. 58, No. 2 (Spring, 2004), p. 259.
6. Ibid, pp. 261-265.
7. Ibid, p. 266.
8. Ahmad Mustafa Abu-Hakima, "The Development of the Gulf States", in Derek Hopwood (ed.), *The Arabian Peninsula: Society and Politics*, (London, George Allen and Unwin Ltd. 1972), p. 32.
9. Patricia Risso, *Oman and Muscat: An Early Modern History* (London, Croom Helm Ltd., 1986), p. 28.
10. John C. Wilkinson, *The Imamate Tradition of Oman* (Cambridge, Cambridge University Press, 1987), pp. 169, 187.
11. G. Atkinson, Political Agent, Muscat, to Colonel Lewis Pelly,

Political Resident in the Persian Gulf, 1st October, 1868, Muscat, Maharashtra State Archives (MSA), P.D., Vol. 83, No. 1130, of 1868, p. 46.

12. Said bin Khalfan al-Khalili, Salih bin Ali, and Muhammad bin Sulayyim al-Gharabi, the Chiefs of Oman to Colonel Lewis Pelly, Political Resident in the Persian Gulf, 9th October, 1868, MSA, P.D., Vol. 83, # 1130, of 1868, p. 226.
13. John C. Wilkinson, n. 10, p. 322.
14. J.E. Peterson, n. 5, p. 258.
15. Calvin Allen, Jr. and W. Lynn Rigsbee, II, *Oman under Qaboos: From Coup to Constitution, 1970-1996* (London, Frank Cass Publishers, 2000), p. 176.
16. Major S.B. Miles, Political Agent, Muscat to Lieutenant Colonel E.L. Ross, Political Resident in the Persian Gulf, 28th November, 1873, Muscat, MSA, P.D., Vol. 83, No. 1130, 0f 1874, p. 226.
17. Francis Owtram, *A Modern History of Oman: Formation of the State since* 1920 (London, I.B. Tauris and Co. Ltd., 2004), p. 139
18. Calvin Allen Jr. and W. Lynn Risgsbee, II, n. 15, p. 37.
19. J.E. Peterson, n. 3, p. 33.
20. J.E. Peterson, n. 5, p. 268.
21. B.H. Ellis, S. Mansfield and Fitzgerald, Political Dept., to Her Majesty's Principal Secretary of State for India in Council, London, 28th September, 1867. Bombay Castle, MSA, P.D., Vol. , No. 1168, of 1867, p. 137.
22. Sangeeta Barooah Pisharoty, "Coast to Coast", *The Hindu*, 28th February, 2009, accessed from http://www. thehindu.com/mp/2009/ 02/23/stories/ 2009022350190100. htm accessed on 26-5-09.
23. Erik Gilbert, "Oman and Zanzibar: The Historical Roots of a Global Community", in Himanshu Prabha Ray and Edward A. Alpers (eds.), *Cross Currents and Community Networks: The History of the Indian Ocean World* (New Delhi, Oxford University Press, 2007), p. 175.
24. Interview with Mr. Chandradutt, Principal, Centre of Science and Technology for Rural Development (COSTFORD), Thrissur, Kerala, India. COSTFORD provides training on technical courses to students from Oman under the pro.
25. Khalid al-Aziri, "Gender, State and Culture in Oman (1970-

2005), in Valeria Fiorani Piacentini and Elena Maestri, *From Tribe to State: Perspectives on Identity, Social and Cultural Dynamics in Eastern Arabia,* Crissma Working Paper, Vol. 1, ISU Universita Cattolica, 2007, pp. 23- 24.

26. The author's family has in its possession photo albums of office parties in Muscat of the late eighties and the early nineties from which it is evident that Zanzibari women were very westernized in their dressing style. Frequent visits by family members to Oman have also confirmed that their former colleagues have now adopted a conservative style of dressing.
27. Jeremy Jones and Nicholas Ridout, "Democratic Development in Oman", *Middle East Journal* Vol. 59, No. 3 (Summer, 2005), p. 385.

Index

Index